ALLENA HANSEN

CHOMP CHOMP CHOMP

How I Survived a BEAR ATTACK & Other Cautionary Tales

CHOMP CHOMP CHOMP © copyright 2014 by Allena Hansen. All rights reserved.
No part of this book may be reproduced in any form whatsoever,
by photography or xerography or by any other means, by broadcast or transmission,
by translation into any kind of language, nor by recording electronically or otherwise,
without permission in writing from the author, except by a reviewer,
who may quote brief passages in critical articles or reviews.

Some names, incriminating characteristics and arcane details have been fudged or outright invented, so do get over yourself and don't take it personally. Except for you. Go ahead and stew in it. I'll deny everything.

Author photo by Starla Fortunato. www.starlafortunato.com

Paperback ISBN 13: 978-1-940014-20-3
Hardcover ISBN 13: 978-1-940014-15-9

Library of Congress Catalog Number: 2014939332

Printed in the United States of America
First Printing: 2014
18 17 16 15   5 4 3 2

Cover and interior design by James Monroe Design, LLC.

Wise Ink, Inc.
53 Oliver Ave S
Minneapolis, MN 55404

www.wiseinkpub.com
To order, visit www.itascabooks.com or call 1-800-901-3480.
Reseller discounts available.

Storytelling is how old ladies avoid being left on ice floes.
Storytelling is how the irascible keep from being rasced.
Storytelling is the refuge of the powerless to the delight of the dispirited.
Its narrative is our history, our collective wisdom, the testimony
of our survival, and our commonality.

Storytelling is what propels our religions and our mythologies,
our social fabric and our body politic.
Our stories survive our monuments, our institutions, our most ancient
and forgotten of cultures.
Stories drive our imaginations, stoke our passions and color the essence
of our humanity.

Here is mine.

To AA and RP and all who've survived *me*.

PREFACE

Even before I get to the hospital, they're photographing me for public consumption. It's obviously a slow news day in mid-summer, because some enterprising news organization has mustered the celebu-copter and a couple of paparazzi to intercept the air-evac. Sure enough, here they are up in the air with us jockeying to get a good shot of me through the window. I can't see any of this, you understand, but the tech, who has been keeping me upright and conscious so I don't drown in my own blood, is cursing under his breath. "Goddamned vultures," he says. "We got a dying woman up here and all they can think about is getting a picture of the bloody stump."

Oops. That's *me* he's talking about. The bloody stump.

I, on the other hand, am secretly kind of thrilled. News cameras? Helicopters? *Now THIS is exciting stuff!*

The pain is blunt and heavy, like I've been smacked in the head by an anvil. I try to concentrate on my breathing, though it is getting harder and harder to draw air through what up until recently had been my nose and mouth. Most of my teeth are gone, and so, likely, is at least one of my eyes. I know that the bear that attacked me has pretty much chewed out the center of my face, and that my scalp—what might be left of it—has been clawed and peeled from my head like the rind from a blood orange.

Breathe! Keep breathing! I tell myself. *You've made it this far, just stick it out a little longer.* If I'm going to live, I've got to remain conscious, because if I pass out, they'll never be able to *find* my trachea in all this mess, let alone intubate it. This much is obvious to all of us, and I'm trying my damnedest to make sure they don't have to.

They've got my face swathed in wet dressings to keep it from falling off, but from here on the inside of it where I'm sitting—all befuddled and annoyed—it just feels wet and cold and . . . alien. I'm still *me* in here, but I know that whatever I was to everyone *else* is gone—and not just my face. Something intrinsic, something soulful has been taken, and I wonder if I will live long enough for that to make any difference—and what that difference might turn out to be. I've no idea if I'm going to live or die in the next few hours, but one thing's for certain. *This hurts like hell.*

By the time we land at UCLA Medical Center, about 150 miles away from my ranch home in California's southern Sierra mountains, nearly a hundred people are massed awaiting my arrival—satellite vans, cameras, and boom microphones at the ready. (They say the news services monitor the emergency radio bands, and when something tasty comes through on the scanner they're on it even before the air evac is mustered.)

"It looks like they've got every news team in Southern California down there waiting for you," says the attendant. "It's gonna be a gauntlet, but we'll try to keep you away from it. You ready?" he asks.

"Just get me into the ER so I can pass out," I manage to gurgle.

They hustle me out of the helo with a blanket over my head for "privacy" and meet me on the landing pad with an intake nurse who sounds, well, *emotional*—and shortly thereafter by a young Asian doctor, who does not.

"Ho-*kaaai*," he says, maybe a touch too brightly to be reassuring. "We going to taking care you now." He pauses, as if to reassure himself that yes, he *is* a trained medical professional, someone well-equipped to take the situation in hand and prevail over the forces of Darkness. But I can hear a hesitation in his voice.

Now, I *know* I am a mess; I've known that since I saw the mangled apparition in my rear-view mirror as I was driving myself down the mountain to the fire station, but I hadn't known just how *bad* a mess. Now, with this quaver in his voice, I have my answer.

"We get all you info from fireman, so you take deep breath now—we starting anesthesia. You count backward from ten to one . . ."

PREFACE

Well THAT was quick . . . sure beats sitting in a waiting room with twelve sneezy kids running all over your feet. I've been in enough emergency rooms in my life to know that getting wheeled in on a gurney with TV cameras and helicopters and reporters is something of a Big Deal—even in the heart of Hollywood. My fifteen minutes are here—and me without a stylist.

Along with the anesthetic, I am flooded with relief. Now I can finally let go, stop fighting, and leave my fate to the pros; there is nothing else to do now but kick back and relax. I have a flickering thought that these might well be my final recollections on this earth, but in all the bustle, I don't have much of a chance to ponder the implications. All I know is that against all reasonable odds, *I've made it!* I've literally looked into the Jaws of Death, pried them off of my face, and snuck out the back! If I die on the operating table, it will be with the knowledge that I'll never again have to prove myself to anyone—for after a lifetime of trying and coming up short, I've finally proved myself to *myself*. This brief moment of victory is mine to savor—and oh are its sirens sweet, even smug.

I feel myself fading away; whatever is going to happen to me now is up to someone else. My last thought as I slip off into oblivion is, *DAMN girl. You actually pulled this one off.* And that little voice inside my head that's kept me going through all of this is telling me: *Job. Well. Done.*

My lips have been ripped off in the attack, so no one can really tell, but I go down smiling.

For the morbidly curious, there is a medical photograph of the meatlump they brought into the emergency room at:

http://imgur.com/bew8pqy
WARNING: Gore. NSFW/NSFL

INTRODUCTION

When in danger
Fear or doubt,
Run in circles.
Scream, and shout.

—Infantry Journal, Vol. 35 (1929)
(Attributed to Heinlein, Wouk, et al)

It's been said that the troubles in our lives can be separated into two categories: "first-world" hardships (those annoyances we grudgingly accept as the cost of living in an advanced society) and "caveman" hardships (those primal nightmares so unfathomably awful, we can only shunt them off to some far recess of our lizard brain and hope they never come out).

There's no denying that my own first-world hardships have been traumatic, even life-altering events. Losing my home to fire, being falsely arrested and jailed, and battling with the predations of the health-insurance industry have been very real and wrenching experiences—certainly nothing to sneeze at. But spirit-sapping as they were, I found comfort in telling myself that these modern travails were piffles compared to caveman hardships like being routed from a cozy rock shelter by a bloodthirsty raiding party, setting out on an ice floe because I could no longer hunt, or huddling behind a meager fire as the saber-tooth tiger waited atop the rock overhang for thirst or hunger to drive me out.

But then I suffered a few of *those* troubles, too—not the least of which was being mauled and nearly killed by the titular bear in the summer of 2008—and I came to realize that modern hardships are basically just caveman ones with money and middlemen added to the equation. The ice floe becomes the rest home. Instead of raiding parties coming to evict us, we have the marshal's office. In either case, our damages affect us with the same cruel intensity; the scars, whether physical or psychic, are just as debilitating, so why bother with the distinction?

By the time the "Ursadent" (as my sainted son took to calling the bear incident) rolled around, I'd been through so many misadventures that it was easier to just ignore society's labels ("bear victim!") and try to look at it all as entertainment while getting on with the mop-up.

Of course simply going numb has its limitations as a coping strategy, but overall, I've found it far more effective than freaking out when confronted with life's "oh shit" moments. Benumbed alacrity has allowed me to brave the sexual minefields of 1970s Playboy mansion, bounce around the dark periphery of Hollywood without losing my humanity, and credibly entertain fallen literary heroes like Alex Haley and monumental whack jobs like Hunter S. Thompson (who once introduced me as "the distaff Hunter S. Thompson," so there you go). It's allowed me to survive a near-drowning under the ice, a serial assault as the featured guest at a gangbang, and a couple of horse wrecks so epic even the saddles had to be put down. Along with a mixed bag of other horrors, I've picked up enough heartache and broken body parts to throw even Job for a loop, but overall, I've found my "WTF? What*ever* . . ." attitude vastly preferable to fretting about things that haven't happened yet and ordering my world around things over which I have no control.

Thumbing my nose at the world's carefully layered conventions may have its unintended consequences, but as I also discovered, there's a certain *purity* in fighting off life's bears without relying on society's protocols and expectations. The scars I've amassed in my battles with the forces of civilization just sit there inside me where they inform no heroic narrative and confer no bragging rights whatsoever, but the Warrior Queen ones, those scars that now crisscross my face, bear undeniable testimony of my small triumph against nature red in tooth and claw—and in These Troubled Times, that's a whole lot more than most of us have to show for our efforts.

INTRODUCTION

Over the course of my long recovery, I came to realize that certain events transcend our personal involvement. The Ursadent was one of those perverse novelties that engaged both media and private imagination alike, for we humans are hardwired for community, and that mechanism in us is triggered by the outlandish and extraordinary. Events such as the baby in the well, the abducted schoolgirl, and the miners trapped in the airless shaft all command our attention and bring us together in ways that flood, famine, pestilence, and pandemic cannot. Thirty, fifty, one hundred years from now, we may have forgotten about the nameless millions who suffered, felled by Pol Pot or the earthquake in Haiti, but we'll still remember the Baby Jessicas and the Donner Parties because the very weirdness of their stories engaged us on a personal level. Most of the time, we are herd creatures self-identifying as Americans, or believers, or vegans, or 49ers fans, but when it comes right down to human catastrophe, we find it less taxing to throw in our lot with the plucky survivor rather than consider the larger human tragedy.

And that, apparently, is where I come in.

I can't count the number of strangers who have approached me on the street and spontaneously hugged me. "I saw you on TV," they say. "You're the Bear Lady, aren't you?" Hundreds, maybe thousands of others have written me letters or sent me posts wishing me well and sharing their own untoward experiences. "You're inspirational," they tell me. "You've given me hope." (Huh? I was dumb enough to get myself mauled by a bear!) And always in the face-to-face conversations comes the inevitable question, the one that defines me and which I grapple with in these stories: "However did you *survive* that?" they ask. And the honest answer is, "Beats me."

Maybe the mental toughness that got me through the attack had its seeds in my early reading list when as a young tomboy-in-training I thrilled to ghost stories, gross urban legends, lurid historical accounts of the ghastly and the grisly. My father's medical textbooks and crime and war photography? I couldn't get enough of that stuff. I was more Wednesday Adams than Nancy Drew, more Richard Gorey than Dr. Seuss. It gave me a certain nonchalance about the grim and gory that inured me to the horror of the mysterious.

Or maybe it's a function of the same ornery streak that once caused my exasperated father to exclaim, "You are the *pushiest* little goddamned broad I've ever met! You just don't know when to quit." While perhaps not the most graceful of character traits, that tendency to persevere has nonetheless stood me in good stead when it comes to first-world challenges like getting stuck in the wrong lane on the 405, forbearing mayhem while awaiting "the next available representative," and prevailing over the perverse nature of inanimate objects—those rusty hinges and leaky toilets, real and metaphoric, that defy with equal perseverance our human efforts to tame them.

But I like to think that my survival has been motivated by an unbounded and lifelong curiosity—the drive to seek out what's just over the mountain and bring it back to share with the pack. After all, that's what scientists and storytellers *do*, and I'm nothing if not an analytical teller of tales.

In any case, I've done it all and chronicled it here for posterity, not because I'm particularly pleased with my exploits but because I believe we also serve who only stand as cautionary examples. I'll even excuse myself further by giving it an altruistic spin: I've lived through this so you don't have to. (You're welcome.)

Nonetheless, if you *should* run into any of the caveman monsters lurking out there in the psychic woods—and chances are, you will—I hope you'll read this and remember: If a little old lady can pull it off, so can you.

So sit back my dears, and let Granny tell you a story. You're not going to *believe* this shit.

WHILE YOU WERE OUT . . .

As that rotten bear was eating my face off, my life didn't pass before me like they always say it will. I didn't take that Final Opportunity to account for my grievous mistakes and misdeeds, nor did I see the flashing white lights that herald the Baby Jesus come to take me home (and presumably reunite me with relatives and once-loved ones I've not the slightest desire to ever run into again—let alone spend my assigned eternity with). Heaven? Hell? Where human interactions are involved, they're all too often one and the same.

No, my dears, the flashbacks came later as I drifted between twilight and infinity, unknowing, unconcerned, and literally faceless in the vast parade of history's unfortunates. No one can really be prepared to meet their death, but somehow when it comes, the act seems so simple one wonders what all the fuss has been about.

My mangled body lies inert as doctors and technicians bark and bustle around me and the tubes that now sustain me. Fantastic machines whirr and hum and shoot their miracle rays while a team of the best-trained scientists and surgeons in the history of our planet set about remaking a person out of a lump of mincemeat. Our most primitive nightmare (being eaten alive by a wild beast) meets our most advanced technology (twenty-first-century Western medicine), all to restore the most superficial yet essential aspect of what defines me as human: My face. My identity. Me.

PART ONE

GOLDILOCKS VS SANTA CLAUS

Today is the red-letter day of my young life. Daddy has just graduated from medical school, Madre has taken leave of her pharmacy practice to birth my new pet sister, and *I'm* on my way to meet Santa Claus! Not some "helper" Santa Claus like Uncle Deforest, who smells like mothballs and stale cigarette smoke and pinches my bottom when no one's looking, but *The Real Actual Santa Claus* who lives at the North Pole. Nearly four years old now and sophisticated in these matters, I know that Santa has his packaging and distribution center up in the Arctic Circle where he keeps his  reindeer, but that after the holiday rush he summers in California—at a place called *Skyforest Santa's Village*—where the light is much better for making next year's cookies and toys, and the weather is decidedly milder.

For reasons that evade me, Daddy and Madre have decided that I'm to be presented at Santa's Court, perhaps even granted a personal audience with the Great Man himself! How they've arranged this is beyond knowing, but my plan is to somehow parlay my parents' distinction into getting an advance look at what gifts and toys Santa has to offer this year, because frankly, they seem to be pretty naïve about what's available out there for kids these days. All Santa's ever left me is a lousy toothbrush and some band-aids. And always an orange. There *must* be more in life. . . .

It's 1955 now, and Grandmother has a big bulbous Philco TV set in her living room. I've *seen* the toys they advertise before the *Lawrence Welk Show* comes on, and I'm betting Santa has too.

Best of all, Santa's reindeer will be there, and I can't *wait* to pet Rudolph! The only animals I've ever seen in person have been behind bars at the zoo or dead in a diorama at the museum, and the closest I have to a pet is the occasional handful of sowbugs I collect from under the stairs of the housing project. (I've named my new sister "Snowball," hoping she'll grow into a furry white puppy, but so far all she does is lie there and gurgle.)

Madre's voice interrupts me. "Put on your sweater, it's cold and snowy up there. You don't want to get another earache." Well, of *course* there's snow. Santa would *melt* without snow. I'm not an idiot. As for earaches, they've tormented me ever since I caught scarlet fever last year; I live in dread of the miserable pain.

"And wear your saddle shoes."

I startle. Madre is in a rush, trying to get the baby swaddled and my father away from his textbooks before he lights up another smoke and starts in on another chapter.

Madre swears by saddle shoes. Clunky, ugly, awkward, the damned things weigh half as much as I do, but when combined with not eating lime Popsicles, saddle shoes are supposed to prevent polio. They say a vaccine is coming, but Madre isn't taking any chances; her concern for my feet borders on the superstitious—as though wearing these expensive talismans will ward off the double whammy of yet another deadly affliction visited upon her stringy little daughter.

Personally, I hate the things. But if I'm going to see the real Santa Claus, it's counterproductive to complain. Fumbling, tongue protruding with determination, I repeat the mantra for a skill that has so far eluded me: *loop the shoestring between your thumb and finger, pinch another loop, wrap it around, and pull it through . . .*

"Hurry up, honey, they're here."

We've hitched a ride up to Santa's place with my cousins, and I'm crammed in the luggage section with the lot of them, nose plastered to the window watching the optical illusions formed as we pass the vertices of the orange groves along the way. I'm fascinated by this orange and green kaleidoscope and the intense perfume of the oranges, but my cousins are engrossed in an even greater wonder.

It's called an Etch-a-Sketch, and if you turn the knobs it makes lines on a screen like a television! And if you turn them at the same time, you can make the lines *curve* and draw pictures! Between the scent of the oranges and this fabulous device, I'm overwhelmed with life's potential.

The mathematical precision of my cousin's toy appeals to the budding scientist in me. There's not much in the physical realm a little girl can manipulate, but this Etch-a-Sketch thing certainly holds intriguing possibilities. If I get the chance, I'm definitely going to mention it to Santa!

When we finally spill out of the car at Santa's Village, the first wave of clear pine and hot gingerbread hits me like the Vicks VapoRub my mother smears into an old woolen sock and pins around my neck to ward off colds. Beyond the parking lot I can see . . . snow! And rough log cottages, and huge spotted cement toadstools, among which scoot grown-up-sized elves in odd pointy shoes. *Can Santa be far away?*

A fat lazy snowflake lands on my eyelash, brushing it like a kiss. No two are alike, they say, but how do *they* know? I bet that somewhere there *are* two that are exactly alike; it's just that scientists haven't found them yet. Someday, I'll prove them wrong! Grandmother has taught me how to search for four-leaf clovers, and when some silly adult tells me there's no such thing, I delight in showing them the ones I've picked from her lawn and preserved in Scotch Tape. I tell them, "You just have to look *really* hard and not give up."

Another snowflake falls on my nose, and crossing my eyes I can see the spiky frozen feathers, like moth antennae under Daddy's microscope. Fascinated, I watch it disintegrate as it melts on my skin.

"There's the candy kitchen over there," says my aunt.

"Let's take the sled up there," says my uncle, pointing to a far summit.

"I've gotta pee," wails my cousin as Madre takes our hands and leads us into Santa's bathrooms and gift shop.

The mass of damp humanity inside is jockeying to get a look at some taxidermy bobcat displayed behind a railing. Green felt booties sit on a table alongside some hand-knit sweaters that my aunt and mother seem especially taken with. There are jack saws and bear traps and woodcraft and furs, all punctuated with the enticing scent of warm candy from a close-by candy kitchen—but nary a toy to be seen.

Someone steps on my foot. Another jostles me into a hewn timber post. I lose my mother's hand and careen into a Christmas tree, poking myself on its sharp needles.

"Can I see Santa now?" I ask, tugging on her coat to right myself. Timid.

"He's very busy, but we'll get in line in a little bit when it stops snowing. Daddy's holding us a place." Madre seems unusually distracted by a rack of painted tea sets. I try to feign interest, but nurse an urgent need to get to the toy workshop before all the good stuff is gone.

Crammed up against a forest of anonymous legs, I sneak a peek outside the window. Santa's hut is at the end of a little arched bridge that crosses an enchanted pond. Festooned with candy canes and pine boughs, it seems the sort of place Santa *would* receive his young admirers. This *must* be the real thing!

A white-picket fence funnels the supplicants toward the candy-striped guard house, and the line to the door stretches back almost to the parking lot. It's snowing hard now, and I can barely make out my father, gamely shifting from one foot to the other and blowing on his hands to keep the circulation going as he shuffles in queue toward Santa's antechamber.

Presently, Daddy's joined by my aunt and cousin. It's becoming apparent that a visit to the actual toyshop probably won't be forthcoming, but at least I might be able to get a good word in with Santa. Madre takes me by the hand and leads me out the door. It's *cold* out here. "Go to Daddy," she says, pointing me in the right direction and giving me a scoot on the butt.

I see Daddy at the head of the line. I see the helper elf beckoning me forward to join him. I see the mass of dark, cold, wet *big* human bodies blocking my path, so I do the rational thing and cut across the snow under the bridge to get to him. I'm not afraid of some snow. And I'm definitely not about to get trampled under any more heedless adult feet.

KEY-RAAACK! SPLASH! Faint yelling from above. I can't see a thing. My skin feels like knives and I can't catch my breath. And it's *cold*!

I am under the ice.

Someone grabs at me and misses. I'm floating away downstream somewhere, drawing into myself, aware of a hard pressure against my ears, but it's more of a roar than the familiar high-pitched thrum I'm used to. I'm not sure what I'm supposed to do, but I know I'm in trouble. Worse, my saddle shoes are wet! Madre is going to have a hemorrhage! Banging into rocks, tumbling, looking up and seeing only darkness, death never occurs to me; it's beyond my scope of experience. More than anything, I'm just curious as to what is happening to me. Numb, yet still observant, I begin to fall asleep. . . .

Then there's a flap and a flurry and the human noise returns as a pair of trousers appears next to my face. Someone is lifting me out of the water. Voices call for blankets and I can hear a lady crying. I don't know the person who has grabbed me, and it's cause for concern; Madre has told me never to let a stranger touch me. I hope she's not mad.

The elf, far from being angry that I've messed up his pretty snow scene, seems to be petrified. I can see him gape-mouthed, flattening his back flat against the door of Santa's hut like a threatened housecat.

Then I see Madre. For the first time in months I have her full attention as she starts toward me as if in slow motion. My rescuer barks something, and the crowd parts to let him through. Madre follows on his heels. "Are you okay?" she asks, anxious, peering into my face. She seems genuinely concerned—I've never seen her anything but unflappable.

Something inside my brain clicks. Never in my life have I been aware of so much attention focused solely on me—and it's all *good* attention. I take a moment to marvel at the sensation of celebrity, the rightness, the simple *power* of it. These people are putty in my hands waiting for me to speak, and after a moment's deliberation, I do.

"I want to see Santa Claus."

And *just like that*, I'm hustled into Mrs. Claus's warm candy kitchen where my icy clothing is removed and replaced with an oversized sweater. Someone rustles up a new pair of dry socks from a wall display and a pair of doll-like leggings from what can only be imagined as a recalcitrant elf. Clucking and bustling with concern, Mrs. Claus wraps me in a warm fuzzy blanket, towels my hair, rubs my feet back into sensation. A candy cane appears (I would have preferred one of those lovely butterscotch clusters) along with a cup of hot cocoa. Madre winces; she's not comfortable with people coddling me, let alone introducing me to chocolate. "Thank you for the candy. Thank you for the cocoa," I recite as the candy ladies coo and fuss. "We're so sorry to have caused you this trouble," says Madre.

I'm basking in all this sugar-spun attention when Mrs. Claus's kitchen goes quiet. Santa himself sticks his head into the room, followed closely by my father who's carrying a stethoscope from his little black bag—this must be one of those "mergencies" he's always alluding to. My father *and* Santa Claus—conferring together in Santa's own candy kitchen! This is working out even better than I'd hoped!

The tableau set, I'm thrilled to be at its center. For the first time in my life, I'm seeded in my element. Madre is right; I *am* the most egocentric little girl in the entire universe, and you know what? I'm *loving* it.

"She'll live," pronounces my father.

"I'm so sorry for the trouble," says my mother. Again.

"Would the little girl like a toy from Santa's bag of presents?" asks Santa.

It's not how I imagined my first meeting with the real Santa, but everything has worked out perfectly. Not only do I have exclusive access to him, it's in the presence of my parents and all these witnesses. It's time for my big play!

"Do you have an Etch-a-Sketch?"

For just a moment Santa stares me down, his snowy eyebrows raised in mild alarm at my audacity. Instead, he rummages around in his bag and pulls out a little knick-knack—a stuffed Rudolph the Red-Nosed Reindeer—which I clutch in a death grip. *A gift from the real Santa!* Okay, so it's not an Etch-a-Sketch, but Madre always says that it's the thought that counts. And it would be hard to snuggle up to an Etch-a-Sketch when I go to sleep tonight anyway.

In these more innocent times, when a near-fatality at a corporate theme park can be bought off with a twenty-five-cent trinket, I'm sure it never occurs to my parents to blame anyone but me for the incident. Strict Methodists, children of the Great Depression, emerging pillars of their community, they're acutely aware of propriety and consequence.

As their eldest daughter, exemplary behavior is my duty, not an option, so I eat my candy cane with chagrin, entirely aware of the stares and whispers all around me. *That's the little girl who fell into the pond.* I think I'm supposed to be ashamed for causing such a commotion. But mixed in with it is a certain sense of triumph. Now Santa knows me *personally*! This can only bode well for Christmases yet to come.

We all leave Santa's Village as inconspicuously as we have arrived and seemingly none the worse for the wear; but with the excitement wearing off and the cold setting in, I start to shiver uncontrollably. My ears begin their familiar throb and stab. I'm too afraid to say anything because I know it will just make Madre mad at me—and I've already caused everyone enough problems for one day. "Your ear is bleeding," says my cousin. He's concerned, even if no one else seems to be.

"Stick some Kleenex in it," says Madre, fashioning a hunk into a makeshift earplug. She's been carrying the same wadded-up tissue in her brassiere my whole life. How it keeps regenerating is a mystery, but when there's a nose to be wiped or blood to be sopped, it's always there at the ready. It's not as though they're going to divert the car to a hospital just because I fell through some ice and nearly drowned.

Against Madre's protests, my aunt persuades my cousin to give me his warm hooded parka and prized Etch-a-Sketch to play with—he's tired of it by now, anyway. *A double triumph!*

Distraction and denial work wonders on earaches, as does the lull of the road and the warm stuffy air inside the station wagon. Still wrapped in Mrs. Claus's blanket and clutching my stuffed toy reindeer, the pain ebbs and I drift off to sleep.

My soggy saddle shoes are nowhere to be seen.

WAS BLIND BUT NOW I SEE

Failure comes hard when you're eight years old, but apparently I've failed my eye test something terrible because the school nurse is in a tizzy when she contacts my parents. "How could you not notice?" she's saying as I stand there in her office trying to decipher the chart from up close so I can memorize the letters for the next time I'm tested. "You're *doctors*! I have no idea how she's managed to do so well in school; without glasses she can't even see the blackboard, and uncorrected, she's legally blind."

But far from being upset about needing glasses, I am elated. *Glasses*, I think, will give me gravitas. Glasses will make me seem older and more serious. Glasses will put me on a more equal footing with my teachers. I've learned that some teachers *hate* smart kids. They seem to resent that we know all the answers to their questions and aren't afraid to correct them when they get something wrong. And it doesn't help matters at all that I'm also the smallest kid in my class. I'm guessing I need all the credibility I can get. Grown-ups wear glasses. Maybe *now* they'll take me more seriously.

I choose a pair of Cinderella-blue cat-eye frames with twinkly silver stars etched into the corners and earpieces. They make me feel so sophisticated, so *adult*. As we drive home that evening, I stare up at my old friend, the moon, and see for the first time that it's round and cratered—and there really *is* a face in it. The street lights aren't just blurs anymore, and they hang from posts and wires with defined shapes to them. I can read signs and tell when people are looking at me now, and even see their lips moving. I can't wait to get to school on Monday morning and show everyone this chic new me.

Instead, my new Coke-bottle glasses complete my transformation from a nerdy little smartass into a total outcast. What few friendly faces once greeted me fade further and further into other cliques until I am left with only my younger siblings, my books, and my piano for company—and I'm not so sure of any of their good intents either.

No one is foolish enough to try to bully me, and no one is overtly hostile, but no one reaches out to me either. Madre compounds my isolation by forbidding me to take part in the wholly routine social activities my classmates take for granted. "You're not old enough to dance," she tells me. "No, you can't go to movies. I need you here to watch your siblings." I don't even bother to ask her if I can get a real haircut or wear tennis shoes instead of these ugly clodhoppers.

"But, Mom," I persist, trying to explain how things work in my world, "the other kids all get to."

"You're not *like* other kids," she tells me. "You're different."

Oh. I hadn't noticed.

I'm nine years old and I'm not allowed to listen to radio (*rock 'n' roll isn't music!*), watch popular television shows (*that garbage*), eat cafeteria food (*junk*), carry a lunch box to school (*use a grocery bag*). I'm forbidden to read comic books (*rot your brain*), wear store-bought clothing (*cousin's perfectly good hand-me-downs*), stay up past eight o'clock at night (*little girls need their sleep*), or go anywhere alone (*ever!*).

Inexplicably, I'm not even allowed to eat butter at the family dinner table, only margarine. "Butter is for grown-ups," Madre explains. "Butter costs too much to waste on kids who don't appreciate it." *But I do. I do appreciate butter!* It sits there in the refrigerator, taunting me, wrapped in its fancy waxed-paper wrapper, but I don't dare sneak a taste. "If you get all the privileges when you're a little girl, you won't appreciate them when you're an adult," she says. I don't yet know how to say "bullshit," but the underlying concept is beginning to take root in my preadolescent lexicon.

My sense of isolation is only compounded by my eccentric home-sewn wardrobe and outdated hand-me-downs; they might as well stick a sign on my back that says "kick me"—in fact, one day someone does, and they do. *Hey,* I rationalize as I nurse my wounded shins, *at least it's some attention.*

Female classmates are already wearing makeup and something called "training bras," carrying purses to school and teetering around on kitten heels with nylon stockings. I'm stuck with my plain little-girl jumpers and saddle shoes with white ankle socks. *They* sport St. Christopher's medals given to them by their boyfriends, and make no attempt to hide their contempt for girls (like me) "retarded" enough not to have one, too. For their part, the boys would rather poke hot needles into their eyes than be caught talking to me, so is it any wonder kids brush by in the halls and sneer, "God girl, you're weird."

Seemingly, it's become the school mantra. Nearly every day, someone, somewhere informs me that I'm outside their range of normal. The Other. Unfathomably freakish.

"God girl, you're weird." Teachers, classmates, random adults I don't even know come up to me and give me their unsolicited assessment.

I don't think I'm weird. I think I'm interesting, well informed, doing my part to advance the public discourse. *What is wrong with these people?*

Maybe it's because I'm so elfin and like to bring in tomato worms for show and tell. Maybe it's because I think Venn diagrams are more interesting than comic books, and prefer Tom Lehrer songs to Elvis Presley ones. Or maybe it's because no one, including the teacher, knows what I'm talking about when I mention Lepidoptera, or wax poetic about the parallax view through my father's binoculars.

Whatever. At ten years old and already a social pariah, I can see my future—staid, cloistered, musty—and it isn't encouraging. As the torment grows worse, my pre-adolescent funk goes into overdrive until one day after school I come across Rusty, a rotten, evil-hearted fifth-grader, tormenting yet another unfortunate outcast like me. For some inexplicable reason, I'm convinced that Rusty has a small crush on me. He asked me to loan him a pencil once and occasionally speaks to me directly instead of behind my back. Something of a social reject himself, he's one of the few people at school I have any sort of connection with.

But today he's cornered a third-grade girl out behind the bathrooms, and the poor thing looks terrified. Neatly dressed, obviously studious,

CHOMP CHOMP CHOMP

she is clutching an armload of books in her soft pink arms and is crying uncontrollably. I turn to assess the situation.

The girl is obese—in a time when fat children are an anomaly—and therefore an automatic target for the Rustys of the world. He towers over us both, ignoring me completely, thoroughly enjoying himself as he taunts and mocks his prey. A long viscous string of snot runs down the little girl's chin and drips onto her ruffled collar. She's sobbing so hard she's having trouble breathing.

"What are you doing, Rusty?" I demand, drawing myself up to my full 3' 6". I'm as offended as a wet hen by this jerk. "Why are you picking on her? She's just a little kid. What did she ever do to *you*?"

"What do you care?" he snorts. "She's fat." Matter of fact, sneering. "Everybody laughs at her."

"Well, I don't. Go away and leave her alone. Shame on you."

He stares at me in astonishment as if I've just commanded him to turn himself into a jelly doughnut. He can't believe what he's hearing, and backs off a few steps to consider his next move. I offer the girl a hankie, and she looks stupefied at this unexpected kindness.

"Thanks," she says. "They're all so mean to us." *Us*.

Overcome, Rusty spits out the only thing that makes any sense to him anymore: "God girl. You're *weird*!" And suddenly it hits me that *yes*, by his dumbass standards—and apparently by everyone else's in this stupid school—I am indeed "weird." And this thought gives me an *enormous* amount of pleasure. It's not an insult, I realize. Coming from a lout like him, it's a compliment!

"Thank you," I say, genuinely flattered. He stalks off in amazement, perplexed and uncomprehending.

I am elated. They can't hurt me anymore. I walk home from school that afternoon, dreaming of the day I can go off to college, a magical place of respect and probity where I'll never have to deal with boors and bullies again. . . .

HOPE AND CHANGE

August 1965

September 1965

I'm sure there are people on this planet who look back on their preteen years with fondness, but I am not among them. Nothing happened during that time to counteract my suspicion that when you're twelve years old, life is just terrible, school sucks, and people are no damned good.

But at age thirteen, two seminal changes convince me that life might hold some promise after all. First, I get contact lenses; then, just when I'd given up all hope of ever pubing, my bony little chest sprouts tits. And not just your little run-of-the-mill, girly knockers, either. In the space of two years, I go from a pimply dwarf beanpole to D-cup Barbie doll, and by the time age fifteen rolls around, no one is more amazed at my transformation than I am. I stand in front of the mirror and just marvel that what once was sere and sinewy at best is now nothing short of lush—voluptuous, even.

Madre finally relents and lets me buy a good bra and shave my legs. I even sneak up to the shopping center after school and buy a tube of mascara at the drug store. People begin to notice this new and improved little blonde. More to the point, they stop calling me "weird."

Even my teachers begin showing me a grudging respect. I've always been an outspoken student, but now they at least make the pretense of listening to what I have to say—and on occasion actually treat me with a certain deference. I am elected to student-body offices and edit our school paper. Folks in the community know my name; church and district officials ask me to speak on behalf of "the youth" of the peninsula at meetings and conferences.

I form a folk singing group that appears in a couple of broadcast television appearances and concert performances around Los Angeles, and my résumé continues to grow. As a high school junior, I am chosen to represent my school as a foreign exchange student. Hippies and jocks alike ask me out on dates. My daddy's rich, my mammy's good-lookin', and I even find myself a hot boyfriend! So why this disquieting sense of misplacement?

Soon I'll be off to France as a "goodwill" ambassador, but I'm not really sure what that means anymore. This spring, in quick succession, every host country I've been assigned has become engulfed in student riots, and the US State Department keeps pulling my student visa and reassigning me elsewhere. Some of my older friends are already fighting the draft call-ups; they'd expected to be going on to college, not off to Southeast Asia to blow up peasant farmers they've no cause against. I can't help but see the irony in our government's skewed policies—trying to keep me safe while doing its best to kill off my classmates.

My parents may be rightly concerned about the escalating political tensions in Europe, but I'm raring to go; I've been working for five years as a church organist, babysitting on weeknights and weekends, and saving every penny I make for this experience. There is *no way* I'm going to let a little anti-American sentiment scare me off.

Besides, after two years on the high-school karate team, I've got a *great* spinning back kick—though I've always suspected that it wouldn't do me much good when confronted with my own complacency and a masher with loaded handgun—or a policeman with a canister of tear gas. I'm not planning to spend my summer ripping up cobblestones and hurling them at gendarmes, but it never hurts to be prepared.

Our karate *Sensei* is a soon-to-be famous master of the art, whose

HOPE AND CHANGE

prowess in the dojo is exceeded only by his rumored prowess elsewhere. He's a cocky son-of-a-bitch to be sure, and enormously proud of his reputation as a ladies' man. His students, me included, hold him in awe—and terror.

When at last it comes time to test for my red belt, we're told that as a special treat, the master himself will conduct the trials. Presumably this means that I'll be sparring against this umpteenth-degree black belt in front of the class, the judges, and one of these new video cameras. The very idea fills me with dread, and by the time we're suited up and seated in a circle around the Sensei, I'm petrified. *Well, if I'm going off to Europe to fight for the running dog lackeys of the capitalist-imperialist oppressors, I'd best confront my demons here first.*

One by one, the master bests my teammates, dispatching them with ever-more-flamboyant combinations and acrobatics. He moves so fast and with such power that his dervish seems to suck all the air from the room. When it comes my turn, it is all I can do to rise, walk into the ring, and keep myself from throwing up at his feet. In his world, girls don't study karate; girls strut around the ring holding placards between bouts, then kiss the winners and hand them trophies. Maybe if I freeze in this bow, he'll show mercy and let me slink away back into the circle?

"And . . . spar!"

The match is on. Gamely, I take a defensive stance and wait for the kick or punch that will propel me across the dojo, leaving me gasping for breath in a heap on the rubber floor mat. Around and around he whirls, thoroughly enjoying this one-sided exhibition. I feel like the sacrificial mouse in a convergence of cats.

And now, he's advancing on me with a dazzling series of front kicks, flying side kicks, spinning flying back kicks, all mere inches from my expensive orthodontia, threatening to end my stage and screen career before it even begins. *This is lunacy,* I think.

For the briefest of moments he pauses, holding a picture-perfect front kick against my ear for dramatic effect, playing to the audience. In the next heartbeat I know he will extend his leg and send me flying across the mat in disgrace. I brace for the blow, and it is in this fleeting moment that I realize he is vulnerable. Without the slightest nuance or technique whatsoever, I cup his legendary heel in the palm of my hand and push it forward with all of my might.

In front of class and spectators, and for perhaps the only time in his subsequent long career on camera, my Sensei falls flat on his ass—bowled over by his own certitude. *There's a lesson in here, and I'd best take it to heart.* Scarlet with embarrassment—and yes, maybe a little bit smug at my unexpected luck—I retake my seat in the circle. He never asks me to spar again.

THE OCCIDENTAL TOURIST

Flying over Hamburg, I'm struck by the orderly green fields below. Unlike America—unlike *myself*—this place strikes me as perfectly planned, sure of itself and its place in the cosmos. "Remember that you are ambassadors for America," says the official who sees us off. "Good luck, exchange students."

I don't need it. The moment we set down in Amsterdam I feel at peace. All the concerns I've had about not fitting in, not being able to find my way or make myself understood, slip away as I fold into the mix of bodies leaving the airport concourse. Unlike anywhere I've been in America, there is an overweening sense of organization here, an elegance that pervades everything I see. The rough edges are smoothed, even polished. It is so easy to blend in.

Eager to immerse myself in this new culture, I don't know what to expect. Will there be wooden shoes? Will I be assailed by oom-pah music? Partly because I'm famished and partly to reassure myself that I've not disembarked into the third circle of Dante's hell, I buy a huge portion of *frites* from a street vendor and realize that while outwardly little but the scenery has changed, something inside me has. Truly on my own, I'm unaccountable for the first time in my life—an American Girl in Socialist Europe, stuffing my face with French fries at the dawn of a new age. Cautious but elated, I set out to meet my destiny.

The hotel where the bus lets me off is sparse and dingy, and my host family never shows up to claim me. I've been sitting here in this fleabag for three days now while the field representative tries to find a family willing to take me in. All the other students have been placed with a motley selection of Netherlanders, the earnest, uncomfortable pleasantries hastily exchanged in the hotel lobby, the luggage gathered as my fellows clatter off on their extended blind date out the door to their summer adventures.

Secretly, I'm relieved when the representative hands me a cashier's check and tells me to hold tight here at the hotel for the foreseeable future until someone contacts me. They'll find me a host family and be back to make belated introductions shortly.

I never see her again.

The hotel overlooks Vondelpark, Amsterdam's equivalent of Manhattan's Central Park, and it's situated right across from the Heineken Brewery. I don't drink, but the milling throngs below me apparently do. The Vondelpark is swarming with people: occupiers and passersby, the boisterous spillover from the May riots in Paris, student backpackers hitchhiking through Europe, random homeless folks, cheerful beggars and junkies, rockers and their legions of zoned-out groupies. All these are encamped amid the radicals and the riff-raff; the tie-dyed, the leather-fringed, and the psychedelicized, crowded into a rapturous stupor. The formal contours of the park are punctuated by nonstop music and dancing, as naked kite flyers and a veritable *Luftwaffe* of Frisbees fill the air with color and movement. I've never seen anything like this!

Future parliamentarian Danny the Red, whose impassioned screeds I've been reading back home in *Ramparts* magazine, lectures in the afternoons, rallying the troops to nothing short of political revolution. Iron Butterfly rips a stony hour-long performance of *In-A-Gadda-Da-Vida* to ecstatic reception as the sweet funky smell of pot, hashish, and Turkish tobacco wafts everywhere—from the storefronts and through the walls of my hotel room—pervading the entire district.

For the first few days, I'm just content to watch the show, soak up the ambience, and spend my stipend drinking coffee and gobbling up *force majeure* Indonesian curries in neighborhood bistros. I've always considered myself an adventurous sort, but I've pledged to the exchange service, my parents, and more importantly, myself, that I'll steadfastly represent my community and my country here on this foreign soil. This means obeying the laws of my homeland: no drinking, no smoking drugs, and no fornication before marriage. I look up from my chicken tikka as the waitress, smiling, offers me a toke from a fat spliff someone has left her as a tip. *Darling, you're definitely not in Palos Verdes anymore.*

As I leave the restaurant, an older man approaches me and asks for my autograph. From what I can translate of his fractured English, he's mistaken me for Barbra Streisand or Doris Day—I can't figure out which (that I'm a fifteen-year-old schoolgirl notwithstanding). As he jabbers, a crowd begins to gather and some Italian guy pinches me on my ass. Instinctively, I whirl and the startled fellow gets the blade of my palm in his temple. Momentarily stunned, he shakes out of it and begins hollering invective at me.

Have I blown it already? I just barely got here, and now I'm about to start an international incident! How were we supposed to know that molesting young women is considered acceptable behavior around here? *Is it?* Someone else shoves me back toward him and I see my carefully crafted ambassadorship crumbling into a sea of bad teeth and angry faces. The Italian guy is calling for the *politie*. Has he mistaken me for a prostitute?

Just when all seems lost, a longhaired hippie-freak breaks through the crowd and rescues me, hooking my arm and leading me off through the rough mob into the Vondelpark. He sits me down on the grass, wordlessly offers me an orange. Later he lets me play his cello and picks up his Martin twelve-string guitar. Somewhere Judy Collins is singing and I find the tenor line beneath her. *Suzanne takes you down . . . to her place by the river . . .*

The crowd that gathers here to listen to us is decidedly kinder, inclusive, communal. They've not a clue who I am, yet they accept me without question—how unlike the insular little social groups I'm used to back in the US.

What am I supposed to be learning here? Aren't these the people Madre warned me about?

I'm truly at a loss, but there is something reassuring in the chaos around me. The vibes are friendly, welcoming, and for once I don't feel as though I have to answer to anyone. It's an odd sensation. When the boy zeroes in for a kiss, I don't push him away. He tastes of tobacco and honey.

After a couple of weeks of this desultory existence comes a cable from the exchange headquarters instructing me to buy a train ticket and head to Rotterdam where I am to meet with a woman who will give me temporary quarter in Breda—*just until they can find me a family*, the exchange is careful to note. I get the sense that I'm baggage to these people. Why does no one want me? Is it something I said or did? More to the point, why did they bring me over here to exchange, if there is no family to exchange me *for*?

I decide not to bother my parents with this detail; the news will take days if not weeks to get to my parents by post, and by then I'll be off to another family, country, whatever. It's my first inkling that perhaps the US State Department is not as well organized as they might have us believe. I could likely disappear here for the summer and no one would ever know who I really am—or where I went. It's an enticing option until I remember my vow to be a good American citizen. Looks like my career as a student radical will have to wait.

Breda, eh? Sure, I'm game. This Mrs. Koch lady can't be any weirder than Purple Tab LSD Guy who markets his wares under the tarp next to "my" spot in the Vondelpark. His pet ferrets keep breaking free and gnawing their way into his stash. (For the record, "electric" ferrets are less charming than one might imagine.) It will be nice to have a stable roof over my head again.

My park-mates tell me that Breda is a gorgeous medieval town and I should definitely go. "We'll still be here if you want to come back," says my longhaired hippie-freak friend.

I meet Mrs. Koch at Schiphol Airport, and am relieved to see that she not only looks normal, she's actually a rather poised and elegant middle-aged lady. She is also quite direct in her expectations. "I am Mrs. Koch. You may call me Mrs. Koch. You will follow me now," she says by way of introduction. Then she turns on her heel without another word and walks off toward the parking lot.

What have I gotten myself into? I pick up my bag and obey. Her

THE OCCIDENTAL TOURIST

Karmann Ghia is waiting. Belatedly, I realize I've not had a chance to empty my bladder since my morning coffee several hours ago. It's a two-hour drive to Breda—in a car with that harsh Volkswagen suspension. I'm too intimidated to ask her to pull over.

IMMACULATE REJECTION

The moment I see Breda's pretty town square, I know I've made the right choice by coming here, although by this point, the only thing that's been on my mind for the last hour and a half is not suffering an internal rupture. When we get to her apartment I excuse myself with as much grace as possible and enjoy perhaps the most satisfying piddle of my life.

Mrs. Koch is listening outside the bathroom door. In she comes as I go out—and ostentatiously begins spraying Lysol on the toilet seat. "You must clean up after you," she instructs me curtly. "It isn't nice." I was sitting down, so I'm pretty sure I've hit the bowl, but ho-kay, my hostess is a neat-freak—I've been warned that the Dutch are extraordinarily tidy. *Maybe I'll learn something.*

I can't wait to settle in and start exploring the neighborhoods around Jan Liebenheiser Stratt, but it seems that first there are important things to attend to; Mrs. Koch hands me a cloth and instructs me on the proper way to scrub out her bathtub. It appears perfectly clean to me, but whatever, I'm certainly willing to adapt to my host family's cultural peculiarities. "Cherms," she tells me conspiratorially, and resumes her spraying.

Next, the kitchen pans could use a good scrubbing, and then the sheets need to be changed on her beds. Apparently, I've been taken in as a housemaid, not an exchange student. But since this is only temporary, why not make the most of it? My little garret in the attic is sunny and pleasant, and Mrs. Koch's apartment is nothing if not "spic und span"— unlike the hotel I'd been staying in. Besides, I have a secret weapon; my younger sister once taught me a great way to get out of doing chores at other people's homes.

IMMACULATE REJECTION

Thanksgiving dinner was always a Big Family Affair for us, with massed generations of far-flung aunties and cousins all gathered for a formal sit-down feast on linen-covered tables at one or another of our homes. Yes, the food was uniformly delicious and the tables were bountiful, but they produced a boatload of dirty china, silver, and crystal to hand wash and dry afterwards. Inasmuch as I was the oldest girl-child and supposedly the most "responsible," the task always came to me to wash the trays full of expensive tableware while the adults enjoyed their after-dinner libations and conversations in the living room.

My younger sister, Laurie, detested the annual chore almost as much as I did, but she was far more devious in finagling her way out of it. Whining worked for the first couple of years, and then she tried employing outright defiance—with limited success. Somehow she always ended up "persuaded" to get out into the kitchen and pick up a dishtowel. *Now!*

Finally, the year she hit puberty, she'd had enough. At meal's end, when Madre gave the signal to start clearing the table, she jumped up from her seat and began gathering Aunt Sally's Limoges with suspicious alacrity.

Delighted to have her help, I set to sudsing and soaking the silver while the womenfolk cleared the table and carefully stacked the dirty dishes and stemware on the counters for us to wash. Then we two were left to the kitchen chores while the little kids went outside to play and our elders retired to their various topics and turbulences.

When Laurie was sure all the adults had left the kitchen, she picked up a Baccarat wine goblet, twirled the stem between her thumb and forefinger, and then with a little flourish and flick of her finger dropped it to the tile flooring where it shattered at her feet. The tinkling of expensive crystal sent several aunties running into the kitchen. "Oops," said Laurie. "Here, let me have the towel," said Madre. And with a sly wink that only I could see, Laurie took off for the library and whatever book she was currently engrossed in. "*That's* how you do it," she smirked to me on the way back home. *Damned impressive* was all I could think.

I'm not about to chance Mrs. Koch's ire with that little stunt, but a few deftly managed fumbles and intimations of clumsiness are enough to get me out of kitchen sink duty. When she learns that I enjoy cooking, we make a deal. I'll cook, she'll clean, and once she tastes my bakery goods, Mrs. Koch actually warms to me as a houseguest. She even invites her girlfriends over for tea so she can introduce me to them and feed them my cookies and ice cream pastries. I can't really complain; it's sure a lot cheaper living here than it was in the Amsterdam hotel, and besides, my afternoons and evenings are free to explore the medieval town and all of Breda's lovely parks and architecture.

Dating back to the 1200s, the gothic *Grote Kerk* is an easy walk down the narrow one-lane streets from the apartment, and after Mrs. Koch's daily clean routine, it's nice to be able to go outside and breathe some city dust and automobile exhaust for a change. One of the oldest buildings in a country of old buildings, the cathedral takes up a whole city block, its stone walls an imposing fortress against the neighboring grocers and milliners should they ever plot revolt or rampage. Over three hundred feet high, with a spire too tall to see from the sidewalk, this ornate-spooky edifice is too compelling for me to pass by without poking my head in to see what's inside.

What is the protocol for entering a cathedral? I bow my head and try to look pious as I pass the long wall of flickering candles in the narthex. It's attended by scary-looking ladies in black I assume to be nuns, but they're busy with their matches and candles, so I'm able to slip along the dark wooden partitions into a cavernous sanctuary. The back wall is punctuated by the coolest pipe organ I've ever seen. The thing is enormous, soaring a hundred feet to the arched ceiling, with literally thousands of pipes that have been newly gilded with filigree and topped with the royal Dutch coat of arms. In contrast to the musty windows and dark woods all around me, the organ looks newly refurbished. And since I'm a pipe organ fanatic just itching to compare its ancient keyboards with the modern console I'm used to, I sneak up to the organ master's chamber and have me a look at this!

Halfway up the stairway, tucked away in a little nook, there's a weathered plaque on which are engraved the names of this cathedral's organ masters—going all the way back to 1492. Ever since I got off the

IMMACULATE REJECTION

plane, I've been trying to put my finger on why I feel so different here than I do in the US. The shops are similar, the food is familiar, even much of the music is the same. But standing here on this landing it finally hits me. There's a *refinement* here that America simply hasn't had the time to burnish. Like a bunch of rowdy bumpkins set loose in an art museum, we simpletons haven't yet developed the background and perspective to appreciate the oil paintings to the cartoons. We may have the money, but we sure can't buy the class.

I've been in dozens of holy spaces in my life, but this is my first honest-to-God cathedral. Sitting up here in the choir loft, the heavy sensation of quietude is nearly overwhelming. And the lingering scent of old wood and granite and seven hundred years of worshipful humanity almost *demand* my reverence. The battered purity of this place speaks to me, though I'm a bit sketchy about what it's trying to say.

It's not entirely welcoming; there's a vague *Frankenstein* air about the place, but it's intrinsically familiar at the same time. Coming from California, I'm leery of huge stone buildings without earthquake retro-fittings, but the inside of this place definitely feels like shelter from the storm—if not so cavernous it's capable of generating its own weather patterns.

It's hard not to be aware of all the lives that must have been devoted to building and maintaining the *Great Church* over the centuries—and all the joys and tragedies that must have passed through here with them. As I watch, another old woman dressed in black scrubs the floor of the aisle to the altar, one small patch among acres awaiting her attention. Even all the way up here, the scent of her lemon and beeswax mixes with the hewn oaken timbers as the late afternoon light streams through the colored glass of the sacristy windows. *Sanctification by charwoman.* Maybe my dirt-obsessed hostess has the right idea after all. Maybe cathedrals are the cities' version of the wide-open spaces where the troubled go to find stillness.

As if in kinship with my frontier forefathers, I look out over the balcony of the choir loft and cup my hands to my mouth. A screech owl imitation would be overkill, but the soft chesty hoot of a Great Horned owl will keep them guessing for months. The acoustics are magnificent. *Whowhoo—whooo, who* comes my brief contribution to the glorification of the Catholic Almighty.

Soon after, the State Department notifies me again. I'm to travel to Paris and meet up with a family on the way to their summer villa in Arcachon, a casino town across the bay from Saint Jean Cap Ferrat. I'm told I'll be spending the rest of the summer with them there on the Riviera.

I can do that.

Mrs. Koch and I make our relieved—and sparkling clean—goodbyes, and on a foggy summer day I make my way back to Schiphol to catch a plane to Le Bourget Airport in Paris, France.

LAPS OF LUXURY

"How do you like zee new car?" asks Monsieur Beaufont, the affable and courtly textile magnate who is to be my new host father. His English is as halting as my French, but we're both doing our best as he leads me from the terminal to his new silver BMW 2800CS in the parking lot. I am enough of a car aficionado to know that this unassuming sedan is something on another level altogether than the Mustangs and Corvettes my classmates drive back home. Daddy's a big Formula One racing fan, and we'd spent the year before I'd left restoring the guts of a 1927 Model A Ford, so I actually *do* know a bit about rolling stock when I reply, "Ah! *C'est marvelleuse!*"

"Do you want to drive eet?" he asks me.

Ohhh yeah. And I do; all the way down the A10 from Paris through the Bordeaux wine country at 200 KPH. This is turning out to be a great summer after all.

"We weel also make you ze capitan of ze speedboat," he tells me. Yes, he has a ski boat, too.

Arcachon is utterly charming, with architecture best described as a cross between Tuscan villa and Victorian manse. M. Beaufort's summer home is close by the beach off a little side road, its stone walls covered with bougainvillea and climbing roses, and its interior rooms whitewashed plaster and polished woods. The family has been coming here for years, he tells me.

M. Beaufort introduces me in turn to his young son, Aaron, and thirteen-year-old daughter, Babette. Dark and heavyset like her father, she looks at me as though I am the most exotic thing she's ever seen. "Zees zwill be her summer to learn En-gleesh," he says tactfully. I am relieved to grasp his true intentions in inviting me here to join them, as no wife is apparent here in the household.

His tall, imperially slim sister, Estelle, is here for the summer too, the acting mistress and hostess of the house. She's a professor of French literature at Brown University, which comes as a huge relief to me as my confidence in my ability to express myself is fading by the moment as I confront all these new faces.

"And this jolly woman," M. Beaufort tells me, "is Cook." He gives her no name, just "Cook," and she, either not understanding a word of English or simply choosing not to be sociable, grunts and goes about deboning some mid-sized creature she's preparing for this evening's supper. "And here are the house maids, and the driver." I've never been in a private home with such a large staff.

M. Beaufort leads me up a wide mahogany staircase to the south tower of the house. An open window lets in the scent of the sea. The sun plays over the crisp white bedspread as gauzy curtains blow against the whitewashed wall. I can hear the village bustling below, and it strikes me that I've stepped straight from Dutch Purgatory onto a stage set from a Luis Bunuel film. "Zis will be your room," he tells me.

As I unpack and dress for dinner, someone is playing Chopin études in the gathering room downstairs. The air is ripe with promise—instead of Mrs. Koch's Lysol.

My days settle quickly into a pleasant routine. I rouse around ten, enjoy a *café au lait* in the sunroom with whoever is up, then walk down to the beach to work on my tan, or wander the narrow streets through town. When I can catch her, I tag along with Cook (I never do get her name) on her twice-weekly shopping rounds. The little specialty food shops fascinate me; there's nothing like this back home. Fine meats cut to order from the *boulangerie*, fresh greens and vegetables carefully chosen from the grocer's open-air stalls, fruits and berries from Madame's garden, breads from the baker, cheeses from the *fromagerie*, and always, *always* some fabulous cake or pastry for Saint's Day desserts—for M. Beaufort has a fabled sweet tooth.

LAPS OF LUXURY

The family takes its Saint's Day celebrations very seriously, each one requiring a "special" dinner—though they all seem special to me. Better still, it seems there are as many Saints as there are visitors to the family table, and *Monsieur* insists that his guests are well fed. Watching Cook shop for these feasts is an education in itself: I learn that the basis of fine cooking is fine ingredients, and there is an art to selecting them. Though she certainly has her schedule full preparing meals for up to twenty people every day, Cook takes the time to show me how to choose an artichoke, how to test fish for freshness, and how to cajole a butcher into selling her that choice cut he's keeping in the back for a special customer.

Sometimes she allows me into the big country kitchen to help her chop, bone, dice, observe; she seems grateful for the company, though she speaks no English. We don't exchange many words, but we don't really need to; kitchens the world over share a common language of taste, aroma, texture, and the pure joy of cooking something wonderful for people who will appreciate it. In this one summer, I learn the culinary foundation that will serve me for the rest of my life.

Our afternoon dinners are a thing of splendor. Savory roasts, soups, and sauces ringing with unexpected flavors, fresh vegetables in combination, beans, salads, and relishes. That fabulous bread. That *butter*.

And Monsieur Beaufort is a wine aficionado. He's on vacation, *par Dieu*, and he's going to enjoy every last bottle he's stocked in his ample cellar. Each meal is accompanied by multiple bottles of at least one vintage—which he pours for children and adults alike. Even the eight-year-old gets a glass or two. I, on the prissy other hand, hold firm to my convictions. As a US citizen, I'm not allowed to drink alcohol until I'm twenty-one, and that's that. That I'm in France now, that the State Department isn't watching, that Bordeaux has just had one of the best harvests of the century, and I'm being *ridicule* notwithstanding. He shakes his head sadly and chides me for my foolishness.

"*Very* dee-li-cee-yews wa-teur," he smirks as he pours my nightly glass of Vichy. In retrospect, I want to kick myself insensate every time I think about it.

CHOMP CHOMP CHOMP

It's Friday morning, and although I've only been here for two weeks I'm beginning to feel like a pampered regular. Yesterday we spent the day on Monsieur's powerboat, waterskiing in the bay over to Cap Ferat, and tomorrow we will be driving *en famille* into town to hear mega pop-star Sacha Distel in concert. All we need is for Princess Grace to show up in a white Mercedes gull-wing convertible—and sure enough, she does, complete with liveried bodyguard. What could possibly be more perfect?

Maybe lying in the sand in my pink and brown bikini? Golden, tanned, nearly sixteen, and as lush as I've ever been? A warm breeze brushes my skin, while the morning sun bakes my covered parts in the most delicious heat. Half-heartedly trying to read French *Vogue*, I'm actually just watching the early risers stumble down to the beach, and smiling at all the late revelers doing the walk of shame in last night's evening attire. (Technically, I'm a bit *outré*; arriving at the beach before 2 p.m. is considered a serious faux pas here.) The only other people around are a few tourists and the bistro staff setting up for lunch on the beachfront patio. I love having this fabled beach all to myself.

As the day goes on, the beach begins to fill with pastel sun umbrellas, boisterous children, slinky models, and well-fatted and hairy industrialists like my host. Other than the skimpy bikinis on the men, folks look much the same as beach-goers anywhere—only sleeker—and I'm totally comfortable sitting here alone among them. Confident, even.

My new woman's body and this soft bikini startled me when I first saw them together, but because this was the more sedate of the only two bathing suits in the whole store that fit both my top *and* my bottom, Madre, who had come along to supervise my travel wardrobe, had no choice but to let me buy it. *It's perfect for me*, I decide, and as I'm congratulating myself there comes a soft voice, "Pardon, mademoiselle . . ."

Before me stands Adonis, a freaking god made flesh. He's backlit by the afternoon sun, and all I can see of him is bronzed abs, caramel eyes, pillowy lips—and his red *maitre de naigeur* Speedos. The lifeguard. I look around; *have I done something wrong?*

He smiles. "You are Américaine?"

"Yes."

LAPS OF LUXURY

"Californie?"

"Oui." *How did he know?*

He haunches next to me, sitting on his heels. I am speechless. My five years of French class desert me entirely. He smiles, and his beautifully chiseled face turns ethereal. What is this jaw-droppingly gorgeous man (*MAN!*) doing sitting here next to *me*? I am genuinely flummoxed. The only naked male skin I've been this close to before has been on high school boys—and sports chums at that. And none of them has ever smelled like *this*. I feel my breath leave me, yet I'm not in the least bit alarmed.

"Tu est etudent au Université?" ("*Tu*," the familiar) he asks.

"Um, non?"

Despite his lousy English and my miserable French, I am able to gather that his name is JeanClaude, and he's a grad student in microbiology at the University of Bordeaux. He's working here for the summer. He finds me attractive. He wants to take me out to dinner with some friends and then to the casino. He doesn't suspect I'm only sixteen.

Well, hot damn!

"I'll have to ask my host," I tell him. Unfazed, he says he will introduce himself to my surrogate father and formally ask his permission to see me this afternoon after he finishes work. I give him the address. He smiles again. I am dazzled.

In the evening, JeanClaude shows up in a crisp white dress shirt, perfectly tailored slacks, and soft leather loafers. I'm wearing the little black dress I've packed away just in case, and strappy gold sandals that match my hair. M. Beaufort beams like a proud papa, and little Babette's eyes pop. I feel like the ingénue in a James Bond movie.

Yes, the evening is elegant and easy and glittering and glamorous, and just as promised, he has me home by midnight.

"I will see you tomorrow, *Fifi*." A statement, not a question.

Those excellent lips brush the length of my cheekbones after a long soft kiss goodnight; he trails one finger down my neck, my shoulder, my forearm. It takes me forever to get to sleep.

CHOMP CHOMP CHOMP

Over the next weeks, I work on my French, he works on his English, and we both work on each other. His little *pensione* on the strand is dark and smells of wet swimwear, bamboo, and grass mats—and us. The tiny room is furnished with a makeshift shelf of textbooks and a little bed covered with a bright cotton throw—and not much else. Hanging wooden beads separate the single room from the bath. There is a towel somewhere. To me, this is what heaven must look like.

To his great credit, JeanClaude respects my technical virginity, but in all other respects, the man is a virtuoso. *If this is what it's gonna be like when I finally get laid, I'm gonna be one happy camper; I was made for this stuff.* The rest of the summer is gone far too quickly; it seems one always falls in love at the journey's *end*. . . .

The day I leave, I realize that all the oxytocin my endocrine system has sent coursing through my veins as a result of this grand love affair has exacted its price. I've said goodbye to my wonderful hosts, taken one last walk through town to the beach, kissed my beautiful lover at the train station and promised to write. But the exhilaration of heading for home is tempered by an awful sense of loss—not of *him* so much, or even of that moment that was *us*. It is the loss of part of *myself*. I've left my childhood in that little grass room by the sea, returning as a woman now—a woman who will neither have this crystal moment of transition nor her first taste of "adult" loss ever again. And this realization makes me ineffably sad.

They say you're not supposed to get this close to someone and then leave their life forever. Suddenly I understand why they tell you to "save" yourself for marriage. Not because of some vague moral compunction, or out of fear of "cheapening" the brand, but because the wrenching away, the sudden physical withdrawal from all those lovely endorphins after having had free access long enough to get hooked on them, feels plumb unhealthy. As to whether the pleasure of the memories they carry offsets the *pain* of the memories they carry, well . . . it depends on my mood.

Yet in the midst of my hormonal snit, the loss of innocence is tempered by something far more profound, something I wouldn't trade for all the world. It's the reassurance that I'm truly not just some geeky little schoolgirl anymore. I'm desirable –and desired by a highly desirable man at that! A powerful realization for someone who's had to rely only on her brains all her life. *Glory be and pass the gravy; now I can finally get by on my looks!*

On the train to Hamburg, I write a pathetic little love letter. I know this has been a summer fling, and I know I'll never see this man again, but I can't stop pining for the romantic fairytale I've left behind. Later, I'll have it edited for grammar and clarity by a sympathetic French teacher—a disappointed one, who understands the language of doomed romance.

IS THAT ALL THERE IS?

I know what I want, yet I'm stuck with these mindless, careless, horny kids in the most superfluous year of our lives. The whole world is happening out there, and here we are just killing time until we can get out and live.

It's late August, and Chicago has exploded into riots, mankind has landed on the moon, Woodstock portends a cultural tsunami, and all I can do is spend the entirety of this autumn pining. My senior year is ahead of me and college applications are waiting to be written and submitted. But I don't care. After my own "summer of love" it all seems so redundant.

My senior yearbook photo shows a self-contained, perhaps-too-serious young woman with sexy eyes and a Mona Lisa smile. I think it suits me.

We all make it through the year, they accept my application to UCLA (along with half my class, it seems), and I graduate with honors and acclaim—my whole future dangling low and ripe for the plucking. But all I want to do is lie on the beach and avoid thinking about the future—and miss my lost love. There's the excitement of going off to university, sure, but why does it just seem like more of the same?

Walking home from the last day of classes, watching my classmates speed off down the hill in their expensive cars, they're all carefree, honking and yelling and full of exuberance, anticipating whatever it is newly liberated eighteen-year-olds anticipate.

Me? Not so much. I've finally ditched my virginity, having decided

IS THAT ALL THERE IS?

that it is of little use anyway now that birth control is readily available to unmarried women—it's just one more thing to get out of the way so I can get on with my life. A friend of a friend is kind enough to do the honors in his cramped and cruddy little apartment near the UCLA campus on Stoner Avenue (of course.) We've made a brief pretext of dating, but both realize we're hopelessly mismatched and have quickly moved back on track with our separate lives.

Having managed to end my high school career with straight As and more listings in the yearbook than anyone before (or possibly since), I'll soon be off to one of the better universities on the planet in certainly one of its most fabled locales. Moreover, I've survived a lonely childhood and privileged adolescence that has already claimed the sanity of more than a few of my peers.

I should be *thrilled*. I should be *proud*. I should feel like I've *accomplished something*. And yet, clutching the remnants of my now-empty locker to my bosom for what I hope will be the last time, all that comes to me is smoky-voiced chanteuse Peggy Lee's dispirited plaint, "Is That All There Is?" Thirteen years—three-freaking-fourths of my entire life—spent in classrooms, and what do I have to show for it? A stupid piece of paper with my name spelled wrong and a head full of redundant information. I can't even find a decent boyfriend.

FLUSHED

Last night while we slept, a group of my youngest sister's friends celebrated the end of summer school by stealth toilet-papering our house, wrapping it 'round and 'round, roof to foundation in multi-colored butt wipe. Ostensibly this is a demonstration of their high regard, but there is also a certain element of terrorism in knowing that a pack of drunken children were able to access our home and defile it so thoroughly without even alerting the family dog. It looks as though some demented carnival troupe has come through and used the place as a rest stop.

My mother has commanded us (meaning me) to remove the offending eyesore, "Before the neighbors see it." But because we're living in Madre's world, we're not to simply pull it all down and throw it in the trash bin. No, because poverty could strike at any moment, we're to save the toilet paper—every last sheet—and stuff it into used grocery bags she's pulled from her pantry. No need to waste perfectly good toilet paper.

I know from past experience that the bags of used paper will be placed in the kids' bathrooms—leaves, grasses, spider webs, and all—to be used instead of store-bought until every last bagful has been flushed into our overloaded septic system. Her reasoning here is two-fold. Not only is this a dandy way to save money and conserve valuable natural resources, it's also inducement to us kids to dissuade our friends from TPing our house—a reminder every time we sit down to "go" that associating with villainous cohorts, however minor their transgressions, exacts its price.

I've commandeered a platoon of very likely the same neighborhood kids who pulled this prank in the first place, and set to directing them in the cleanup. They'll do this because they know that if they don't, my retribution will be terrible the next time I babysit for them. Neighborhood pranks are one of those anthropological phenomena I hope to study next month when I get to UCLA and finally leave this madness to join the Real World—the world where rational thought and *normalized* behavior are ascendant, and where most likely no one is forced to gather up used toilet paper unless it's as an initiation rite or political statement or something *meaningful*.

Usually this sort of imposition would grate on me, but on this lovely morning, life is almost cheery as the kids hop-to under my orders. I'm nearly done, and the late-summer beach is calling my name, so I stuff toilet paper and stack the bags in the garage without undue resentment. By the time all this paper is gone, I will be too. Besides, when we're through, it's a simple matter to grab my ten-speed and bicycle off down the hill to the ocean.

Once I get to Redondo Beach, it's clear sailing all the way to Santa Monica—provided I can avoid the drunk drivers who follow on my tail and try to sideswipe me, or grab at my ass and yell out the window, "Hey honey, it's illegal to pedal pussy on the street." *Oh. These. Wags.* Like I've never heard *that* one before.

I've taken to carrying raw eggs in a little pouch on my handlebars; eggs, I've discovered, are highly precise projectiles that make both a satisfying *splat* on rear windows and an effective distraction while I swerve off into the nearest escape alley. Creeps in cars notwithstanding, I love the long, strenuous ride to and from the beach, and the reward once I get there is mile after mile of the graded bike route that's recently been constructed along the South Bay coastline. Maybe one of these days I'll meet someone attractive out here riding along the same bike lane, and we'll connect, ride together for a while, stop somewhere shady. . . .

So far, my fantasy remains only that—a fantasy. I pedal alone with my diminishing expectations, but today the surf is up, so I park my bike on the sand and spend a couple of blissful hours bodysurfing the pier break at Hermosa. Here in the water, propelled by the force of the waves, gravity made liquid, the same mindful mindlessness returns—at least it does until I misjudge timing a giant set of breakers and get swallowed up in the churn.

Wave after wave rolls me along the ocean floor, sandpapering my flesh, sucking the blood from my brain and the breath from my lungs until mercifully tossing me ashore to hurl my pizza and lie gasping in the wash. I crawl back to my bike, shaken and humiliated, and curl up on my towel in a miserable little ball of nausea. *Please don't let anyone have seen that.*

Eventually the hot sand brings me back around, but newly sobered and wondering what ever compelled me to venture out alone into eight-foot surf! It's been a long time since I've confronted death this immediate. The ocean has always been my friend, my solace, the place to go to let my brain go numb when things get too complicated. But that was just *mean.* The damned thing betrayed me. Not sure who else to blame for my bravado, it only makes sense to take it out on the ocean. *Stupid ocean . . . I'm never going into you again.*

My paperback copy of *Atlas Shrugged* is stashed in my bike bag, waiting for me to finish it—someday. This seems as good a time as any. Existential objectivism has certainly had its more scholarly proponents, Sartre and Nietchze among them, and Ayn Rand can reduce even the most elegant argument to sophistry, but somehow after my shake-up, I prefer the potboiler to the profound. Let's see what John Galt has to say about the whims of King Neptune. *You seek escape from pain. You exist for the sake of avoiding punishment.* Oh *puh-leeeze.*

Half engrossed and half grossed out, I notice a jogger out of the corner of my eye. He's running up the beach toward the pier, his hyacinth trunks blue against his golden tan and the misting surf. As he comes closer I can see his perfect musculature, his flowing blond hair, his dazzling white teeth. All around me other people are noticing him too.

Oh my GOD! It's Robert-freaking-Redford jogging along the tide line of Hermosa Beach! What is he doing down here?

It's all I can do to keep myself from getting up and following him down the beach, but along with everyone else in the vicinity I simply stare slack-jawed as he approaches, willing him to veer in my direction—and stare after him as he passes, oblivious to my mental entreaties. I fixate on his perfect ass as he runs away and out of my life.

I swear by my life and my love for it that I will never live for the sake of another man. Sounds reasonable enough on its surface, but I'm betting Ayn Rand never met Robert Redford. Better to lose myself in the pages of this goofy novel than fall for another handsome stranger I meet on a sunny summer beach.

The afternoon deepens and the sand gets hotter. I am half-dozing over my book, chin to forearm, elbows propped in the sand, when I notice those hyacinth-blue trunks coming back my way again. This time they stop and speak to me: "The ultimate dénouement of free-market capitalism is monopoly, of course. And arguably an aristocracy."

My eyes follow the trunks up the torso, past the golden chestly curls and the impossibly broad shoulders to the beaming face. It's him! Redford! He sure *looks* like Redford anyway, but of course my common sense tells me he's not. For one thing, he's talking to me. I jerk to attention.

"Johnny M.," he introduces himself. "You're sitting on my spot."

"No, this is MY spot," I protest. "I sit right here every time I come down."

"You're stoned?"

Huh? Oh. "Every time I come down *to the beach*. I live up there on the hill."

"Ahh. One of *those* girls . . ." As I'm soon to discover, the hill people of the city and the hill people of the country are of two different social orders. In this iteration, I'm perceived as part of the privileged, sophisticated one, not the inbred one beset with unresolved dental issues.

"I noticed you're reading Rand. Don't you find her a little pedantic?"

As a pick-up line, it's original if a bit lame, but I'm not put off in the least. In fact, this guy is so aesthetically compelling that I'll forgive him anything, even innate intelligence. I stammer something about the writer's imperative and mass audiences or something equally indisputable and hope for the best. *Clever* eludes me in the presence of such rampant testosterone.

"Well then," he's saying as he plops himself down onto my towel, "scooch on over, we'll just have to share our spot while we resolve this dichotomy."

And resolve we do. All the rest of the afternoon and well into the evening, pontificating about anything and everything that occurs to us in our philosophically starved brains. A fellow collegian, I tell him about my experiences with the student radicals in Europe and he tells me about his experiences with Viet Cong radicals in Viet Nam. We bond over our mutual disaffections, our disdain for hierarchy, and our open desire for each other's hotness. That we end up in bed rutting like a pair of crazed weasels is an existential inevitability. And we still have the rest of the summer to go!

DOWN FROM THE HILL

My first day at UCLA is something I've dreamed of since I was a little girl in pigtails. The chance to be with smart people who *want* to be here, committed to the pure joy of learning unfettered by small-minded teachers, or disruptive students, or politically dictated curricula—or so I imagine.

Oops. I've not even begun to unpack in my dorm room when Gil Scott Heron's spoken-word rant, *The Revolution Will Not Be Televised*, comes blasting through the quad. Fascinated, I listen to his intricate, angry poetry, thrilled to be with like-minded scholars, at long last!

The first day of classes sees me fairly traipsing down the 1,663 steps from Hedrick Hall to my first seminar. "This is the first day of the rest of your life," says the little voice in my head, and for once it's not being snide or sarcastic. So a-tingle with anticipation I can hardly sit, I find a place near the front and wait for the class to begin.

Survey of Cultural Anthropology. Images of Margaret Mead dance through my head, and I'm half expecting her to walk through the door and pick up the chalk. This is going to be so good! FINALLY, someone who truly knows and loves their subject; someone who's actually *written* the books we've been assigned to read. Someone whose very *mission* is to impart knowledge with grace and good wisdom. I can hardly wait for my new, real, actual life to get started.

The hour comes. We wait. And wait. And wait. Yes, this is the right room. Yes, all these other people here seem to be waiting for the same class, pens and notebooks poised at the ready. The hour passes. No professor. A few students get up and leave as others begin to gather in the hallway for the next seminar. Then, at the very last moment, a sweating, disheveled grad student comes bursting into the room, looks around in confusion, and asks, "Where this is?"

Is the fellow Punjabi? Yemeni? Serbo-Chinese? I wonder if even *he* has a clue. "Am Ydjelbda Hrunumg (*approx*)," he mutters in helpless, nominal English. "They tell just now me suppose teaching section. What is subject?"

Sometimes the signs are just all wrong; the stars align in the wrong direction or the chicken guts foretell disaster. When your spaceship explodes the day before you send your armies to invade—*that's* a portent. When the ravens roost on your towers or the wedding wine is sour, *these* are portents. Today is one of those times, and true to the portents, my college experience goes downhill from here.

My roommate likes to shoot bullfrogs with her shotgun after hours. "Ya'll shine a flashlight on 'em and those big ol' eyes are just shinin' up at you, then *BLAMMO!*" she explains, patiently and unbidden. My psychology professor is very publicly arrested for sharing marijuana with his students. In class. My cheap typewriter jams so many keys I have to retype all my papers three times just to get them legible, and my English professor accuses me of plagiarism because I've turned in a paper encompassing a short piece I just published in Los Angeles's storied free press, *The Freep*.

Throughout this, my sweet Johnny stands steadfast, interrupting his own classes to ferry me back and forth from his place in San Pedro to UCLA. After our weekends of bliss, I love tooling back up the San Diego Freeway in his snazzy little roadster, but the drive is taking its toll on us both—and then his car dies. We try bicycling the thirty miles each way to see each other, but it takes up so much time and physical energy that it's obvious we're going to have to make a choice if we're both to stay in school: either move in together, or break up—and I'd sooner blow Richard Nixon than betray the man I love.

When I tell my parents I'm moving out of the dorm and into Johnny's mother's house in working-class San Pedro, their reaction is immediate and sure; I'd fully expected them to cut me off financially, but not to cut me off from my family itself, forbid me to even *try* to contact my siblings for fear I'll contaminate them. "Living in sin," they call it.

"Shacking up without benefit of wedlock."

(Yes, people really used to talk like this. As in, "You're going to pick up this phone right now and call all your relatives and tell them that you're *living in sin*." Um, o*kaaaay*. Imagine the conversations I'll have. "Hi Uncle Torvald, you probably don't remember me but I'm Bob's oldest, Allena . . . You know, Bob? Your nephew on your wife's younger brother's side? Yeah, Bernice's brother. Well, anyway, there's this guy I met, see, and . . .")

How can I tell my folks how much I need to be with my lover while tackling this brave new world that's calling me to help mold it? I'm bouncing around so many genres right now—citizen, scholar, hippie-chick, church-lady, temptress, naïf, artist, agitator, peacemaker—I feel like a pinball in a parlor game. My parents' reality and the one I'm living in are so far removed from each other that we might as well be on different planets. I'll not survive on theirs without renouncing everything I believe in—just as they'll not compromise with mine.

Besides, it's really not *me* they're worried about. It's how all "this" will look to their friends. "Why are you doing this to us? Why can't you just get married like everybody else?" wails Madre.

I've been waiting for this moment for eighteen years. *Take a deep breath and wait a beat or two for effect.* Not with rancor or snottiness, but enormously satisfied I say, "Because I'm not *like* 'everybody else,' remember? I'm *different*."

"Harrumph," harrumphs my father. "You've made your bed, now lie in it."

So we do, Johnny and I. As often as we possibly can, and wherever we can imagine one—stairwells and parking lots, golf courses and libraries, in grocery aisles and church sanctuaries. Movie theaters, construction sites, hilltops and beaches, ski lifts and streetcars, all become our bower. And, of course, there is always our little house in San Pedro.

Johnny's widowed mother, who was pregnant and married at fifteen, is certainly more supportive than my disappointed parents are. Gracious as well as generous, she opens her home to us in spite of her own religious misgivings, and welcomes me into her family without the slightest preamble or question. I cannot even *imagine* my parents taking a heretofore unknown boyfriend or girlfriend into their household, let alone allowing us to share a room together. But Iris is kindly, nonjudgmental, and sincere in her Christian beliefs, and she treats me as an equal and a valued friend. In return, I adore her. And when she gives me the run of her kitchen and shows me how to bake her famous cinnamon bread, I know I've been accepted.

Living in Iris's home is like living in another world; instead of books and classical music, there is non-stop country-western and daytime television. Instead of formality and decorum, there is happy chaos. And instead of being treated like a second-class citizen, I sit at the table as an adult. In the wake of banishment and exile from my own family, I react like an abandoned pet that's been rescued from the pound: grateful, enthusiastic, eager to please and fit into this exotic new tribe—and *tribal* it is.

Johnny's two sisters and their families live just around the block, and at least one of them is always here for coffee and gossip in the mornings, or en masse with kids, friends, husbands, and coolers on the weekends for barbecue and beers. I'm just another face in the crowd to them, and I'm learning to fit in.

Johnny has a night job as the clerk at a ramshackle little liquor store out by the tracks off of Western Ave. A standalone shop on the outskirts of a decaying industrial park, it's the sort of location where desperate souls come to sit in the parking lot and swill a pint of cheap vodka after a long night out drinking—or dump dead bodies out of moving vehicles.

Yet Lanny, the owner, has only been held up once in the twenty years he's had the place—and that was by one of the "regulars" who'd chickened out after he'd had Lan empty the till at gunpoint. The fellow apparently had had second thoughts about sullying his own best haunt. After apologizing to Lan, he'd returned the money and broken down in tears. "You're the only friend I've got," he tells him as they wait for the police to show up and take him away.

Johnny functions as sort of confessor-counselor to the sad losers who frequent the store. In between stocking the cooler and shelves, and amusing me back behind the soft drink cases in the storeroom, he sells small containers and six packs to the sort of people who buy their booze late in the evening.

During these transactions, I just sit on a stool behind the counter and listen to the conversations they have with him. From what I gather, before he was drafted into the Army, Johnny was the local football hero and all-round golden boy, the one people thought would go away to college and make something Big of his life. It seems that everyone who comes into Lan's Liquors knows him from "before"—when he went off to Vietnam as a military police officer, not as this stranger who came back a long-haired, bearded hippie-freak.

Yet despite all that hair he's still the charmer they remember, and these hardened rednecks open up to him in ways I could never have imagined, sharing their hearts over the scuffed Formica countertop that separates their succor from their wallet. These hundred nights at the liquor store teach me how to talk to anybody about anything, make me realize that people, even the most depraved and intimidating, are still just people. Johnny's teaching me how to be fearless.

Compared to the posh gentlemen farms of Rolling Hills where I grew up, Johnny's rough-and-tumble working-class neighborhood is a real eye-opener. My parents have worked so hard to keep me *out* of places like this that the change is almost as exotic for me as my sudden appearance in their midst must be for my new neighbors. The first thing I notice are the sidewalks and streetlights—we didn't have those in the residential areas of the hill. But here, they're extensions of people's living rooms—a place where kids can play and hang out because their front yards are mostly full of defunct car parts. The streets, too, are playgrounds and gathering places, more the province of people than vehicles.

The second thing that assails me is the *noise*. Blaring television sets and radios, shrieking children outside and battling adults within. Above drone police helicopters, beyond is the dull roar of the freeway interchange. If I close my eyes, the road noise almost sounds like breakers on the shore—but for the semis and un-muffled motorcycles.

The lack of privacy in this neighborhood is stunning. Compressed chaos. In Rolling Hills, all the homes are set back from the road and posted with discrete white lawn signs with the street number and the family name carefully painted in red script. Here, that information is spray-painted on the cinderblock fences separating one tract house from the next.

Each morning, I awaken to the bathroom sounds of our next-door neighbor, whose stylized wall art informs us he is known as "El Loco Melvin." From what I can glean, El Loco Melvin is in the last stages of lung cancer, because I can hear the literal chunks of him hacking up through the phlegm as I rouse from my sleep.

On the other side of our house live Tootie and Bea. Tootie is a grizzled junk collector whose body is as lean and battered as his beat-up old truck. Years of sun and alcohol have left him wizened and leathery, the perfect Jack Spratt to his obese old battle-axe of a wife. Their domestic warring is so enthusiastic and so predictable, it's almost as though it's been staged for our daily amusement; a real-life Punch and Judy show just outside our kitchen screen door. When excitement gets slow and money gets tight, Johnny and I (and frequently our friends) like to huddle on the other side of the cinderblock fence separating our houses, ears to the cracks, just reveling in the improvisational riffs of their mayhem, as if through their bickering we can somehow assuage our own mounting sense of disenchantment.

I've only settled into the noisy rhythms of this place when Iris announces she's marrying Dave, a kindly sort she's met at church, and will be moving into his home downstate. With her bedroom and sewing room freed, Johnny's younger sister Leanne, Leanne's husband, Mex, and their three young children move in. "No sense in them paying rent if they don't have to," says Iris. She has a point; the mortgage on the house is all of $53 a month, and even on unemployment Mex can manage his share of *that*. Johnny buys a lock for our bedroom door so we can study in a semblance of peace, and what was once our quiet retreat from the chaos of the big city becomes a suburban madhouse.

By pooling our various and paltry incomes, at least we have plenty of food, even in the midst of an economic recession. Friends and friends-of-friends gravitate to our house for the company and the good home cookin'. And since this is the sixties, when, as the saying goes, "Dope will get you through times of no money better than money will get you through times of no dope," it's inevitable that at some point, *someone* will show up with a baggie of cannabis as a hostess gift.

This presents something of a moral dilemma for the household. Imagine, if you will, four reasonably hip young adults, longhaired, tie-dyed, and socially aware—none of whom have ever smoked pot. Not only that, we're all wary of taking that first step down the road to moral ruin.

Our excuses are myriad: we're health nuts, it's Mom's house and we don't want to jeopardize our occupancy, it's wrong and illegal, *think of the children!* But mostly we're all just afraid we'll get addicted and go insane. We've seen the hollow-eyed red freaks who skulk around the neighborhood waiting for someone to leave a door unlocked so they can pillage the house for booty. We've physically rescued our television set from them on two occasions—Johnny and friends simply visited the offending party and took it back, because the drugged-out slacker lacked the ambition to pawn it. None of us envisions a future locked up in the company of these zombified miscreants just because we were dumb enough to smoke marijuana and end up brain damaged.

The bearer of this contraband house gift is Johnny's old army buddy, a great hulking lummox now employed as a police officer, who most likely has procured said baggie from one of the local *cholos* his department routinely harasses during traffic stops. His wife, Julie, is a soft-spoken redhead of almost unearthly beauty and piety. She's the very *last* one of us I would have expected to deftly roll a doob, fire it up, and pass it to her cop husband as he beams in adoration. It would be rude not to at least take a toke.

I've never so much as *touched* a cigarette, let alone puffed on one, but if Carlos Castaneda can eat peyote, turn himself into a crow, and work a best seller out of it, I guess I can try some pot. *What the hell, it's just one more lost virginity.*

Joint to lips, inhale as instructed, count to thirty, exhale through the nose. *There. I did it.* Johnny and Mex do the same. We all look at each other expectantly, waiting for horns to appear and fangs to sprout, but nothing happens.

"What am I supposed to feel?" asks Johnny.

"Just go with it, man."

Julie rolls another joint, then another. Presently, the room erupts in contagious laughter. Faces relax and distort, lights dim, the music carries us to a velvet place where colors meld and boundaries blur. "Wow," says Mex, with his usual laconic paucity.

Somewhere, a redneck beats his wife in outrage. Somewhere, children cry out in hunger while rich men curse the poor. All I'm aware of is Miles Davis blowing pure and honed and insistent, *Here come de Honey . . .*

And it does. I catch Johnny's eye and he takes my hand and leads me to our room. It's the start of a beautiful affliction.

THE MORE THE SCARIER

Money issues being what they are and affordable housing being scarce, our urban commune is soon joined by another couple who is willing to pay some rent money, pool their food stamps, and help out with the mounting chores. Gregory is a singer-songwriter, and his lady, Bettyjo, is a part-time dancer and party girl; they bring just the right artistic mix our white trash family needs to attract even *more* hangers-on and psychedelic jollity.

No rank neophytes to this stoner thing, Gregory and Bettyjo take up residence in the illegal back addition of our crumbling tract house and promptly set up an equally illegal pot garden along the cinderblock walls of the yard. "You take care of them, and they'll take care of you," sings Gregory in between tokes.

Suddenly every helicopter overhead is a potential prison sentence, and every strange face in the neighborhood a red freak waiting to snatch our resinous "children" from the garden. When I come out to the kitchen one night for a midnight snack and a person I've never met is smoking a hookah in our living room, the idyllic façade begins to crack, and my patience along with it. Our refrigerator seems to empty as soon as it's filled. Plants disappear from the backyard, and cash vanishes from my purse. The situation is becoming unruly, and apparently I'm not the only one adversely affected by it.

It's been a long, hard morning of classes and a trying afternoon at my campus job afterwards. Someone has spilled hydrochloric acid in the lab and used the fire extinguisher to neutralize it, so I've spent the last six hours trying alternately to vacuum it up and mop it off my skin—with only marginal success. It's nearly sunset by the time I come bicycling up the block toward home, and here's Jimmy, Mex and Leanne's angelic four-year-old, sitting in the middle of the street in front of our house to greet me. He has a hammer in his hand, and he's surrounded by a pile of bright plastic toys, dolls, cars, laughing happily as he smashes them to bits against the asphalt. It's not a particularly busy street, but this is hardly a reasonable scenario for a sweet little blond-haired boy. "Jimmy . . . ," I begin, hesitantly, not wishing to alarm him. "What are you doing in the middle of the street?"

He looks up and smiles at me, his little face calm and suffused with a radiant happiness. "I'm breaking my *toys*, Aunt Allena," he explains patiently.

His older brother, Chris, is eight. Enamored of what he calls his "army men," Chris has battalions of these molded plastic things stationed all over the house where they occupy every empty surface of every open room. End tables, toilet tanks, under the beds and along the bookcases—these little soldiers end up in my backpack and in the vegetable bin of the refrigerator. Child has staked his claim to the house as surely as if he'd systematically peed in all the corners. A phalanx of GI Joes, Incredible Hulks, and toy tanks guard the television set, their weaponry pointing toward the sofas where we ersatz grown-ups gather in the evenings to enjoy supper and whatever communal substance any one of us has been able to score that day.

Our motley group delights in getting loaded and watching old *Dragnet* reruns on TV while we work our way through dinner. Stoned and convivial, we giggle helplessly as officers Joe Friday and Frank Gannon plod their way through leaden dialogue and implausible plotlines to bring the bad guys of Los Angeles to justice.

The officers are particularly vigilant about ridding our streets of "hippies" and "marijuana addicts" and "student radicals"—just like us. We criminal troublemakers need all the yucks we can get in our reduced circumstances, so we make it a point never to miss this nightly dose of irony, because even unintentional comedy is frequently still quite funny.

So we're settled in one evening, totally engrossed in the idiocy before us, when Chris comes racing into the room, plops himself down

THE MORE THE SCARIER

in front of the television set, and before anyone can say a word, spins the dial to cartoons, eliciting a moan of extreme disapproval from the six of us. We're all too stoned to get up and switch the channel back—let alone take on the seething mass of self-involvement that is Chris.

"Hey Chrissy," says one of the guys. "Change it back, dude."

Chrissy bristles. Facing us, the enemy, he crosses defiant arms over his chest and growls, "If you make me change this channel, I'm gonna *break* this TV set."

The room goes deathly silent while six stoners contemplate this declaration. No one has the slightest doubt that Chrissy is serious in his intent. Then from across the room, little Jimmy, fresh from his toy-bashing, pipes up. "I'll break it, Mommy," he offers helpfully.

Chris is undeterred. He plays his trump card. "If you make me change this channel, I'll tell the police you all smoke bari-jewana!"

Now, this is a new one. Operation DARE has just hit the public schools, and authorities are encouraging school children to rat out their scofflaw parents. We've tried very hard to keep our illicit activities away from the children's attentions, and smoking of any sort is only allowed outside in the backyard and under cover of darkness. But apparently those little eyes haven't missed a trick. I wonder what would be the public good in putting six nominally tax-paying adults in prison and three little kids in foster care, but our concerns here are more immediate.

"Chrissy," I remind him, "you climbed the refrigerator and snuck that whole plate of marijuana brownies, remember?" A dose of Ipecac and a good night's sleep had ensured that Chrissy came through none the worse for wear, but the commune is out an entire batch of electric brownies, and there are still some hard feelings from both the heads among us as well as the chocoholics.

"Which means," I continue, "that *you* will have to go to jail, too!"

A brief murmur of approval from the sofa contingent. *Well played!*

Chris considers the logic of this, but being eight years old, he's still pretty easy to fool. It's odd to see such an aggressive child in and amongst a commune of pacifist flower children, but I have to admire his style. No less puzzling is his insular hostility toward anything that isn't a plastic army man; his family is uniformly giving and gentle, and there's certainly no abusive uncle lurking in the attic. I decide that Chris is just one of those people who prefers not to share his limited spaces with other human beings. I'm sympathetic, of course, but too much in love with his uncle to identify with him . . . yet.

BURN BABY BURN

By the time spring quarter rolls around, I realize I cannot stand to spend another minute in UCLA's cramped, windowless classrooms—where everyone including the instructors chain-smokes cigarettes of varying composition. I get enough of that at home, and certainly not indoors. Just stepping into the stench of an empty classroom is enough to stimulate my gag reflex, rendering concentration on the class discussions impossible.

Folks who grew up after smoking in public spaces was forbidden will never know the special hell waiting for those of us with sensitive eyes and lungs back then. Mine rebelled at the merest whiff of burnt tobacco and smokers were everywhere—on planes and in theaters, in classrooms and restaurants—with absolutely no way to escape from them). It was like having bug spray blown into your face for hours on end, or being stuck in a lunchroom full of elderly women all vying to out-perfume each other.

At first, I try sitting in the back near the door. Then, when this proves ineffective, I sit hunched on the floor with my nose in my lap, as close to the ground as possible in order to pick up the stray wispy current of fresh air coming in from under the doorway. I try wearing a wet handkerchief tied around my nose and mouth as a filter, try listening to lectures outside in the corridor. When all this fails I try asking everyone to consider the lungs of those few of us who do not smoke, and get hooted out of the classroom for my troubles. Then when avid Marxist professor Angela Davis comes to town and anti-war protests close down the campus for a week before finals, I give up the ghost. This august university thing is not going to work for me anymore.

The decision to drop out and enroll at Johnny's new CSU campus close to home is surprisingly easy. Instead of imposing brick edifices, classes meet in an old apartment complex. And instead of smoke-filled classrooms and impersonal lecture halls, the professors prefer to hold forth outside on the grassy quads whenever the weather permits. Instead of hundreds of classmates, there are usually only a dozen of us or so, and the seminars here are diverse and lively. In reality, I'm just sick of school—and I like getting laid.

I've just told my UCLA advisor I'll not be returning, when Johnny seeks me out in the sculpture garden where I'm waiting for him to come pick me up for the last time. He's ashen and somber when he takes my hands. "Chrissy was playing with matches," he tells me. "They got him out, but he was burned pretty badly. And he burned the house down."

This is terrible news on so many levels that I am seized by nausea. Johnny and I sink to the grass in each other's arms, too stunned even to cry. We both know what this means for us. We'll have to find another place to live, and on our combined wages that's just not going to be possible if we're to stay in school.

I am eighteen, estranged from my family, about to drop out of school, and flat broke in a terrible economy. So I do the rational thing: I get married.

Johnny and I are newlywed and homeless, about to start searching the alley behind the liquor store for a two-bedroom washer/dryer box to live in when we are invited to take temporary refuge in a neighbors' guest house. It's really just a converted garage with a window and a door, but it looks like home to us.

Our would-be landlords, Hal and Sara, are as straight as we are radical, and although we've always been friendly, we certainly never expected an offer like this from them—or anyone, really. No one in our social circle even rents their own *apartment*, let alone owns their own home, let alone owns their own home with a detached guest garage! I'm so relieved at their kindness that I barely even wonder at their motives.

It can't be money, because they've not asked for rent, and they're not particularly religious, so I don't think we're going to be proselytized. Besides, they're sharp and funny and their little kids are delightful. Maybe they're just fascinated with our eccentric academic lifestyle? Maybe they want us as pets? Johnny and I discuss the matter for about thirty seconds before yelping our grateful acceptance.

Sara is a product of small-town Alaska, buxom, bountiful, and savvy to the point of cynicism. A brunette morph of Marilyn Monroe and Auntie Mame, there's nothing naïve about this gal, despite her isolated upbringing. *I can learn a lot from her*, I think.

Hal, on the other hand, is sweet and nerdy and recently discharged from the Coast Guard where he met and married this prize. Tall and thin, all limbs and Adam's apple, he is clearly besotted with his voluptuous wife and perfect children, as though he gets up every morning and can't believe his good luck.

He's an electrical engineer, and to my great delight is building a computer in the garage workshop where we will be staying. Having studied FORTRAN and data processing in high school using the nearby TRW UNIVAC to run my programming, I'm eager to see if my rudimentary skills can transfer to a privately owned, transistorized system. Home-built computers are still in the geeky province of ham radio and photographic darkrooms in the early seventies, so this is a very cool development indeed.

Grabbing what's left of our books and our bedding, we move into our new household within the hour. It may still be a commune, but at least this one is a step up the social ladder.

Johnny and I waste no time trying to corrupt them, and it doesn't take long.

"So," says Sara, that first night at dinner, "do you guys have any marijuana?" Hal is appalled, looks to me seeking denial, and finding none, capitulates. "Yeah," he says dubiously, obviously coerced into this quest by his strong-willed wife. "We'd like to try some." Johnny and I are only too happy to oblige them.

These are Troubled Times for sure. Dicky Nixon's deep into his dirty tricks; as the bloody war in Vietnam continues to rage, the political rift between young and old intensifies, threatening civil war here at home.

CHOMP CHOMP CHOMP

Kids like us are being blown up in Southeast Asia, *and* on streets and college campuses all around the USA, rendering fewer and fewer of us of fighting age particularly interested in defending the system that's killing us off.

We *aren't,* however, reluctant to *fight*—if only symbolically. In futile but headline-grabbing retaliation, homegrown revolutionaries take to bombing war-industry offices and torching the banks that support them, making folk heroes out of the likes of Bill Ayres and Eldridge Cleaver, and living legends out of Yippee pranksters like Abbie Hoffman, whose *Steal This Book* has inspired tens of thousands, if not millions, of beleaguered baby boomers to do precisely that—and a great deal more.

Hardhats and rednecks, in turn, take perverse delight in beating the crap out of unwary longhairs and making life generally miserable for anyone with facial hair or unfettered breasts. For the average hippie freak on the street, all is not peace and love—in fact, the nation threatens to tear apart under the specter of civil war.

But there *is* a sort of wartime camaraderie that makes the growing urban tensions bearable. Like most of our youthful fellows, vets Johnny and Hal, and indignant pacifists like Sara and me, are caught between the two cultures and discomforted by the increasingly shrill political rhetoric emanating from both sides. Here in our congenial little blended family, there's a sense of continuity and trust that takes the scarier edges off the culture wars raging just beyond our door step. Our sustenance is in our friendships.

Memorial Day weekend is a time to relax, make homemade pizzas, and fire up a fattie, pretending that the nascent summer won't be long, hot, and violent. Folks have gathered and uncorked a few bottles of cheap Italian Chianti, the effects of which are highly convivial, judging by the rowdy laughter coming from the living room. I barely hear the telephone above the merrymaking, and answer it flippantly, *"Yeeeeessss?"* The voice on the other end isn't up for jollity. Leanne's voice is trembling and nearly inaudible. "Mom and Dave were killed in a head-on collision on the way to Utah for their anniversary. Can you please put Johnny on the phone?"

BURN BABY BURN

I watch my husband's face as he gets the news, and though his expression hardly changes, something familiar goes out of his eyes. I know without him saying that whatever love we shared, whatever plans we set out for ourselves, are all finished. The house quiets and empties along with my heart.

We go through the motions of being a couple, say reassuring things to each other, even make plans to move out of Hal and Sara's garage and into an apartment of our own. But I'm not really surprised when I return home from work one day to find my beautiful husband and my bounteous landlady locked, as the saying goes, in passionate embrace on the kitchen table.

Sex, drugs, rock and roll; we all take our comforts where we find them. Mine were in my family. Sara and Johnny's apparently come from seducing other people's spouses. We'd been married for all of a year.

KEEP ON PUMPIN'

I'm sure there are more discouraging ways to end a marriage—lose a family, give up one's home, friends, and livelihood—but they don't come immediately to my mind. To make matters worse, Johnny's in the same program as I am in school, and I've not the slightest desire to keep running into him there with his new girlfriend. Finding another job is proving far harder than I would have imagined, for Johnny's left me without a car. And worst of all, my parents are madder at me for the divorce than they were about the marriage. I can't seem to get anything right.

Desperate to clear my mind, I decide to ride my bike down to the beach for some exercise. Since I've traded smoke-filled classrooms for smog-choked freeways in my search for gainful employment, my poor eyes and lungs can use the break.

I always feel disassociated when I'm riding along the beach, as though someone else is bent over these handlebars, cranking away on the pedals, counterbalancing these hips with this ribcage. The parkways, all the pretty houses, the street traffic passes as if in a movie, and I am just watching it go by while someone else does all the work.

Occasionally, a burning in my heart and lungs interrupts to let me know that, *Hey, we're going to need some more concentration here or we'll be taking a short pause to dump you into the curb.* But mostly, it's a time to let me be alone with my body, humming along in alpha mode—that dreamlike awakening where everything is acute, yet muted through a veil of non-reality. It's a lot like dope, only with a full-body workout thrown in for good measure.

I've just turned onto Pacific Coast Highway when the pickup truck that's been dogging me all the way down the hill comes close up behind. Mindful of the creeps who've tried to run me into the curb before, or sideswipe my rear tire and knock me over as they speed by, I try my best to ignore the looming presence, moving to the far right edge of the road, varying my pace so he doesn't try to spook me, thinking I'm unaware of his presence.

He's right on my rear wheel now, slowing to match my speed, and he holds it there for a few long moments, leering across through the passenger-side window trying to catch my eye—edging over just enough to let me know he has me cornered. He's staring at me hard now, smiling a thin smile that makes the skin of my back bunch and crawl.

By now I've played this game with a hundred clowns just like him—the predatory yobs for whom beer keggers and county lock-ups were invented. Never once has a longhair pulled this sort of stunt. It's time to brace myself for what's coming next.

When he lays long and deafening on the horn then accelerates and pulls away laughing, I don't even break stride as I pull the raw egg from my bike pouch, wait until he slows for the red light up ahead. Then I take careful aim and splatter the shit out of his rear window, hang a hard right at the corner, a quick left up the alleyway, and *zooooom*—off down toward the beach to the bike path. The egg will bake into epoxy in the hot summer sun. Maybe next time he'll think twice before he tries menacing a hippiechick on a bicycle.

Safe along the beach, the pathway is nearly empty of tourists. All the dog-walkers have gone off to work and the surfers have long since staked out their encampments along the high tide line. The place is all mine; mile after mile to sit back tall on the seat, hands free, steering with my hips, and give myself over to the comforting numbness and the glorious shimmering seaside.

Past the mansions and the teardowns, the retirees and the voluntarily unemployed are enjoying coffee and newspapers on their beachfront patios—separated from the passing riff-raff like me only by their low brick walls, their carefully trimmed hedges, and the presumption of their exclusivity. A few recognize me and wave, or call out a pleasant "Mornin'."

CHOMP CHOMP CHOMP

It's hard not to feel cheerful.

Redondo gives way to Hermosa, Hermosa to Manhattan, and now I'm well into Co-pilot-ville, the stretch before Marina del Rey where all the lower-level airline personnel hole up on layover. It's not unusual for a dozen people to share one of these houses, rotating through available bedrooms and kitchens as their schedules require. Pro athletes and club crawlers like to hang out here too, the better to take advantage of the ever-changing crop of stewardesses and exotic dancers who room here while methodically working their way toward a mistress apartment in one of the ritzy Marina Towers just up the coast.

On this particular morning, there's a beer-fest going on, kegs tapped, outside speakers blaring, already in full swing though it's not even noon yet. Guys in trunks and T-shirts line the walls, sprawl on lawn chairs, block the sidewalk. All the stews are apparently still asleep—or in hiding. I have no choice but to slow down to avoid plowing someone over, or more likely, given the size of these hulks, colliding with one and landing myself in a thorny wall of bougainvilleas.

"C'mon and join us," someone calls out. I smile. Say nothing. Keep pedaling and dodging bodies.

Someone holds out a red plastic beer cup, sloshing its contents onto my tank top. Cheers erupt. I smile again. Say nothing. Keep on pedaling. I'm nearly past the spillover from this drunken congregation when I feel someone take my arm. My bike goes forward, I do not.

He's not really grabbed me, just kind of "helping" me off my bicycle, so I'm not particularly alarmed—after all, there's a pretty large audience. I look up, up, up into the face of a smiling blond giant; he's beautiful, actually, and friendly.

"Here, let me help you."

This guy must be six-foot-six, and I'm all of five-foot-one.

Another behemoth appears on the other side of me, takes my other elbow, and together they lift me up off my bike—my feet still pedaling helplessly against the air. They carry me off into their lair, and deposit me on a sofa in the living room. Someone offers me yet another beer.

KEEP ON PUMPIN'

"No thanks," I say politely. "I don't drink."

There are four or five guys in various stages of dress seated around the living room. A football game is running on a video screen and people's attention is about evenly divided between the game and this new arrival.

"I'd like you to meet Darrell," says one of them, formally introducing me to the fellow who has first accosted me. "He plays wide receiver for the Dallas Cowboys." I look him over; he's definitely big and wide. It's plausible.

"So why aren't you at practice?" A reasonable question.

"I'm on waivers," he says. A reasonable answer. "You wanna fuck me?"

Now, I've been propositioned before, and without preamble, but this is the first time anyone has put the question to me so simply: blunt and inarguable, like a turd on a table. Moreover, this is the first time I've actually given it serious consideration.

It's a lovely day and I'm newly dumped by the man I've set my future with, given up my birthright over, squandered my dignity for. What could this handsome stranger possibly take from me that hasn't already been taken, betrayed, and pissed upon?

A lighted joint appears under my nose and I take a long, satisfying hit, hold it, let it out through my nose. I notice that someone has closed the front door. As if in a trance, I'm astounded to hear my voice. And it says, "Sure. Why not?"

The bedroom is brightly lit by the big west window that faces onto a cinderblock retaining wall. It is furnished with the bed, a dresser, and a chair, and on the wall in front of the bed is a black-and-white poster of a Siamese kitten clinging to a thin bamboo pole by its chin and its little front paws. Its toes are splayed and its eyes look determined if not particularly comprehending. "Hang In There, Baby," says the caption.

There is a lesson in here, and being one of those people who tend to look for signs when confronted with a challenge, I decide that this one is self-apparent.

I remove my top and cut-offs and so does he. He lies down atop me, nearly squishing the breath out of me. There is not the slightest connection between us . . . well, maybe a *slight* connection, but that's it. He's finished before I can even get started.

"Well!" I say, anxious to be on my way and up the coast. And before I can speak another word, his accomplice is standing there next to the bed spitting on his fingers. I can see where this is going, and I'm not in any position to stop it. He takes his partner's place between my thighs and gets to work. I notice someone else standing in the doorway, watching, patiently waiting his turn. And another. Then another. I can hear someone on the phone in the living room, "Yeah, come on over . . ."

The kitten stares down at me.

I can either go along with this and try to stay the good sport, or risk things getting seriously weird—and let's face it, this is plenty weird as it is. On the plus side, I'm in good enough shape for this sort of work out; Johnny and I have spent literally days at a time in our pursuits, so marathon sessions aren't unknown to me. Physically, I should be okay as long as no one gets kinky.

The psychological toll doesn't even occur to me. Right now what I have to do is survive this without serious injury—maybe even try to appreciate the novelty. I know instinctively that the best thing I can do is let my body go numb, try to keep my wits about me, and keep on top of the situation, so to speak. I need the balance of power tipped to my hand, not theirs; to give them permission, and by extension, retain the option not to do so. I can worry about all the penicillin I'm going to need after I get myself out of this.

Lying there, I think about all the times my parents used to take turns spanking me when I was growing up. I never really understood their

KEEP ON PUMPIN'

reasons, or what I might have done to upset them, and they were never very specific about it either; more intent on beating my scrawny little-girl ass than explaining the source of their *real* frustrations.

Far outsized, outweighed, out-maneuvered, all I could do was lie there and let them be finished. Sated. When one would tire, I'd lie there and wait for the next one to come in and pick up were the first had left off. "Wait 'til your father gets home," had the force of sentence and execution in my family. And my father rarely wavered from my mother's edicts. "I'll give you something you can really cry about," he'd say. "I'm going to blister your butt until you can't sit down."

Frequently, they did. Then, the final absurdity, "We're doing this because we love you." No wonder I turned out so warped. . . .

So in the interest of getting it over with, I try to be nice to these impromptu rapists. When one of them wilts inside of me—perhaps in a fit of conscience, perhaps concerned at the gathering cesspool of microorganisms he's stuffed his membrane into—I give no indication to the others waiting their turn. I catch his eyes, telling him his secret is safe with me. I can sense his gratitude, and know I've found an ally here.

Four or five couplings along, a sort of contest has begun to emerge— *How long can she keep this up?* A few guys are standing around the room, watching, even cheering me on. When a new participant starts to get a little rough, I make eye contact with one of them and my nascent fan club discourages him in no uncertain terms.

"Hey, take it easy, man. She's a guest."

Damned straight, Jethro. . . .

The kitten stares down, urging forbearance. *Hang in there, baby.*

Around the time suitor number eleven starts into the room, I've had enough.

Gathering myself, I move to leave.

"Okay boys, game's up. I'm tired." I mean it. I reckon I've fucked in excess of my own height in erect penises today. That's more than enough for any girl—especially one who's facing a twenty-five-mile bicycle ride back home.

The guy waiting his turn in the doorway moves to stop me from leaving, tries to push me back onto the bed. He looks to the group in the bedroom for assistance, but they are on my side now. He's quickly restrained by the flaccid fellow I've befriended. I learned early in life that it's important to get the audience on your side before you lead them to the punch line.

"Let her go. She's been a good sport."

The kitten smiles its benediction upon us.

In this brief moment of crisis, I stare down my would-be assailant. The situation is on the cusp of no-longer-voluntary, and though the element of struggle and triumph might be exciting to him, I think he realizes that I'm not going to be the only one fighting him off. He backs away, grumbling, zipping up his pants as he goes.

Breathing a short sigh of relief, I know I am going to be able to leave in one piece now. The party's over.

"Help me find my clothes?" I ask my rescuer. He nods and herds everyone out of the room, closes the door, comes over to me, gives me a big hug, seemingly as shaken and depleted as I am; maybe his folks hit *him*, too.

"I'll watch the door while you shower," he says. "You can go out the bathroom window if you want, and I'll meet you outside."

"That's okay," I say. "We're okay now." *We're.* He looks at me for a long moment, almost grateful, it seems. Maybe this has been an ordeal for him as well?

I shower in the dingy little stall, wash the stink and funk out of my hair as best I can without touching the slimy walls, marvel at the whacky fates that have led me to this state, and wonder what my part has been in bringing it about. After all, I was simply riding my bike in a public place, certainly not anticipating this outcome when I started out this morning. Should I have screamed? Made a scene? Tried to fight? What about that joint? Should I have slapped it away and tried to break out through the door?

No, I did the right thing. It could have ended a lot worse. When I make my way back out into the living room the guys are still all there, staring at me. For a moment I'm concerned all over again, and my heart sinks.

KEEP ON PUMPIN'

Then they do something I'm *really* not expecting. They stand and begin clapping, cheering for me. A few come up and thank me. A couple invite me over later for a "private party." Phone numbers are pressed into my hand. It's an odd moment, but in a strange way, a triumphant one. *It's not what I'd envisioned for my day's activities*, I tell myself, *but at least I'm leaving in one piece with a semblance of my self-respect intact.* And all the while, Johnny and Sara's perfidy hasn't crossed my mind even *once*.

Someone brings me my bicycle, stashed, no doubt, by the side of the house after my abduction, and before I can mount and start the long slog back up the hill, *gingerly*, my new-found champion has taken it from me and begins pushing it alongside as he walks me out and away from this testosterone-ridden den of jag-offs. A few steps up the strand he turns, stops next to a gleaming chocolate brown Jaguar XKE convertible parked on the street corner. The top is down, and the cream-colored leather is buttery and new-car fragrant. He hoists my bike into the back behind the seats. "My name's Goldie," he says, "and *you* are one amazing lady. At least let me buy you dinner."

One would think that after such a sobering encounter I'd grab my bicycle and flee back up the hill as fast as my legs can pedal. But no . . . I'm seduced by the Jag and Goldie's sweet apologetic smile. Sensing my hesitance, he throws his hands up in the air and takes a step back. "You have my word I won't touch you. Promise. I just want to buy you a nice dinner somewhere and talk. Please let me apologize? I'm not like that." He looks at me beseechingly, as though my acquiescence might somehow grant him absolution for his sin.

For a moment I'm actually tempted; it will be getting dark soon and it's an awfully long ride home. I'm crazy hungry after all that, and hardly in condition to bicycle all the way back up Palos Verdes Drive North. But today's experience has left me uncharacteristically wary.

"Goldie," I say. "I know those aren't really your friends, and I appreciate you coming to my rescue and all, but . . ." and here I take a deep breath and let it out in a long, weary sigh, "not tonight, dear. I have a headache."

ADVENTURES IN HOLLYWEIRDLAND

I've moved out of Johnny's life and into a sparse little apartment across town, where unable to find any kind of legitimate work that pays a living wage, I take to baking cinnamon rolls and taking them around on my bicycle rack to construction sites, offices, nearby mom-and-pop convenience stores. I have a steadily growing customer base and a contract with a popular hamburger joint when the local food mafia reports me to the city health department—who threaten me with arrest.

What a freaking joke. I'd seen the dreck they serve in those taco wagons, and I wouldn't grow a science project on it. But heavens forefend a pretty young woman in cutoffs and a straw hat is allowed to sell wholesome snacks as an alternative to their industrial slop. The inspector intimates that he could arrange to be on the other side of the hill during lunch hour if I were to "make a few concessions." *Eeeech.* For this kind of sleazy harassment, I'd rather be in Hollywood.

Hollywood . . . ? Hmmmm, why not?

It takes all my courage to approach my father for a loan to buy a car, but when I do, he's surprisingly supportive. He's seen me perform in front of an audience before, singing, pontificating from pulpit and lectern, acting in school and little theater productions, and he knows I have a knack for this sort of thing—certainly I can't screw it up any worse than I have my marriage. When I'm offered an assistant's job with a Hollywood public relations firm, he's actually excited for me. What a great chance to learn the business from the inside out! I'll save some money and get a roommate in town.

I call the agent's office and tell them I'm in. The receptionist tells me to be there at 8:30 Monday morning. ("And wear sometin' *cleassy*," she says.)

I show up for work on Monday morning as instructed dressed in my best adult office-wear: a long-sleeved white cotton blouse, pencil skirt, low heels, and stockings. My makeup is clean and simple, my hair is in a prim little bun, and I'm ready to type, file, compose letters, and answer phones, everything the employment agency has prepped me to expect. My new boss, Eddie, gives me a cursory once-over and suggests I spend the day getting the "feel of the place," because next week he's starting production on a big TV awards show. "We've got to get organized and get to work."

Sounds good to me. I'm more than ready to be this producer's right hand, his "Gal Friday" as the ad put it. I envision myself sitting at the big glass reception desk crisply fielding calls, discreetly covering for his oversights, fetching coffee, and chatting up clients as they wait for him to finish an important meeting behind the heavy rosewood door. So when I get there the next morning at 8:30 sharp after two hours of battling morning rush hour, his reaction comes as a bit of a letdown.

"Good Morning, Mr. Ricks! What would you like me to do today?" I say.

What will my first task will be? Organizing his celebrity gift lists? Getting some bigwig from Paramount on the phone for him?

"Yeah. Go pick up [insert-very-famous-celebrity's-name-whom-I-cannot-mention] at the airport, and keep him happy, if you know what I mean."

I do. And I won't.

When Eddie says the guy's name, I'm horrified not only by the suggestion, which is creepy as all hell, but because ____ is my old sensei, the same person I set on his ass when he made me spar with him in front of his karate dojo back in high school—and he's very publicly married by this time. The whole idea of servicing him—*especially* him—is just too unseemly for words. Probably not what *he* is expecting either. In any case, better someone "cleassier" picks him up and "keeps him happy."

"Um, I don't think so, Eddie."

"Hey, he'll give you a tip."

"That's not what I signed up for, Eddie," I say. Truth be told, I'm livid. I'd honestly thought he'd wanted an office assistant, and I had gone to considerable trouble to arrange my new life around this job. Worst of all, I'd involved my parents—who are already beside themselves over my previous ill-fated decisions. It's all I can do to keep myself from crying—or strangling Eddie right there on his orange shag carpeting. Instead, I say, "How would you like it if someone asked that of *your* daughter?"

"I wouldn't let my daughter anywhere *near* this joint," he says.

Maybe he's a little nonplussed by my hesitance. Maybe he's not used to girls who actually *do* want to do office work and don't have some ulterior motive. Maybe this will all work itself out if I just try to be nice and professional. *Businesslike.*

"Eddie," I say in the voice people normally reserve for very slow children, "when you interviewed me, you told me you needed someone to run your office for you. Someone to write letters and keep you on schedule. I didn't take this job to fuck your clients for 'tips.'"

For a moment he seems flabbergasted, likely wondering what kind of foolish young girl from the provinces *wouldn't* jump at the chance to have sex with his stable of C-list celebrities.

"Okay," he concedes. "I'll send Benoit." Benoit is either his connection or his brother-in-law—maybe both—and I'm pretty sure he's the same guy who tried to get me to pose nude for him after work yesterday. Eddie brightens. He'll try this another way. "Tell you what," he says, flipping through his Rolodex. "I'm gonna send you on up to this guy. He's been bugging me to find him a new assistant; maybe *he* can put you to work."

Let's call this character Jackass. He's a hot young comedy writer who's made a big name for himself shilling for the marijuana lobby. His home in Laurel Canyon is a hangout for "new" Hollywood, and scoring an invite there is considered something of a coup in certain hip social circles. Even *I* know his name, have been watching this guy's work on TV for several years now, laughing my head off, and I'd *love* to meet him. I don't even think to ask why he needs a new assistant. Surely people are *clamoring* to work for him?

"*Thanks*, Eddie," I manage sincerely, as he copies down the address. Maybe this situation can be salvaged after all. Working for Jackass would be a dream come true for a smartass like me.

Driving up the long, winding canyon in my new old car, full of myself and my exciting future, I can almost see the credits rolling with my name listed prominently among the writers. Maybe I'll even get an on-camera spotlight on the show! *It's happened before....*

Halfway up Laurel, I'm almost expecting to see Joni Mitchell strumming a twelve-string in one of the driveways along the road. After a few backtracks up and down the narrow lane, I find the address, press the buzzer on the gate, and after some confusion about my name and my business (Eddie hasn't bothered to call to let anyone know I'm coming), I'm admitted to the grounds.

The place looks like Merlin's tree house would look if it had been designed by Robert Nutria. All glass and wood and interior tree trunks and limbs winding in and out of the buildings. And hookahs. And lolling stoners *everywhere*. And ladies strolling around the grounds with their breasts out. Noticing my unconventional attire (clothed) and sensing my purpose (official), one of them directs me out to the pool.

Jackass is bent over someone's glossy stomach, snorting from it what I assume to be cocaine while another naked lady fluffs his massive Jew-fro with a blow dryer. Somehow I'm not all that surprised when I recognize my psych professor from UCLA stretched out on a lounge chair nearby. Like Jackass, he is butt naked. I hope he doesn't recognize me, because I have no idea what sort of etiquette governs this sort of thing.

"Um, Mr. Jackass? Eddie Ricks has sent me to talk to you about an assistant's position?"

Jack's far too entranced with his blow and his blow dry to take any notice of me standing there in my skirt and blouse and sensible shoes, but a well-clothed woman I assume to be his wife takes an instant liking to me. "You'll do fine," she purrs after giving me a quick up and down. "You can take that cabaña over there." She motions to a largish guesthouse adjacent to the pool. "You'll do windows, *yes*?" She nods up and down emphatically.

Wha?

It quickly dawns on me that the *assistant* he's looking for will neither write for him, nor manage his appointment books. What he's looking for is either a housemaid or another girlfriend—or both.

"Come back tomorrow night around eight. We're having a party."

Am I supposed to work it, or work *it?* I've no idea, but I'm not taking any chances. "What would you like me to wear? What will my duties be?"

She stares at me as though I have beetles crawling out of my ears. "It's a *party*!" she says, nearing exasperation.

She abruptly returns to her ministrations with Jackass's hair, relieved to be rid of this annoyance, *me*. I get the impression that I'm hardly the first young woman she's "interviewed" on her husband's behalf, and look around for someone, *anyone* who might be able to clue me in as to what is going on.

A trim ebony man with what appears to be a dueling scar across his cheek taps me on the shoulder. "Excuse me, miss," he says. "Your car is ready."

How unsubtle. I just barely got here, and now apparently it's time for me to leave.

I drive back down the San Diego Freeway with my head in a fog. Is everyone in Hollywood crazy? What's missing here? Who *are* these dreadful people? My parents may have been socially repressed, but at least they were dependable. And intelligible. And their friends' families were intact—and clothed. The Hollywood Hills must be where the divorced people go to lick each other's wounds.

Well, dearie, now you're divorced too; you better figure out how to fit in.

Eddie dismisses my concerns with a curt admonition not to take everything so seriously. "But they never even got my name, let alone told me what they want me to do." "Aw, don't worry about Jackass," says Eddie. "I've told him all about you—he *loves* you. It's always a little free form up there, but you'll be just fine. You should go. You'll meet somebody."

For once, Eddie is right. There are more famous faces per square foot crammed in this living room than at an Oscars after-party, and those faces I don't recognize, I probably should. Our host and hostess are nowhere to be seen, but here's the *real* Robert Redford, and the *real* Warren Beatty. Hal Ashby is chatting up Bob Altman while a goofy blond groupie in a micro minidress passes a joint between them.

"I've got this great new singer," some chest-hairy guy is telling another chest-hairy guy. "You should sign her." A young Donna Summer hangs behind him shy and rainbow clad, exotic and extraordinary. It's dazzling. *What am I doing here?* Trying to blend in with a glass of wine I have no intention of drinking? Maybe over here by the kitchen . . .

"What are you doing *here*!?" comes the voice from my left, echoing my very thoughts. It's my host. "I thought Dierdre told you to hang out in the Jacuzzi tonight. She's out there waiting for you to show up."

Well, that solves my quandary. Jackass gestures me out the sliding glass doors toward the pool where I gather I'm to make myself useful. He takes the wine glass from my hand as I go. Maybe he wants me to serve drinks?

The hot tub is in full bubble, alight and a-steam. Disco thumps from the outdoor speakers and a fire burns in the fire pit. At this moment the Jacuzzi is unoccupied, a fact which has Deirdre in a tizzy. "Get your clothes off and get in there," she hisses. "And *be friendly.*"

My bountiful derriere has sat on its share of nude beaches by this time in my young life, so the idea of being naked in front of strangers doesn't faze me, but the idea of being naked in a hot tub with fat old hairy ones does. *Oh well, at least it's chlorinated. Maybe one of the famous "Bobs" will drop in for a dip.*

No such luck. I'm quickly joined by some mid-level artist's rep who looks much like my now-former boss, Eddie. I gather that Jackass has the Hugh Hefner spillover concession and seeds it with a string of hapless young women like me: sort of like a feeder team for the Playmate brigade—and this is to be my audition.

CHOMP CHOMP CHOMP

A has-been television announcer joins us and wastes no time with formalities. "I need a massage," he informs me, shucking out of his designer briefs. *Well, so do I, Bub.*

The way he strips is so perfunctory, so *entitled*—as *if* I've dressed up, made up, and driven across town specifically for the privilege of servicing his blubbered, withered old carcass—that I'm seized with revulsion, momentarily rendered speechless.

Ewwwwwwwww. Do you have any idea who you're talking to, you skeezy coot? I'm not one of your little starlet wannabes. And I'm sure not gonna massage THAT!

"Um, no thank you," I manage to stammer. "I was just getting ready to leave."

And I do.

Say what you will about cats, but they have an uncanny ability to detect human tears. Even if you're on the other side of the house weeping silently in the back of a closet somewhere, any cat who knows you well enough to sleep on your bed will seek you out and insinuate itself onto your lap as surely as its fur sticks to your throw pillows.

Shortly after Johnny left, a cat showed up in the hedges by the door to my apartment. A bedraggled little Siamese, the poor thing looked as woebegone and abandoned as I felt, and because I'm big on portents, I took him in. A good call, as it turns out. The thing becomes an instant friend and therapist, and the mid-sized rodents that have been raiding my larders soon find other quarters to pillage.

All things considered, "Cat," as it insists upon being addressed, is 90 percent of the good parts of Johnny (warm, furry, companionable), with only about 3 percent of the bad ones (it, too, farts under the covers). And since I had it neutered, it can't go out philandering on me, or surprise me with the news that it's had kittens by three different lady cats that it forgot to tell me about. Plus it uses the toilet *and* leaves the seat down. (Cats are a whole lot more charming if you teach them to use the commode instead of having to mess around with a litter box.)

Anyway, Cat is now purring in my lap as I wrench the last few tears from my broken expectations. After my latest fiasco in Hollyweirdland, I've been doing some serious soul searching. The mercenary undertones of any human interaction in that town are enough to suck the joy out of even the happiest of occasions. A new baby? How *wonderful!* Who's her rep? You sold your screenplay? *Love it!* Let's do lunch, I'm syndicating this new project, and . . .

Obviously I'm not cut out for this scene, no matter how many people tell me I should give it a serious go. There's just no way to subordinate an ego as rampant as mine long enough to remain civil in the company of such predators and degenerates—I'm simply not that good of an actress. Some people are okay with taking orders from inferiors, readily exchanging their self-respect for a bi-weekly paycheck. Others are adept at faking passion or admiration in exchange for little dribs and dabs of access. I, alas, am not.

More to the point, I'm constitutionally incapable of having "business sex" with people I wouldn't normally have voluntary sex with—and "business sex" is seemingly mandatory for anyone trying to break into the industry without benefit of brother-in-law or "benefactor."

True, I could cut off my long blond hair, start wearing my coke-bottle glasses again, don hideous over-sized clothes that disguise my body, and work the character actress angle. Or change my gait and posture, cultivate my zits, coarsen my voice and demeanor, and play the scary redneck chick who always lurks in the background during the convenience-store scene.

I *could*, but why should I *have* to? I'm a child of the sixties, dammit. The same thing that's working against me—the physical lusciousness that prevents anyone from taking me seriously—can also work *for* me—if only I can figure out the mechanism to keep it in check. When you're twenty years old and gorgeous, the world is full of temptations.

Our generation of women has come of age at a time of enormous transition—we're the first group of young unmarried women in the history of the planet to have unfettered access to reliable birth control—and a certain flexible morality is not only acceptable to us, it's essential. We can either throw in our lot with the God and Country housewives still gamely holding onto the authoritarian mindset of the 1950s, or join the vanguard now defining a new social order—one in which women are accepted as fully functioning members of society, and not just as breeders and helpmeets for a hierarchy of men.

It's important to think on this carefully, as I'm not fully comfortable in either role, but not fully alienated from them either. Madre has certainly given me a good example of how to be a working wife and mother, simultaneously pursuing a career, supporting her husband in his, volunteering in the community, steering her family. And yet, look at all she's given up to do so. The woman has no life of her own. I doubt she's ever spent a night by herself, let alone ever had a place she didn't have to share with someone.

That's not the life I want for myself. I'm *sick* of sharing my spaces with other people. Sometimes I even resent sharing with this unobtrusive cat. *Time to retreat and regroup,* away from predatory men and mercenary women, away from the mindless pursuit of money and the ruthless chase after power. Away from the traffic and the sulfurous air, and the too-many people on the too-mean streets. I've failed and I'm feckless and I'm fed-up. GET ME THE FUCK OUT OF HERE: away from *everything* except from *me.*

I get methodical. There must be someplace reasonably nearby Los Angeles close to what's left of my family and friends. Someplace where the air is clean and the town is vibrant and marginally civilized—because electricity and grocery stores are still nice things to have around. A happy place that will attract the kind of men I want to meet (sporty and adventuresome) and repel the kind of women I do not (fussy and wimpy). Smart people would be nice, with enough money to have some free time on their hands and the inclination to enjoy it. Someplace where I can fit in . . .

The family ski house in Mammoth sticks in my mind. Something about passing over the spectacular Sherwin Summit on our way back home to Los Angeles has always left me in tears, though I can never figure out exactly why. But even as a little kid I know it has to do with leaving a place that touches something profound in me—only to return to one that makes me frustrated and melancholy. It's as close to spiritual longing as anything I've ever known, and it's calling to me now. It may be the coward's way out, and it's as hugely irresponsible as everything else I've gotten myself into since leaving the bosom of my respectable family, but my mind is set; I'll move to Mammoth, get a job—any job—and become a useful member of the community there.

Someday I'll build a house, perhaps even run for city office . . . and maybe I'll find my future there in the snow and the sun and the Sequoias.

OFF TO SEEK MY MISFORTUNE

Highway 395 up to Mammoth is a stark and dramatic drive through the high northern border of the Mojave Desert. Death Valley is off to the east and the temperate coastal ranges are just over the peaks to the west. The Owens Valley through which it passes speaks of capacious greed and environmental rape at the hands of the water barons and the ranchers who sold out to them during the 1930s.

The once-verdant Owens River Basin, its lakes and aquifers, has been drained into the aqueduct that brings water into the semi-arid desert that is Los Angeles. I've been watching this region dry out and die since my family first started coming here in the 1950s, and by now, Mono Lake is nothing more than a vast bed of dust. It's not hard to feel a kinship with this bruised and ill-tended land.

Everything I now own is packed in the front bonnet and the rear jump seats of my little sportster—blankets, pots, books, shoes, my big flokati rug, all crammed and crushed into a passenger space meant for two adults and their weekend luggage. I've sold or given away everything else, the remnants of the life I'm leaving, left. Cat sits on the headrest next to my ear, yowling his disapproval as Bach's "Organwekes" thunder through the sound system and the car's well-tuned engine blends with the bass line of the pipe organ. I'm unconsciously playing the accelerator along with the organ score: C . . . let up on the gas, F# . . . accelerate slightly, G. . . .

By the time we get to the straightaway leading up to Sherwin

OFF TO SEEK MY MISFORTUNE

Summit, I'm so oblivious and so caught up in the music of engine and open road that the tachometer is approaching redline. *Probably time to switch to James Taylor so I don't kill myself before I even get started*, I think.

It's high noon when I pull into town and head straight for the condo where I've rented a room and bath—the upper floor of the unit—for four months at peak rate, all paid in advance so I don't have to worry about anyone's opportunistic whims leaving me looking for new quarters at the height of tourist season. It's cost me the better portion of my meager savings, but by springtime I'm sure to be settled in, well employed, and able to afford a place of my own.

Cat will like that. The guy I rent from assures me that his dog is cat-friendly, but I can hear it barking in the background on the phone as we arrange for the bank transfer, and it doesn't sound all that hospitable to *any*one—particularly not a fussy cat. Still, I was lucky to find this place so close to the start of ski season, and the transfer went through without a hitch, so I'm feeling pretty confident that this is going to work out just fine.

"Hey, how ya doin'?" my new landlord greets me at the door. "C'mon in. You're upstairs, right?"

"Um, yes?" He'd been pretty specific in his ad. Doesn't he remember? Two big unruly dogs pounce on me from under the kitchen table. Cat digs his claws into my upper arm and growls. Then a male voice calls down from upstairs, "Is this the broad I'm supposed to be sharing my room with?"

What? "I rented a private room and bath for the season," I remind the guy at the door. "I have the receipt."

"Oh, that must have been Dan you talked to. He's in Manzanillo now. This is Aaron, by the way," he says, pointing to a sullen-looking fellow blocking the stairway to my bedroom. "I'm Zack. I'm the owner."

I'm aghast. Dan has my money, but Zack is the owner? What have I gone and done?

"So," says Zack, "how do you want to handle your rent? Week by week, or month by month?" All I want to handle right now is Dan's throat, but I guess he's in . . . Manzanillo. It was all budgeted so carefully, right down to the cat food, and now I am not only skewered, I'm broke as well.

These two are probably in on the con together, but what am I supposed to do? I don't want to share a room with this grungy lout—even if I *can* get my money back. For a long moment I look Zack in the eyes trying to find one shard of human charity, but none is forthcoming; if this is a scam, he's not about to relent and confess. His face betrays nothing; he just shrugs and smiles a snide little smile. There's no point trying to argue with him—and who can I complain to? Dan has my money, and Aaron has my room. "Yeah. Thanks anyway," I say, too stunned to be outraged, thinking of the Donner Party, survival in the frigid mountains—I'd cannibalize these two asshats in a second if it came to that, and feed their lousy gizzards to my Cat.

I decide I'm lucky to have found out what sort of people they are right at the onset. And I'm sure I'm not the first person who's ever had to seek quarter in the passenger seat of an old sports car. I'll set up camp here in the parking lot tonight, and tomorrow see if that job at the restaurant is still open—at least there will be food and a warm kitchen.

My car isn't warm, but it's dry. Snuggled into the heavy flokati rug, parka zipped, watch cap over my head, it's almost cozy in here. Tears wet my cheeks, and Cat curls himself into a warm ball at my neck, a small reassurance in the uncaring night. I crack the window for air, and search, unsuccessfully, for sleep.

It's still dark when I am jostled awake by a tremendous lurch and an ear-shattering crunch. It takes me a minute to register where I am—*in a car, in a parking lot in the mountains.* I cannot see a thing but white and cold, although the car and Cat and I are all definitely moving. An earthquake? Avalanche? Apocalypse? Wet, heavy snow fills the car, covering my legs and parka. The glass of the window shatters, the door is hanging by a bolt from the body. Then I hear the roar of an accelerating snowplow barreling down on us. *WE'RE GOING TO BE KILLED!*

The driver probably hasn't even noticed that the dark lump he's just battered isn't a big rock of ice; why should he? The tires of his snowplow alone are bigger than my car, and he's twenty feet above me in a cab, probably listening to Creedence Clearwater on headphones while he clears last night's snowfall from the parking lot. I lean on the horn, hoping it will alert him to our presence, bracing for the next impact.

"What the hell do you think you're doing?!" The driver has seen us, his headlights shining directly into what's left of the car. His face is purple, distorted in the headlights. He is screaming at me, pointing. "Can't you read the fucking sign?"

NO OVERNIGHT PARKING—ABSOLUTELY NO EXCEPTIONS

Well, no. I hadn't. No wonder it was so easy to find a spot.

"Get the hell out of here before I call the sheriff!" I don't know what scares me more, the monstrous snowplow idling like a beast of prey ready to mow us down, or the driver, murderous at being interrupted.

Will the car even start? Will it run in this mangled condition? Mercifully, the engine turns over, and hugging the door closed as best I can, we lurch out of the parking lot and onto the empty street. My fender is smashed into the wheel well, dragging against the tire—I can smell rubber burning. Everything I own is soaking wet. My car is ruined. And oh yes, I've just been cheated out of a place to live for the winter. This is *not* the best day of the rest of my life—and it's only just begun.

THE HANDMAIDEN'S TAIL

The handwritten sign in the motel office has seen better days. Torn and crinkled, its lettering is faded in scratchy ballpoint, only hinting at the parsimony that awaits on the other side of the window. "Maid Wanted" it says. "Inquire within." Well, I *was* just going to rent a room for the night so I can take a hot shower and get some sleep before I try to figure out my next move, but maybe this is fortuitous? It's not what I'd pictured I'd be doing today, but then neither are the straits I find myself in.

"I can pay you a dollar a day and one of the rooms," says the manager when I inquire about the salary. "And your towels and linens, of course." He's leering at me slightly. I get an inkling of why he's seeking a maid in a town full of likely prospects.

"I have my cat," I begin. Cat is a deal breaker. No Cat, no motel maid.

"The wife and me love cats."

So it's settled. I'll clean and tidy thirty motel rooms a day in exchange for a pittance and a place to sleep in between my round-the-clock shifts. Hardly the deal of a lifetime, but what choices do I have? Given the circumstances, I'm grateful for the job. There is something to be learned in scrubbing out toilets, I'll wager.

THE HANDMAIDEN'S TAIL

<u>MAID SERVICE</u>
START AT 9:00 A.M.
<u>CHECK OUTS--COMPLETE CLEAN</u>
CHANGE LINENS ON BED--CHECK UNDER THE BED--CHECK ALL DRAWERS.
PUT CLEAN TOWELS IN-CHECK KLEENEX--CHECK TOILET PAPER--SOAP
CLEAN DRINKING CUPS.
CHECK COFFEE TRAY-WIPE OFF-SUPPLY OF COFFEE, CREAM, SUGAR,
    SPOONS, NAPKINS--CHECK COFFEE POT.
EMPTY ALL TRASH PUT NEW PAPER BAGS IN BASKETS.
THOROUGHLY CLEAN THE TOILET, PUT SEAL ON TOILET.
CLEAN SHOWER.
CLEAN ALL THE COUNTER TOPS AND MIRRORS.
SCRUB BATHROOM FLOOR.
DUST EVERYTHING, TABLE, CHAIRS, HEADBOARD, PICTURES. IF TABLE
    NEEDS WAXING WAX IT.
VACUUM REAL GOOD ALWAYS CHECK UNDER THE BED TO SEE IF IT NEEDS IT.
TURN HEAT TO LOW
TURN OFF ALL LIGHTS
CLOSE DRAPES
CHECK TO SEE IF ALL DOORS ARE LOCKED--UPSTAIRS TWO DOORS.
SPRAY THE ROOM WITH SPICE SPRAY.
    BEFORE LEAVING THE ROOM CHECK BACK ON THE LIST TO
    SEE IF EVERYTHING IS COMPLETED.

<u>DAILY MAID SERVICE</u>
DO MAID SERVICE BEFORE COMPLETE CLEANS.
CHANGE SHEETS IF NECESSARY AND ALWAYS AFTER THREE DAY STAY.
MAKE BEDS, EMPTY TRASH, TAKE OUT DIRTY TOWELS REPLACE WITH
CLEAN ONES.
CHECK COFFEE BAR- REPLACE SUPPLY FOR THE AMOUNT STAYING IN THE
ROOM. REPLACE DRINKING CUPS AND COFFEE CUPS.
TURN HEAT TO LOW. TURN OFF ALL LIGHTS. SPRAY THE ROOM LOCK ALL
DOORS.

What I learn is that I don't mind scrubbing out toilets so much as I mind scrubbing dried vomit off of walls, stuffing mite-infested pillows into clean pillowcases, and fending off Clyde the manager's clumsy advances in the upstairs rooms while his wife handles the office work down below. I also learn that any cash tips for the maid should be folded and placed under the lid of the toilet because that's the only place the manager doesn't look when he comes in after checkout to scour the room for loose currency or edible foodstuffs. Ostensibly to "check for damages," he's actually just scavenging for booty before I get the chance to do it first.

I hate him for snagging *my* leftover cheese and crackers, orange juice, doggie bags, cereal boxes. I also hate that he forgets about the $30 he promised me when I press him for my first month's wages. What's left of my savings is disappearing at an alarming rate. Exhausting as my "main" job is, it's obvious I'm going to have to get another, so on my afternoons and one day off, I clean additional toilets at a nearby condominium complex. "Why yes, I *do* have experience," I tell the manager. "In real life, I'm a motel maid." Sure it's hard work and I hate it with a passion, but at least *this* one pays me cash at the end of the day.

LOSE WEIGHT & KEEP IT OFF WITH THE POVERTY AND DEPRESSION DIET!

The November storms have left a nice base of hard pack on the slopes, much to the delight of the locals who've been suffering through a tourist drought. But now as winter finally arrives on the mountain, the place is packed with skiers, and the town is besieged with traffic. It's finally stopped blizzarding enough to allow a brief peek of sunset to break through the storm clouds, but *dang*, it's already dusk, and after a day of vacuuming, sanitizing bathrooms, scrubbing dirty dishes and cookware, and changing the sheets on what seems like a hundred rumpled beds, I'm still not finished with all my work.

Currently, I'm wrestling a ninety-pound ball of dirty towels and linens across the crowded parking lot to the laundry room, fighting the stinging ice that's blowing into all the exposed crevasses of my sweaty body. The condo manager drives alongside me in her shiny new Jeep, splashing slush from the gutter.

"It's almost dark, and we've got eight check-ins tonight," she yells out the window at me. "I need those units cleaned and ready to go."

"I'm doing my best," I tell her, but what I'm thinking is: *You could get out of your warm car and help me, you supercilious twat.* . . .

My stomach growls along with my unkindly thoughts. On top of everything else bedeviling me, I'm hungry. Lunch was a handful of stray peanuts salvaged from the several bags of shells some thoughtful weekenders had scattered throughout the carpeting of one of the three-story units, but my own makeshift pantry back in the motel room is currently as barren of food as my wallet is of money to buy some.

As I struggle on through the sludge with my mound of crusty sheets and crud-stained towels, my shoes soaked through and my fingers numb, lights begin to come on inside the toasty warm condos all around me. Outside, the peachy glow of the early evening turns to gray. *Now aren't you sorry you dropped out of college?* I think to myself.

Alone in the mountains in the cold snows of winter, surrounded by self-centered assholes, I've no money, no car, and my life is neatly containable in an old canvas backpack. Two days earlier, I literally gathered pennies from the floors of motel rooms to collect the $1 needed to buy my monthly allotment of government surplus foodstuffs. After hitchhiking the fifty miles to Bridgeport to the distribution station, I'd packed up my backpack with the designated brick of "American cheese product," a box of powdered milk, an industrial-sized package of dried vegetable soup mix, and a bag of pinto beans. Then I'd lugged it back down Highway 395 to my hovelette, so at least *that* much is waiting for me for dinner tonight. My stomach recoils as the peanuts begin their transit into methane; the wind blows hard and the snow stings cruel. I am most definitely *not* a happy camper.

Then I smell it. Wafting through the parking lot on the icy winter wind is the unmistakable scent of roasting turkey and baking crescent rolls. *Today is Thanksgiving.* In all my travail, I'd completely forgotten.

All around the town people are sitting down to tables laden with food and drink, and amidst convivial laughter are giving thanks for their warm houses and fine meals with beloved friends and family. And here I am cleaning everyone's dirty dishes. Again.

I think of my own folks, no doubt gathered at this very moment around the dining table, fighting over who gets the drumsticks and who has to walk the dog after dinner. I wonder what Johnny and Sara and all my one-time friends are smoking and drinking and reveling about now that I'm no longer there to prick their consciences with my presence. Then I look down at my ropey arms and hitch my jeans back up a notch over what had once been my hips. And in this moment I realize there is actually an *upside* to poverty and depression—and that's a twenty-three-inch waist. Of such epiphanies are diet programs born.

I stuff the laundry in the wash machines, flip the secret switch behind the panel to turn them on, and march into the condo manager's office to pick up my ten-dollar paycheck. "Do your own damned laundry," I tell her. "I quit."

SCREW U

Of course I'm still going to need that extra ten bucks a week, so against my better instincts, I answer an ad in the local paper for an afternoon position as a guest "hostess" at the ski area. I'm told that this entails babysitting bigwigs and guests of the mountain; watching their kids, running their errands, and acting as a concierge for them during their stay—exactly the sort of thing I expected to be doing for Eddie. The ad says they're looking for "confident, attractive, and well-spoken young women." Well, that's me . . . I think . . .

After vacuuming the fourteenth hotel room of the day, there's barely enough time to brush my hair before setting out to interview with Rick, the guy who manages operations for the ski complex. A quick spritz with the spice-scented room spray I use to "freshen" the units after they've been cleaned of their tortilla chip fragments and cigarette butts should help disguise the fact that I've spent the day with my head in other people's refuse. A dab of mascara, a pretty scarf, and I'm off to the mountain to change my luck.

Rick is everything one might expect of an up-and-coming ski mogul: tall, handsome, entitled, and imperious. In any other scenario, I would probably have gone out with him in a heartbeat, but as every poor supplicant who comes through these offices discovers, there's always a price to pay for that minimum-wage job. He barely even bothers to acknowledge me before he starts unbuttoning his jeans.

GAAAAGH! If predatory men are to be my lot in life, I'm going to be preyed upon on *my* terms and not yours. Why bother to hide my disgust? My upper lip is snarling over my teeth even before the tears start their course down the side of my nose. *If you think you can buy my attentions*

SCREW U

for a lousy $2.50 an hour, you've got another think coming. I already *have* one shitty job.

Drawing myself up to my full five-foot-one, I look this smarmy punk straight in the eye and muster as much disdain as I can summon. "No thanks, R-*ick*," I purr in my best Bette Midler snip. "I don't fuck the locals."

Once again it's time to confront my reality. If the Powers That Be saw fit to make me voluptuous and plop me down smack into the center of this carnal circus, then by golly, I'm going to avail myself of the opportunities that present themselves.

I know that in fifteen or twenty years, the second law of thermodynamics will kick in and entropy will mock my pretentions every time I look in a bathroom mirror. *Everything put together falls apart, so screw you, Ricks of the world.* (Or *un*-screw you, as the case may be.)

I may not be able to find the one lasting love of my life, but I can certainly make up for it in assortment. I don't want their money or their favors. I don't need their credentials or their authority, and I certainly don't want their "protection." I'll settle for being appreciated for being what I am—generous, unexpected, and excellent.

It's time, I reckon, to start auditioning men; heavens know this place is full of them. You want to be an anthropologist? Fine, *be* an anthropologist. Get out there and start studying! You can choose from doctors and lawyers, engineers and entrepreneurs, athletes and artists, and all of them healthy, affluent, and at least temporarily available. I can learn as much in one weekend in bed as in a whole quarter's worth of sitting in a classroom. Men of letters, men of the cloth, men of the soil, men of action, men of the arts. *Everyone*, I realize, has something to teach me, and all I have to do is ask them.

So I do.

I meet professional athletes who want to be artists, and business executives who want to shuck it all and open bait shops. All these variations and permutations, and always with the unstated understanding that this is the only shot we're going to have at each other, so let's do the best we can to make our time together memorable.

With a young computer professor, I brush up on my FORTRAN and am treated to a late-night session on one of the very first "Internet" connections—a fantasy game, he calls it, being played in Boelter Hall down at UCLA with a similar team hooked up to a WATS line at MIT. "It's called Dungeons and Dragons," he tells me. "Someday you'll be able to sit down at a computer in your home and play a game with anyone in the world." Then he shows me some animated pornography he's programmed. I'm impressed.

A glorious baritone is all too happy to demonstrate that not all opera singers are fat (they get barrel-chested from their expanded lung capacity and the stomach muscles needed to produce all that volume). Then he sings me a lullaby while he cuddles me to sleep.

A Formula One mechanic teaches me how to accelerate through a turn and shows me how to do a 360 in an icy parking lot (yank up the hand break while simultaneously cranking the steering wheel hard to one side). Against my protest, he sponsors me in a local demolition derby. (I'm not the last man standing, but I do survive.)

From a master woodworker I learn how to secure dovetail joinery (use Elmer's). An NBA center tutors me on the finer points of down-court tactics (hide your hands). A pediatric oncologist teaches me how to cope with spiritual helplessness (good wine and long-distance running).

I learn how to communicate enthusiasm in a commercial voiceover (big smile while you read your lines), how to stay on key and in rhythm singing complicated jazz improvisations (follow the bass line), and what to do if you're surrounded by a pack of wolves (sniff their butts). *Now how could I have learned any of this from a textbook?*

Matching the naked to the clothed is a fascinating pursuit. It's almost like getting two men in one, as the person beneath the haberdashery is often wildly at odds with the one presented to the outside world. I'm getting pretty good at discerning the difference. Some I'd consider spending my life with; most turn out to be stinkers. But I can honestly say that I made *love* to each and every one of them, and every last one of them thanked me when the time came to say goodbye. A veterinarian as furry as the creatures he ministers to has even offered to let me live in his condo while he's away studying predators on the African veldt for the year. *Finally*, I can get out of this awful motel. I quit as soon as I can.

A local hotelier sees some of my doodling at the local art fair and commissions me to paint decorative detail in its rooms and in the bar—and actually pays me for doing so! On the weekends I play piano at one of the nicer restaurants in town and sing cabaret at another. Life is definitely starting to look up.

With all the spare energy I have now that I'm not a motel maid, I've taken to spending my evenings writing in the jazz lounge at Whiskey Creek, a restaurant where the older and more affluent skiers tend to congregate. There is a quiet corner where I sit nursing a mug of tea and scribbling in my journal while I enjoy whatever combo is in town this week. It's the closest thing I have to a living room, so I make good use of the space, turning it into my own private little salon.

I'm never averse to chatting up anyone who cares to sit down and tell me a good story, and if he's lively and witty—and has an original pick-up line—there's a good chance he'll also get an invite back to the condo when the bar closes. One fellow in safari jacket and chukka boots gets my attention with, "Hello. Has anyone ever told you you look like Theodore Bikel?" Since I'm about as far from resembling the grizzled old Yiddish folksinger as anyone on the planet, I'm piqued enough to invite him to sit and chat. He proves so clever and engaging I end up enjoying a late-night supper with the guy *and* his twenty-something son.

Another wins me over with, "How would you like to come back to my condo and let me make you my world-famous Grand Marnier soufflé?"

But my favorite is the dapper old gentleman who taps me on the shoulder and says, "Excuse me, miss, but is you deaf?"

"I beg your pardon?"

"I asked if you was deaf."

"Why no, sir. No I'm not."

"*Damn* girl," he replies. "There must be *some*thin' wrong wif you. . . ."

If nothing is going on at the Whiskey, I'll hike down into Old

CHOMP CHOMP CHOMP

Mammoth to a nightclub they call Mill City. Dubbed "Smell Shitty" by the locals for obvious reasons, this old warehouse has been converted into a huge open dance floor with a busy central bar. A hangout for those who prefer their evening entertainment loud and rowdy, it's home to traveling rock 'n' roll bands, country-western bands, juke rhythm bands, and sundry studio musicians up from LA who flock to the place for its rafter-rattling acoustics and its highly marginal dress code.

With all the sweaty bodies and the sub-standard ventilation, the club turns into a sauna about fifteen minutes after it opens. Usually it's too damned hot to wear much clothing at all when you're dancing (and after all, this *is* the early seventies). Consequently, a lot of illicit skin ends up exposed during the course of the evening—on occasion, mine is among it.

In addition to the swarms writhing on the dance floor, there is always a large contingent of rednecks who show up just to get plastered on cheap beer and watch the topless hippie-chicks dance the night away. I'm pleased to count myself among the regulars, dancing my brains into a groove—alone, with couples, singles, or the odd hound who wanders in to escort its over-reveled master home. It doesn't matter, I just love to dance—and love to watch the mix of people *watching* me dance.

Although I'd never go home with anyone from Smell Shitty, it's a wonderful place to get mindless and let off steam. Literally. In the cold mountain air, the steam rising from dancers taking a breather outside looks like a roiling human cauldron on the verge of boiling over. In a sense, I suppose we are.

When I was a little girl, I'd invent these fanciful ballets for myself, leaping and twirling about to the strains of Tchaikovsky or Rossini coming from my scratchy little record player. Neither grace nor talent colored my movements, but in the privacy of my bedroom I was a famous ballerina, a magical creature flying across a far-off stage. There I would spin and twirl until my mind went numb and reality became something glittering and expansive rather than the drab confines of the room I shared with my more practical younger sister.

"Stop spinning," she'd yell at me over the strains of the *William Tell*

SCREW U

Overture. "You're making me barfy. I'm telling Mom." Then she'd run off and tattle on me, and Madre would appear in the doorway to spank me, confiscate the record, and return it to my father's library. "You're going to make yourself crazy doing that," she'd say—and maybe I did. But in any case, I eventually stopped dancing, too self-conscious to even try to do it in the presence of anyone else besides my bedroom mirror.

By the time I got to high school, it was all I could do to stand against a far wall of the gym and watch my cronies out there on the floor, twisting and frugging and gatoring away as though it were the most natural thing in the world to move one's body around to music. Music as *I* knew it was supposed to be serious and sacred, approached *methodically* and *scientifically,* processed through the mind, not the spirit. Dancing was as unfathomable to me as quadratic equations would be to a sled dog, and the very idea of doing *that* in public made my body start to curl inward on itself. The few times I *am* asked to dance, I just stand there like a dork, too self-conscious to move. Dancing, I decide, is just not my "thing."

Then one day a drummer I've met in town asks me if I've ever "done it" to Ravel's "Bolero." I can honestly say that I've not, though I know the score from my childhood twirlings. I'd never associated its tense, anticipatory passages and insinuating transitions with the act of intercourse. *Sex to a soundtrack! Of course!* Suddenly it's all clear to me, and with this realization I discover that I'm really *good* at dancing.

Moreover, my newfound lack of inhibition on the dance floor encourages the hesitant to join me out here, maybe even work up the courage to ask someone they've been eyeing to dance with them. Afterward, they come up to thank me. *Thank you for dancing like you mean it, Thanks for making my evening,* or *When I saw you dancing, I just wanted to run out there and follow you around the floor.* I get this one a lot.

I've just finished a particularly enthusiastic set and am sitting at a far table, sweating profusely and guzzling ice water while the band takes a break. A distinguished-looking man in an expensive leather jacket and a Greek fisherman's cap is standing near me, scanning the room. He's older than most of the patrons here, far too elegant for the surroundings. Towering over the stoners and fake lumberjacks milling around the bar, he catches my eye and zeroes in. By the time he reaches the table, I'm spellbound. Looming, he bows slightly and says, "Pardon me for asking, miss, but—are you in *love*?"

I've heard some doozy pickup lines by this time, but I have to give this guy points for originality. Smiling back, I gesture to the empty chair next to me, and he sits, elbow to table, leaning back slightly, chin resting on his thumb. He never breaks eye contact.

"What if I say yes?" I ask.

"I'll say, 'I *thought* so, and I just wanted to tell you how radiant you look tonight.' Then I'll tip my hat and move on."

"And if I say no?"

"Then I'll say, 'Then perhaps you'd be free to have dinner with me this Thursday night? Say around seven o'clock?'"

"I'd *love* to be in love," I tell him.

"Meet me at my place?" he replies and presses a card into my hand. It's a heavy, handmade stock with intarsia print; very European, very expensive. "Rod Roddewig: Epicure." On the back he had written the address of one of the swankiest houses in Mammoth Lakes.

How on earth am I supposed to decline an invitation like this?

"I'll be there, Mister . . . um, Roddewig," I say, sizing up those knowing eyes, his perfectly trimmed beard, that *cap*.

"Call me Rod."

He touches the brim of his cap with his forefinger, rises to pull out my chair, bows slightly as I leave. As I dip, whirl, and do-si-do, I notice him watching me from the far table—alone, and out of place in the raucous beer hall. He's nursing a scotch, smiling. While I dance, I muse on the absolute genius of his opening line. He hasn't asked me if I'm here with anyone, or if I'm seeing anyone, he's asked me if I'm "in love." If I say yes, he comes off like a gentleman, and if I say no, he comes *on* like a gentleman. But in either case, he's left the decision entirely up to me.

I don't notice when he leaves.

BOWLFUL OF PORRIDGE

Cat watches from his perch on the bookcase as I dress for dinner. My inclination is to go ladylike, posh, maybe even wear pearls for this evening. But Rod Roddewig was attracted to a sweaty dervish in fringe and tie-dye, so I'm having a crisis of identity. Who am I, really? The refined academic or the decadent sybarite? *You're a retired motel maid looking for a good time*, says the lesser angel of my desires.

It seems that no matter what situation I find myself in, I'm required to choose one or the other. Maybe my sense of alienation, of not ever quite fitting in anywhere is informed by this conundrum? *Or maybe you're just a pompous twit on an ego trip?* (I *hate* that little voice. . . .)

The little black dress and pearls win out, but I throw on a hippie scarf and an embroidered Afghan sheepherder's coat for detail. And my snowmobile boots for traction. That seems about the right mix.

The night air outside is clear and cold, and the stars envelop me as I walk. It's easy to lose my equilibrium in the mountain darkness and succumb to the sensation of flying, skimming the ground rather than being anchored to it. By the time I get to Roddewig's stone mansion, the sensation of suspension has become so surreal, so detached, that I'm nearly hallucinating. I'm not brought back to earth when he answers the door wearing a thick Norwegian sweater and that cap, smoking a pipe. The man is breathtaking.

From somewhere beyond him comes the warm scent of roasting game bird, savory herbs, something toasty and cheesy baking in an oven, all punctuated by the mellow earthy smoke from his pipe and a flute solo floating in the background. As I walk in, the house is cavernous, diminishing me—like it must all the non-giants who walk among us. A fire burns in the center of the room under a massive copper hood that extends up to . . . somewhere.

He takes my coat, notes my attire, nods approvingly. With his finger and one arched eyebrow, he motions me to twirl around for him. I do. "You look amazing tonight," he says. "I'm so glad you could come. I thought I'd take the liberty of cooking for you here. You strike me as the sort of lady who could appreciate that sort of thing."

Why yes, I can.

He sits me down on a vast leather sectional facing the open stonework kitchen, bids me to make myself comfortable, and brings me a glass of wine. The sofa could easily seat a dozen people—I've never seen anything like it. "I thought we'd start with a Sancerre," he says, raising his glass in toast. "To you."

I'm lost, entranced. It's like the disorientation I feel when the night sky meets the earth, and the dimensions meld under my feet. Now I've brought it *inside* with me, and the same thing is happening. I'm disambiguating into this wonderful house, the décor, the intoxicating smells coming from the kitchen.

He returns to a skillet of something pungent and fruity sautéing on the big cast-iron stove and begins stirring it with a whisk, then beating in chunks of butter from a stoneware crock, chatting amiably. " I just returned from a jaunt to France with Gael Greene, the food critic from the *New York Times* . . . ," he's reciting. "A guest of Baron Philippe to mark the inclusion of his Mouton Rothschild into the Grande Cru Classe. Twenty-one days, twelve hundred and fifty-seven miles, seventeen three-star restaurants, all five first-growth wineries, one million, three hundred forty-three, five hundred and eighty-six calories . . ."

Whatever he's cooking smells heavenly. I fixate on a splendid Two Grey Hills Navajo rug slung casually over the sofa, a fur throw folded over the ottoman, Etta James is purring something low and seductive from speakers hidden somewhere inside the hewn-stone walls. This is like something out of *The Thomas Crown Affair,* only I'm sitting here in the

BOWLFUL OF PORRIDGE

middle of it instead of watching it from a theater in Westwood Village.

Roddewig carves the roasted pheasant, dresses it with the fruity reduction, portions out the wild rice and mushroom risotto. I'm about to swoon. "We'll have this with a '66 Lafite I brought back," he says, uncorking the bottle and decanting it into a thin crystal carafe as I finally forgive myself for my austerity back when I was staying at Monsieur B.'s villa in Arcachon. "Everything's better with a bit of age on it," he says with a sly little wink. I'm about to drop to my knees right here and now, a slave to his bidding, but he's all about the food. And so am I, I realize.

Over dinner I learn that Roddewig is a wine critic, a restaurateur, and a nightclub impresario. He likes to throw parties, "swing parties," he says matter-of-factly, for the wealthy and famous. *So that explains the playpen sofa.* But what he loves most in life is cooking. "And discovering exquisite bottoms. Like yours. When I saw you dancing, I nearly lost my marbles."

Ahhhhhhh. So Roddewig is an ass man....

Dinner is extraordinary, the wine superb, the conversation far-reaching and witty. I am, in every sense, delighted. *My first raconteur!* And headier still, I'm holding my own with him. This is the sort of person I came up here to meet. Finally. My destiny has arrived.

We finish off the evening with a fine old port—which he pours into oversized snifters the thickness of my thumbnail—and cigars, which I never knew I liked. Utterly satiated in body and spirit, I sink back into the leather sofa, ready for whatever he has to give to me, do to me, exact from me. I'm putty, I'm aspic, I'm a blow-up doll, lifelike in every detail. Do with me as you will....

"I never fuck on the first date," he says cheerfully, taking my hand and leading me to a guest room. "Why don't you sleep in here, and I'll drive you home in the morning? I'm right across the hall if you . . . need anything." He pauses here, unexpectedly flirtatious. I realize he's giving me the option to come to *him*, knowing I will eventually, allowing me the initiative here as well. Ever the gentleman.

I'm so charmed by his nonchalance, his easy assumptions, that I stand on tippy toes and kiss each of his furry cheeks goodnight, his cap still immobile on his head. Then I turn and flash my perfect arse at him before slipping into the well-appointed room and the best night's sleep I've had in months.

A WHOLE NEW WORLD

Roddewig and I spend every day skiing while he's here, and every evening cooking for each other. But cooking *with* each other? Not so much. We had sex once—it seemed the right thing to do—but what we've really found in each other is a friend. We both know we can get laid anywhere, but finding a companionable gossip is a real treat—especially when it's a companionable gossip who can ski like a banshee and loves great food and wine.

Everywhere we go, he introduces me to people—*fabulous people*—of the sort I've only read about in international society magazines. People who aren't striving—because they don't have to. The ones who congregate in places you never knew were there. People so sleek and so self-assured they surely must have been born that way. Young people, old people, people of indeterminate gender, but all people with a certain *je ne sais quoi*. An inner light, if you will, and that warm, buttery skin that separates the stellar from the merely spectacular. *I think they've confused me with someone else. . . .*

"This is my good friend, Allena," Roddewig says, like he's known me forever. "She has a great . . . [peering over my shoulder at my backside] *personality*." His women (and I call them that because, in reality, we're *all* his girlfriends), far from being catty or condescending, seem delighted to meet me. As do the men. Roddewig is so upfront and open about his love life that there's no room for jealousy or possessiveness. He's just . . . Rod, and he belongs to everybody.

I think of all the chicanery and double-crossing that I've been dealt in my relationships with men, and decide that his is by far the best policy. Be honest and straightforward from the very beginning, stay cheerful and matter-of-fact throughout, and no one will have false expectations. Or claim to have been misled. Or have an excuse to cast aspersions when another variable enters the sexual equation. For solipsists like me who are too lazy to keep track of our lies and too self-centered to even bother coming up with them in the first place, it's a policy that makes perfect sense.

Thus I learn a great life's lesson from one of the masters:

Thou shalt be upfront.
And its corollary:
Thou shalt not apologize for it.

VOICE OF THE SIERRAS

Springtime in the Sierras is not all it's cracked up to be. For one thing, there's mud—lots of mud, icy and ubiquitous. It's the kind of mud that finds its way onto every clean surface and article of clothing you own, then dries into pollen-laden dust and takes up quarters in your airways. For another thing, my spring hormones are kicking in and there's nothing for them to kick *into*. Mammoth is *dead* in the springtime, which is why all the locals (those who can afford it, anyway) take their unemployment checks and head down to Cabo San Lucas until the summer tourist and construction season starts in June.

I'm wandering around town on a fine spring afternoon, aimlessly checking my post-office box for advertising circulars when I hear a familiar voice coming through the radio on the PA system.

Looking for a good time? [Over a nasty *BUM PA-pa DUMP* stripper's blues.] *Come on over to The Naz's house tonight after nine, and get ready to par-TAY! Forty Mono Street in the blue A-frame. And bring your own herb.*

That voice. It's unmistakable. I've heard it a thousand times as a kid, a teen, a student. Back when AM radio was *the* social medium for young people, this voice accompanied me on dates and consoled me in their aftermath. That creamy-dreamy bass had been with me as I resented my way through homework, wandered lonely beaches, and stared for endless hours into the bathroom mirror, trying to will myself into a state of hipness worthy of the velvet patter coming out of my red transistor radio. Later on, it provided a sexy-soothing backdrop to my earliest backseat fumblings, a familiar touchstone as I ventured forth into the brave sexual frontiers of the sixties.

No doubt about it, this voice belongs to Leroy Joseph, the undisputed

CHOMP CHOMP CHOMP

king of Los Angeles AM rock, and judging by the fact that he is reading the local weather report, he's just across the parking lot from me in the studio of the local FM outlet. Live and in person. *That does it. I'm going over there right now.*

Now, I'll admit this is a purely groupie move on my part; the mere sound of that voice is still enough to make me squirm. What Leroy Joseph might be doing in this tiny start-up radio station in Mammoth Lakes, I don't even care to guess, but one thing's for sure—I'm going in, and I'll likely gush like a star-struck teenybopper when I do.

One of the sadder truisms in this life is that radio personalities' looks never match up to their voices. You can almost count on the sexiest purr coming from the pimpliest pipsqueak. Leroy, however, is the happy exception. I march into the office of the tiny broadcast studio, and there he stands—a tall, dark, half-Lakota Sioux with mint-green eyes and a killer smile. His thick black hair is tied back in a ponytail and he's wearing blue denim everything with perfectly scuffed cowboy boots. His jeans are tight and his presence is massive. Man doesn't even have to open his mouth and I'm lost.

The connection between us is instant, the chemistry volcanic. We're ready to jump each other and we haven't even met. He locks eyes with me, touches the tip of his tongue to his upper lip, eyes narrowing like a mountain cat about to drop from a tree onto the neck of its ungulate prey. I'm frozen and galvanized all at the same time.

"Do you have any . . . *requests?*" he asks, heavy on the insinuation. His voice is so deep and so resonant that I'm ready to collapse into a puddle at his feet, my knees heavy with lust. I've got to think quick, or I'm a goner. Anything. Anything for a bit of distance between those compelling eyes and the last shard of my common sense.

"Um. Play 'Misty' for me?"

The new Clint Eastwood movie's just out, so that's not as much a cliché as it might seem. In fact, the implied sense of menace is just enough to give us the breathing room to introduce ourselves.

"I've noticed you dancing," he says.

"I love your music," I say.

VOICE OF THE SIERRAS

"Do you need a roommate?" he responds, his eyes settling over me like an eiderdown comforter.

In retrospect, I probably should have taken this query as cautionary, because as it turns out, it's not hyperbole. He really *does* need a place to stay, and he really *is* this impulsive and flighty. But at the time, all I can think about is the electric *zzzip* of those 15,000 watts of clear channel crackling through the studio and my own lingering hunger for a voice in the night. *His* voice.

It doesn't take him long to move in. My vet has returned from Africa with a new wife, and I've relocated to a small room and bath behind the laundry room of an apartment building in the center of town. It's a small room, *very* small, and certainly illegal, but it's within walking distance of everything, and it's only $90 a month—including all the electricity I can eat. Not only this, it shares a wall with a bank of dryers, so the coming winter promises to be warm and cozy, if perhaps a bit vibratory.

I've made a bed of my flokati rug, lined the window wall with plank-and-cinderblock shelving for my makeshift kitchen, and strung a length of heavy chain across a corner to hang my clothing from. I do my dishes in the bathroom and my laundry in the laundromat just outside my front door. All in all it's a nice, tight little cabin—like a sailboat, I tell myself. I keep my skis in a small locker in the garage, and the window cracked for Cat to come and go as he likes. Cat immediately takes up residence in the big Jeffrey pine just outside the door, where he spends his days snagging blue jays and his nights tormenting the neighborhood dogs. There's not enough room in my room for the both of us, you see.

It is here that I bring my sweet Leroy, with his backpack full of clothing and his brain awash with a bewildering collection of dissonances and discrepancies. And it is here that we make our little love nest. All 170 square feet of it.

Fortunately, the majority of our time is spent down at the radio station, troubleshooting. The owners, a couple of enterprising-if-clueless brothers, have decided that what Mammoth really needs is an FM profit center. They obtained the permits and the financing to build the structures, but ran out of money before they had a chance to hire an actual staff to get and keep the thing on the air. Their business plan, apparently, is to let the local kids come in and fill up the airtime (for free—the brothers *graciously* won't charge them a cent for the privilege) in exchange for their use of the kids' time and record collections. All they need is an engineer with a first-class radio operator's license to oversee everything and keep the station in compliance with FCC regulations.

Enter Leroy. He's been a racetrack announcer, worked the carnies and the supermarket openings. He'll hitchhike across the country to take a two-week fill-in in South Dakota, or lend his name to a radio lineup that's in need of a little bit of star power in exchange for a few hundred bucks and a snootful of blow. That's just the way things are in this business, as I soon discover.

In the world of on-air announcers, Leroy is widely acknowledged as one of the Greats. A bordering-on-genius talent with a knowledge of the library that is second to none, his segues between selections are a thing of beauty and his groupies are legion and legendary. But he is also widely known as a complete flake, prone to taking off for points unknown on a moment's whim, never to return as the record tracks into dead air and the phone banks light up with advertisers on the verge of apoplexy.

This time Leroy blew into town on a fishing trip, or a backcountry pub crawl, or on the lam from an angry ex-wife—I never do find out—and happened upon the Inverness brothers in a local tavern. A few drinks were exchanged, contracts were produced and signed, and Leroy is now in charge of putting together a syndicate of ski resort radio stations playing what he has proposed be called "album-oriented radio"; that is to say, he'll put on an album and let it track through a few cuts, just short of BMI copyright infringement, and use the time he doesn't have to be on the air to do production, traffic, and janitorial services. This innovation saves the Invernae the boatload of money they would otherwise have had to "waste" on hiring actual employees to run the place.

In exchange for all of this Leroy won't take a salary, let alone union pay scale, but he'll get slightly more than minimum wage and an undefined "percentage" of the company. I cringe when he tells me this. The

VOICE OF THE SIERRAS

Inverness brothers are renowned for this tactic; half the people in town have a percentage of one of their defunct operations or another.

Leroy proposed he make tapes of hour-long sets and rig up the station to play his prerecorded content so it can operate through the night with only a "babysitter" to keep an eye on the equipment and alert him to any trouble. This is an entirely new concept at the time, and one whose cheap simplicity appeals to the brothers' well-honed sense of thrift. All he needs is a record library. The Inverness brothers balk at buying anything, so they make do with donations from local collections and whatever they can scavenge from Salvation Army record bins. It's an eclectic mix—with Montovani strings and Country Caterwauling predominating—but it's a start.

Because I'm now Leroy's *old lady*, it comes to me to procure "content." He gives me the lofty title of "music director," and tells me to go out and find some. So here we are, Leroy and me and a couple of star-struck locals, organizing, chasing down advertisers, tracking FCC compliance, trying to keep the station running and on the air.

Our transmitter is located on the top of Mount Morrison (elev. 12,241') and when it blows a tube—which is frequently—it requires an organized mountain assault to repair. We recently lost our mechanical engineer to a squirrel-hunting expedition, which—in combination with the significant number of brewskis he'd consumed while toting around his shotgun—left him minus a few toes. They saved his foot, but he's not going to be scaling any mountains for awhile, so that leaves the task to us.

"You haven't lived until you've climbed a two-hundred-foot transmission tower in sixty-five-mile-per-hour winds to replace a busted magnetron," says Leroy. *And I guess my life is destined to remain unlived.*

As we approach from the highway, I take one look at the lonely tower oscillating on the side of a foreboding flint-strewn mountainside and decide I'll take my chances with the marketing end of this production, though that, too, promises to be no less a threat to my well-being.

Soon, I'm holding a belaying rope and trying my best to avoid hypothermia while Leroy fiddles with a vacuum tube twenty stories above me. He's perched on flimsy metal scaffolding, secured only by this rope I'm holding. As I watch the lightning strikes arcing blue off the transmission lines not so very far down the valley, I'm acutely aware of the humming metal superstructure towering above me while bracing myself against a sign that reads, "EXTREME DANGER FROM RF EMISSIONS. STAY BACK!" No LSD trip I've ventured has topped this for situational-induced paranoia. I feel like I'm in a Frankenstein movie, and the monster is about to animate. A crack of lightning hits closer to the tower, lighting the scene in an eerie metallic blue.

"Get down here right now!" I scream up through the wind. I'm so agitated I'm about to lose my sphincter; have never been so scared for anyone in my life. It's at this point that I realize I'm hopelessly in love with the man. If he dies up here on this mountain, I'll throw myself from a precipice! I'll dash my brains on the rocks!

No need. He rappels back down the side of the tower, grinning like the mental case he is. "I got it!" he proclaims to the Owens Valley below. "We're back on the air, people." I fling myself at him and cling like a bush baby, terrified, relieved, horny as hell. My hero.

When we get home to the hovelette, far from tumbling directly into bed with me as I had expected, Leroy is uncharacteristically quiet. He busies himself in the bathroom as I hang up our coats, stash our boots, and unpack the groceries. When he emerges, he is somber, and again I feel terror—the same sinking hopelessness I used to get when the Big Bad Wolf invaded my nightmares and in my dreams prowled the perimeter of our house, pausing with each round to peer into my bedroom window with those burning red eyes and those big white teeth. *I don't like this one little bit. Something is definitely amiss. . . .*

"I'm going out for a drink," Leroy announces, avoiding my eyes altogether.

I'd expected we'd celebrate tonight. It's been a long, scary day and I feel like whooping it up, sharing our adventure with friends, maybe even getting shitfaced and crazy. *We've been together for six months and we've been inseparable. Leroy doesn't even go to the bathroom without giving me a goodbye hug first.*

VOICE OF THE SIERRAS

"Shall I come with?" I ask, more beseeching than offering.

"I need to talk with the Inverness brothers about the transmitter. I'll be back later. You don't need to wait up."

Well, of COURSE I'm going to wait up. What the hell is going on?

Without further preamble, he takes his coat from the door, shrugs it back on, and walks out, leaving me standing there in the middle of the room without a clue. I've just seen a man I don't know. Pride and good manners prevent me from following him, confronting him, but my body feels like it's about to combust and turn to ashes, and my mind is racing back into blackened recesses I thought I'd locked away forever. *Plus ça change, plus c'est la même chose.* The more things change, the more they remain the same. I'd done it again. I'd gone and fallen for a philanderer.

It's way past midnight and Leroy still isn't back. He's not back the next morning when I wake up, and he's not back that night. Or the next. For three days and nights, I sit, holed up inside the little room, not eating, motionless but for the sobs racking my body. My helpless misery is only compounded by the sense of humiliation. I'd thought we were a couple. I'd treated us as something committed and honorable, been proud to be seen with him, introduce him as my partner. I'd worked my ass off to keep him sober and professional, and now everybody and their dog knows it was all a sham.

That's what you get for having been such a slut, I allow myself.

Comes the other voice: *Bullshit, lady! He's been twice the cunt you have and people CONGRATULATE him for it. It's not fair!*

And . . . ?

When Leroy finally *does* come back, I'm lying on my tummy, fast asleep in our bed. It barely registers that he's home until I feel something poking me in the back, sliding down to my bottom, pressing against my anus. There is an arm around my throat, and a hand pushing my face down into the pillow. Roughly, anonymously, he enters me—or tries to, I'm a virgin here, and I've not the slightest inclination to lose that status. I can smell bourbon on his breath, and cigarettes, and someone else—maybe several *someones*—on his skin. But I'm so depleted, so *defeated* that

111

CHOMP CHOMP CHOMP

I don't even move. I just lie there, tearing, punishing myself for his sins as he expatiates them into my bowels. He's killed more than my love for him. He's killed my spirit.

He's snoring there in my bed now. When he'd finished, I'd let him roll off and fall into his drunken stupor without even confronting him—without even reacting, in fact. I acted just as dead as I felt, but now in the aftermath, I'm very much awake, and my resignation has morphed into murderous outrage. This man, this unmitigated *asshole* has moved into my house, availed himself of my comfort, my support, my honest adoration, and he has the *gall* to betray me like this? Betray *us*? Shame on him, and shame on me for letting him.

I steal over to the "kitchen" eyeing the fat-free fryer—a flat, round, cast-iron griddle with heft and a handle. Just like Grandmother's. Just like an old mountain hillbilly lady's. . . .

It has perfect balance and the perfect weight for my purposes.

Leroy Joseph has fucked his last floozie.

I stand there over him for a long minute debating whether or not this is worth spending the rest of my life in prison over. I figure I've got a pretty good case; I'm bleeding from my rectum, and I'm sure a dozen people saw him out drinking tonight with whomever he was out drinking with. Maybe I'll get off with justifiable homicide.

I raise the frying pan over my head and smash it down on his skanky-ass skull with all my might. There is a dull *thud* as the blow dissipates into the pillow and the bedding—hardly the mayhem I was expecting. Leroy only grunts and returns to his snoring. Whatever damage I may have done to his cranium, it hasn't registered on him . . . yet.

In the morning he wakes, groggy, rubbing his head.

"Damn," he says, exhaling three day's worth of toxicity in one miasmic yawn. "That was *some* bender."

I say nothing and continue scrambling his eggs—on the fat-free fryer.

VOICE OF THE SIERRAS

The early seventies are awash in hippie scammers bent on "liberating" everything from shop goods to the toilet paper in public restrooms, so record companies are loathe to send us free albums just because I'm claiming to be a "music director." Procuring "content" requires a certain degree of imagination and daring these days, like showing up at the record company offices in person carrying a large snake or a trained ferret, and giving out copious sexual favors. And that's just to get in the door. "Back in the days of payola, it used to be the other way around," Leroy tells me. "Record reps would make the rounds of the *radio stations* trying to get their product on the air."

He tells me about a singing duo who used to ply the Central Valley when he was working Bakersfield in the early sixties. The guy would show up dressed like a pimp, and his fifteen-year-old girlfriend, eyes a-glop with makeup, would get to work on the disk jockey and music director while he made sure their forty-five RPM singles were included in the playlist. "They weren't very good, and everybody thought they were a joke, but they went on to become huge stars," he tells me. "TV show, politics, the whole shebang."

I'm not quite ready to go that far, but I'm not opposed to looking up some of my old *associates* who might have contacts in the recording industry. Tentatively, I dial Jackass's number. Gregory from the commune. Goldie from the gangbang. Rod.

I guess it really *is* not what you know but who you blow.

"Ah—*leeenna!*" says Roddewig when I finally get him on the phone. He's in the corporate offices of a giant public relations firm now, employed as something he calls an "event planner." "I've just been thinking of you," he tells me. After running down an impressive list of celebrity clients he's working with these days, he says, "I'm throwing a fortieth-birthday party for the managing editor of *Playboy* magazine next week, and I think you ought to meet him. If you're looking for industry contacts, lots of recording and literary types will be there." He goes on to praise the man's intellect, talent, and wholesome goodness. "We've been friends forever. I think you'll like each other a lot."

CHOMP CHOMP CHOMP

Roddewig will fly me down, pick me up at the airport, and whisk me off into the Hollywood Hills for the party. All I have to do is show up and be charming; *he'll* do the rest.

I mull this one over. Leroy has put on his backpack and boogied again, this time "to go fishing," but I'm pretty sure he's either visiting an ex-wife or off somewhere with a new honey he's met in town. What I'm fairly certain of is that he's *not* fishing, because he's left his tackle box in the garage next to his snowshoes. I'm more concerned about the pretense than what he's doing because I know he'll be back. He always comes back—usually a day or so after I've scraped up enough money by myself to pay the rent for another month. Every month.

As I sit here with the telephone receiver in hand, listening to Roddewig extol the virtues of another man, I have an epiphany. I realize that I just have to go about my life as best I can, go cold turkey on Leroy, and wait for my addiction—my *physical* addiction—to him to be over. To literally get him out of my system.

I'm still in love with the guy, I'll admit it, and he loves me back—insanely at times, and certainly passionately. He's even asked me to marry him, but that's not going to happen. He's just too flighty and I will need to be with someone steady and faithful if I'm ever to raise a family—not that I'm so inclined, but still . . . I've resigned myself to his infidelities, but I'm never going to commit to him.

What I *have* committed to, though, is making "resort radio" a reality. We need new albums and artists in the worst way and I figure Roddewig's invitation is as good a chance to get a foothold onto the industry's list of "approved" stations as I'm going to get. Might as well go see the boy, meet his friend Murray, and see what I can pull off—*for the station.*

"Absolutely, Roddy," I tell him. "When do you need me to be there?"

DESTINY CULLS

I'm standing cliffside on the edge of a perfect lawn looking down over the city from the Hollywood Hills. I used to stare at these hills from the opposite perspective of my bedroom window in coastal Palos Verdes and wonder what sort of strange and exotic people inhabited them. So *this* is what was out here all that time!

There is something both surreal and circular about this moment, but I can't dwell on it because Roddewig has just snapped me back to reality, interrupting my reverie with a plate of canapés and a glass of something splendid, then excused himself to "go mingle"—which I know means he's off to rate women's derrieres and gather phone numbers.

I've just taken a mouthful of pâté when a voice accosts my thoughts. "You look as though you're lost in quiet contemplation," it says. "I'd like to think you're not planning to jump; surely the company isn't as bad as all that . . ." I turn, and come eye-to-sternum with our host. Looking up, up, up into the most compellingly masculine face I've ever seen, his bearing, his confidence, his unabashed *amusement* fairly command adoration. Literally rendered speechless, I burst out laughing instead. "No, hardly suicidal—quite the contrary. I was just gathering my bearings for what promises to be the onslaught ahead." My eyes narrow flirtatiously. *Will he take the bait?*

Now it's his turn to laugh, and I'm rewarded with an infectious baritone so hearty it's impossible not to join in. More a roar than a laugh; with his majestic profile, his leonine mane of hair, his lordly manner, this man is every inch the literary lion Roddewig described him as. He looks at me more closely now, seemingly more delighted than surprised at my response.

Nothing more needs be said between us. I've passed the initiation.

We chat a few moments about this and that, and then he passes me off to a couple of "his" writers, two blasé-looking guys in their early thirties who have just published an expose of Howard Hughes. I've read it, and was blown away by its solid research and tight authoritative prose. They, like many investigative journalists—or so these two tell me—are feeling underappreciated tonight and devastatingly horny. We'll have plenty to talk about.

The rest of the evening is a blur, but I'm struck by the difference between this Hollywood party and the ones I'm used to. The home is the same modernist, open, wood-and-wall-of-windows-on-the-hillside style, the same shimmering pool and city lights, and the same rarified atmosphere of cozy inclusion, but the company couldn't be more diametric from those old parties. For one thing, the people here appear to have read a book in their life—and more than a few have actually *written* one. The conversations are subdued and intense, witty and ranging instead of loud and braying and self-congratulatory. It's as though the Manhattan "literati" has been transported to LA, given a tan, a workout, and a sense of humor—dinner-party company, not disco-party company—and I couldn't be happier to be here.

As it turns out, Murray has thrown this bash to announce his engagement to Barbara, the editor of an up-and-coming feature magazine just relocated to the West Coast. She's every bit as smart and vibrant as he is, and they make such a perfect power couple, it's hard to feel disappointed that he's already spoken for.

Roddewig was right about the energy between Murray and me, but wrong, alas, about the timing. No big deal, however, as I'm sure he'll remember me, and there are more than enough intriguing people here to keep me busy for months. It's as though half the city's celebrated journalists, pundits, and novelists are gathered here in this living room just waiting to scintillate all over me and welcome me into their fold. Another swallow of wine, a deep breath, and I'm off to join Roddewig on his mission to fill his Rolodex. It promises to be a most productive night.

DESTINY CULLS

When I return to Mammoth with several cartons of new-release album pressings and a notebook full of industry contacts in tow, Leroy is nowhere to be seen.

"Oh, he and Bobby took off for Sun Valley, to set up a new station there," says the kid who's working the engineering room. "The syndicate decided to try out this new 'cable' thing to sidestep the FCC. Clever, huh?"

Why am I not surprised? "Uh, did he say when he'd be back?"

"Nope. But he said you know how to run the station and you should take over until he does."

"And he didn't tell you when that might be?"

"Nope."

"Did he leave a phone number? Or anything?"

"Nope."

A week later, I still haven't heard from Leroy, but the other Inverness brother finds me in the office and tells me the new station is going great—and they're in talks to start up another one in Aspen.

"Cool," I tell him. "Then how about paying me some of the back wages you keep telling me you don't have?"

"Don't have 'em. Sorry."

I look at him, then I look out the front window at the new four-wheel-drive pickup truck parked in front of the station.

That does it. I've had it with these free-form "businessmen." I've brought in enough sponsors and albums now, and gotten us on enough influential mailing lists to ensure an indefinite flow of new product for airplay. My work here is done—*and* uncompensated.

When Leroy finally does call me from Sun Valley, it's too late; I'm already back in LA, writing a sex-advice column for one of Murray Fisher's Euro-*Playboy* associates. Leroy can go pound Sandy.

RESEARCH FELLOW

The terrible thing is that after a few months, I *miss* the guy. Yes, he's a flake, and yes he's a philanderer, and no, I can't count on him for anything except to be a flake and a philanderer, but *ooohhh* what beautiful music he makes, and *ooohhh* how I miss that honeyed voice in my ear. Every now and then he sneaks me a three-minute toll call from the Sun Valley station, but it's the worst kind of tease—just enough time to say hello and put our minds into the groove before the operator clicks us off. To compound my ambivalence over our separation, Leroy has taken to sending me taped air checks of his radio show—in which he dedicates set after set of plaintive love songs and meaningful ballads to me, his "special lady in the Big City." I can't tell if he's courting me or taunting me, but it's driving me crazy with want—which I'm sure is his intent. Lonely and hormonal, I throw myself into my "advice" column, pouring my frustrations into my words. Murray says it's some of the best raw jack-off material he's ever read—and as both an editor and connoisseur of such matters, he should know.

Since I'm in the sex-biz—if only peripherally and in the second person—Murray urges me to do continuing research, "To bring authenticity to your writing." Personally, I think he just enjoys indulging his fantasies through my written narrative, but it's a fun creative exercise, and it pays my gas bill. "So, what have you got for me today, Murph?"

"Okay. You're a pregnant truck driver, you like girls, and you're drunk in the stall of a rest stop bathroom. And . . . *GO!*" Or, "Give me a five-hundred-word treatise on bug worship."

But if I'm to write about raunchy lesbian encounters or people who get off on large hairy insects, there's only so much my imagination can bring to my work. I'm going to have to go into the trenches and get my hands dirty.

Through a friend, Roddewig gets me invited to a gourmet "swingers" party at the fabled home of an eminently recognizable sports legend. I'd be a fool not to go, if only for the food and the fun of seeing the *who's who* of the international food and wine community stripped of their Gucci and their pretenses.

As promised, the home is splendid, the company stellar, and the atmosphere anticipatory. After drinks and introductions in the sunken, fur-lined living room, and a fabulous array of "nibblers," we all move to the owner's "playpen"—a large upholstered chamber (like an enormous padded cell, I think) dedicated solely to orgies. The lighting alone is remarkable, with changeable color schemes, and spots for highlighting action of note. Tiny opera lights are embedded along the floors for effect, and to guide the inebriated to the adjacent bath, sauna, and Jacuzzi complex. There is a superlative sound system for atmosphere, and on the wall flashes a custom "Walk/Don't Walk" signal that reads instead, *"Love/ Don't Love."* It's all very conducive, although I have to wonder at the uncharacteristic restraint in the wording on the sign. Perhaps the legendary reputation of its owner belies some inner sentimentality?

I've been in multiples situations before, of course, but this is the first time I've done so in the company of other women. I've always been the main attraction in any threesome, and have never had occasion to share the spotlight with another lady. I'm not sure if it's a power thing inasmuch as I want to direct all the action myself, or if it's the last vestige of my prudery begging circumspection. But I've never had sex with a woman before; never even touched one like *that,* and I'm not thrilled about starting now. The scientist in me says I should probably take this opportunity to find out what it feels like. But the "good girl" in me says that if I cross this boundary, I can truly count myself among the depraved.

I close my eyes and listen. The leather walls mute individual voices but the cumulative musk and music is overpowering. Every now and then, the high staccato of someone's ecstasy pierces the low thrum of moans, pants, and croons of encouragement.

In spite of myself, I have to clear my throat to keep from bursting out laughing. *This is plain GOOFY, people!* All these fine, powerful movers and, um, shakers, *fearsome* to some, naked—and let's face it, mostly *ugg-a-ly*—rutting away like grunion on the high tide at full moon. It's too wacky to be repulsive, and the anthropologist in me is transfixed. The elite of Los Angeles in their native habitat, and *I've* been allowed to witness their secret mating ritual!

Our host is working the light switches, Roddewig is staging the scene, the actors are all on their marks and the director has called "action." I guess it's up to me to play the ingénue. I take a deep breath and wade into the crowd of writhing, bouncing, barking bodies, crawling over and among them on hands and knees, careful to avoid soft underbellies until I can just lie prone and sort of snake my way through the squirming mass.

With as much dignity as I can muster, I wriggle over to the pretty brunette with the Vidal Sassoon bob who's been motioning me to her patch on the floor. As I take a deep breath, she smiles encouragement, and I reach out to touch her breast. It looks soft and inviting—not too big, not too small, the nipple friendly and perky and inches from my nose. *I'm going to suck my first lady's titty in twenty-two years,* I think. I cup her breast in my hand and squeeze it tenderly—and it's as hard as a freaking rock.

Fakefakefakefakefake, screams my head, and the spell is broken. I may go through the motions and make the appropriate grunts and moans, but I'm never going to make it as a lesbian. Discreetly, I allow the copulating mob to carry me over, under, away 'til I'm once again settled on the periphery—where I belong. Just watching the show, thanks.

HERE KITTY KITTY KITTY

Cat is an old hand at this relocation bit by now, so he's ensconced in the back of my friend John's Opel GT (a vehicle widely acknowledged as smallest and crappiest sports coupe ever produced). John is off to medical school in Arkansas, and all his worldly goods are packed into the back of this awful little machine. Leroy has finally gotten himself "set up" in Sun Valley and wants me to come and "be" with him (which I take to mean he's either tired of banging the local strange, running out of money, or both), and for some reason, I've answered his call. Leroy may be a flake, but he's *my* flake.

John has kindly offered to detour the seven-hundred-odd miles from Little Rock to drop me off in Idaho, and lacking any better option, I've accepted. There's no way my little Austin Healy bug-eye Sprite will make it past the LA city limits, let alone across the Great Divide.

I've brought all I expect I'll need for an indefinite stay in the wilds of Idaho, and poor Cat is stuck on top of the pile with the last cubic inches of space that will hold his litter box. It promises to be a long trip.

We make it to the badlands beyond Elko, Nevada, before the little guy can't hold it any longer, and our airspace is saturated with ammonia and toxic sulphur compounds. "Amines, mercaptin, methylates . . . ," recites John, working his biochem prereqs. It's freezing outside, but we've no choice except to open the window, as all three of us are becoming cyanotic and threatening to pass out. After sixteen straight hours on the road, Cat has had it. He jumps out the crack in the window, and encountering nothing but open space for the next thousand miles, boldly tears off into it.

I'm stuck with a dilemma. I can either leave my good friend, Cat, to the cold and the coyotes, or I can take off after him. Good sense suggests the former, but loyalty demands the latter. Reluctantly, I pull my parka tighter and step out into the icy desert. Cat disappears behind a hillock with me hot on his tail. I don't blame him for busting the coop, but I'm not at all pleased to be chasing him out here, in this icy cold in the middle of nowhere.

I'm tromping through snow and sagebrush, calling his name at the top of my lungs when I hear Cat's familiar little *raaaaauwww*. "You *idiot*!" I scream. "Do you have any *idea* what's out here waiting to eat you?!"

The noise comes again and I follow it to a little gully, but I don't see Cat anywhere. Nor do I see the cougar until it comes flying past me and launches itself into a piñon pine one short bound from where I stand. It crouches there at eye level, glowering at me. *Holy crap!*

I back slowly, purposely toward the car, never breaking eye contact with the beast, praying it's as scared of me as I am of it. Cat the Kitty is as far from my mind at the moment as whom I plan to vote for in next year's State Assembly election. I raise my elbows and spread my arms to make myself look as big as I can. *Isn't that what they say to do? And never turn your back to them? And get the hell out of there?*

As I near the car, John notices something is amiss, and reaches over to open the door for me. I throw myself into the passenger seat and slam the door closed. "Cougar," I gasp. My heart feels like it's spewing blood.

"Maaaaarrr," says Cat, perched once again on his newly emptied cat box. Little dude is swollen up like a puff adder—every hair standing on end and at full attention. John is laughing. "He came hauling ass back here like a bat out of hell. I figured you wouldn't be far behind."

"That's not funny," I pout. "I could have been killed."

"In four years I'll be a doctor," he says and smiles. "We'll come back here then and try it again. When I can fix you."

I sense a certain tenderness in his voice. After all, *he's* off on a grand adventure, too. Neither of us has the slightest idea where we'll be the next time we meet, but we're both pretty sure it won't be in a rusting Opel GT in the middle of the Arco desert with a cat box balanced behind our necks.

Another portent. I'm having serious misgivings about traipsing off into the unknown again, and to be with a man who's proven himself time and again to be a big ol' peck of heartache. But it's an *opportunity*, I tell myself. And I'm an anthropologist. It's just another tribe to study. John coaxes the Goat into gear and sets out into the late afternoon sun. By tomorrow morning, I'll be in Sun Valley making pancakes for a scout troop of oversized adolescents, and pretending that what I'm doing here on this planet actually matters to someone.

NOT TO WORRY

Back in the 1920s, Sun Valley was envisioned as a Malibu Colony set to snow, and in a way, fifty years after its founding, that's still true. It's still full of the same rich film folk and their trust-fund heirs—and more bulk cocaine than I've ever seen in my life, the snow on the mountain slopes rivaled only by the snow dangling from the little snot balls in the locals' over-entitled noses.

Less than a week after John drops me off with Leroy, it becomes apparent that actually keeping the radio station on the air is secondary to its acting as a link in some Peruvian drug cartel's distribution chain. People I don't know come into our house and leave at all hours of the day and night. Conversations hush when I walk into the station. Calls go dead when I answer the phone. Leroy lives in a state of perpetual arousal.

Personal safety and legal issues aside, and speaking as someone who gets nauseated and panicky from the caffeine in one cup of coffee, I've never understood cocaine's charm as an aphrodisiac. How a monumental headache and an impending sense of doom can enhance the sexual experience is beyond me, but then who am *I* to judge what gets other people off? All I know is that this situation is bad *juju* and I want out of it *immediately*.

Even Cat, who is normally the feline soul of graciousness when it comes to obscure living arrangements, has fled our room in the cabin for the sanctuary of a nearby pine tree. The psychic buzzing in the station-house is palpable and incessant—like being stuck in a swarm of bees that never alight, never allow the air to still—I'm going crazy and I haven't even been here for a month.

"We've *got* to get out of here," I tell Leroy one morning. I'm in the kitchen washing the detritus of last night's community bacchanal, and there are wispy little coke trails on every flat surface I see. Leroy is licking one of them off a dinner plate. "Radio station or no, these guys are serious trouble," I tell him. It's time to play the paranoia card. "What happens when we get raided by the sheriff, huh? Do you really want to spend the next twenty years as some bubba's *special friend*?"

"Don't worry," he tells me. "The sheriff's not going to let anything happen to us. Who do you think put up the money for the permits?"

That does it. I'm heading for my room to start packing my stuff, and I'm fuming with indignation. This is the last time I'm letting this nitwit talk me into *anything*! Leroy watches me, aghast, then angry. I guess he figured that tidbit would reassure me.

"I'm going out for a drink," he says. "I'll be back in a couple of days."

I don't even try to stop him as he walks out the door.

My stuff is nearly packed and I'm wondering who I'm supposed to call to come rescue me from the middle of Idaho, when I'm intercepted by three or four of the guys from the radio station. Big guys. Guys who don't look pleased. They're blocking the doorway to my bedroom and the largest of them is wearing a khaki uniform and carrying a shotgun—the *sheriff*! "Leroy's not going anywhere, girly," he says calmly, "but *you* are." This officer isn't asking me nicely, he's *threatening* me nicely. "This isn't a good place for you to be. Better call your daddy to come get you."

Up until this moment I've been perfectly content to take up my bags and walk as far from this place as I can get, but something happens when people try to bully me. Even people with a badge and a gun. *Especially* people with a badge and a gun. I believe in America, damn it, and when officials abuse our freedoms, I believe in it all the more strongly. Suddenly I know that I'm not going *anywhere* without Leroy. These creeps are just using him for his talent and exploiting him for his gullibility. With me out of the picture, they're free to feed his addictions and reap the profits that should rightly be his—and by extension, ours. If Leroy's staying, so am I.

I just look up at the officer and smile sweetly. If this guy isn't feeling threatened, why does he have three henchmen with him? Far from being intimidated, I'm feeling empowered.

"I'll think about it," I say pleasantly. (*I have, and I'm not budging, you assclowns.*)

"Look," says one of the henchmen, sensing my recalcitrance, "we'll give you gas money."

This clinches it for me. As *if* I can be bought off so cheaply! (*Although I have to admit that the idea of being bribed by a cop is oddly appealing.*)

"Your syndicate now has ten thousand dollars' worth of new deejay pressings I had sent to you," I remind him.

I've worked my tail off to procure that product for their cruddy little stations. Without it, they'll be stuck with whatever they can cadge from the townsfolk's attics, and they know it. Technically, it belongs to the syndicate. But since the syndicate hasn't paid me a penny of the money they promised me, or signed the contract granting me a percentage of the company, I can make a good moral case that they're shit out of luck.

Four sets of eyeballs are trying to bore their way into my cranium, but I don't dare back down now. The testosterone level in the room is approaching boil-over, and these yahoos are one smart-ass crack away from clobbering me. Better to stay passive-aggressive and play the dumb blonde. My pride can assert itself when my teeth aren't at stake.

"I told you I'd think about it," I repeat, nicely, trying to keep my voice steady.

The sheriff's hand tightens on the stock of his shotgun, but his eyes don't waver. "We'll be back tomorrow morning," he says evenly. "We'll need you gone by then."

Utterly alone in this world, I'm left with this as their trucks crunch off down the gravel road outside the cabin. It's started to snow again, and Cat is yowling to be let in. He's shivering and covered with snowflakes that are beginning to melt into his coat—leaving him as wet and woebegone-looking as I feel. I hug him to me and, for maybe the hundredth time since we've known each other, cry bitter tears into his warm, furry belly as he licks the drops from my cheek, purring, trying to reassure me. Trying, I imagine, to reassure us both.

Leroy, of course, is nowhere to be found. I've called all the bars in town and left messages with those I hope are still-friendly acquaintances. We don't have a telephone at the cabin, so I'm stuck walking between the house and the phone booth at the little market up the road. I daren't go to the radio station, because I know that's where the cartel is hanging out, plotting my demise, plying Leroy with cocaine and Jack Daniels and bad women until they can get rid of me. I haven't a clue whom to call—I certainly can't tell my parents, and none of my siblings are in a position to rescue me anyway. My friends are spread out all over the country doing Big Important Things, and everyone here is invested in Leroy staying with the station. All my eggs are here in his basket and he's off scrambled somewhere where I can't find him. I am, I realize, well and truly screwed. *I'm being run out of my first town.*

There's nothing for me to do but go to sleep and hope a solution comes to me in a dream—before the posse returns in the morning. So I'm not expecting to wake up in the middle of the night with Leroy sitting next to me on the bed, his hand on my shoulder, soft and urgent. He shushes me, finger to lips. "Get your stuff," he whispers. "We're leaving." He has Cat in his arms, and his watch cap on his head. He means *right now.*

Once again, I am reminded why I love this guy like crazy. He's as invested in this place as I am, but he's also as fiercely independent, and *no one's* going to coerce him into anything—or mess with his lady behind his back. He hustles me into his pickup truck and we stash my gear in the camper shell on the back. I notice it's packed full of boxes—all the record albums I've sent to the station over the last year. *All* of them. "Every last one," Leroy assures me with a snort. "I snuck them out while everyone was off partying last night. They were all congratulating themselves about how they'd railroaded you out of my life and I just thought, *Fuck 'em. I'm outta here.*"

Had he gifted me with a diamond necklace, I couldn't be more pleased. The man had finally chosen *me.*

As we make our escape down the gravel road, we giggle like lunatics, imagining the looks on the faces of our tormentors when they realize they've been snookered at their own game. We're so pleased with ourselves that all we can do is snort and smirk. Every couple of seconds, one of us starts to guffaw and the other joins in. As we reach the sprawling ranch homes of Gimlet, I think, *Gimlet eyes; what a perfect description. This place never liked us to begin with.* Right before dawn, the town is the color of bile.

An hour later, we're free of civilization, born again on the macadam wings of the open road. We both sense that we've escaped something dark, something evil and soul-sucking, and that for once, our love for each other has come through for us in a tangible way that's made us temporarily whole, symbiotic. Bigger than the sum of our parts.

There's something about the Arco Desert that's hallucinatory and grounding all at the same time. As the morning dawns corral over the scrub and the sage, we are giddy and gleeful like naughty children who've outsmarted the wicked witch; and now we are fleeing through the forest bearing great chunks of her gingerbread house—to be savored at leisure in the safety of a far locale.

"So, where are we off to this time, partner?" I ask, not really caring what he answers.

I know that my cred as a music director is blown forever—all my hard work and hustle down the drain. By next week it will be all over the industry that we've absconded with the inventory. On the other hand, some Podunk station is bound to hear of our booty and give us a midnight-to-six slot just to get their hands on it.

"I've got contacts in Colorado Springs," says Leroy. "Let's see if we can pitch camp and set up a production studio there."

Then an awful thought occurs to me: we've just crossed not only a gang of cocaine thugs, but a crooked sheriff as well. What if they come after us? My tiny sense of triumph turns to dread. "Leroy . . . what about the sheriff? What if he decides to retaliate and makes our lives a living hell?"

"Oh, don't worry about the sheriff," says Leroy, as nonchalant as if I've asked him the time of day. "I let him suck me off in the engineering room."

NOT TO WORRY

I guess the revelation that my Prince Charming is a part-time polelicker shouldn't surprise me, but it does. Indeed, bisexuality is as rampant in the music business as it is in the other arts—as my travels through the bedrooms and bathrooms of Hollywood have so aptly demonstrated. I've been the bottom crust of enough boy-boy-girl sandwiches not to be shocked by this, but somehow the idea having to compete with groupies of *all* genders for the attentions of my lover casts a pall on the exquisite tenderness I'm feeling toward him at this moment.

"Oh yeah," he continues, first noting, then ignoring my discomfiture, "Tweedledee and Tweedledum will hire me on as talent. Those guys just *love* me."

"Who are they?"

"They own an AM/FM/TV conglomerate in the Springs; I'll give them a call when we get into town."

"Why do you call them Tweedledee and Tweedledum?"

"You'll see."

We check into a cheap motel close to the Air Force Academy and Leroy sets to working the phone. Apparently word of our caper has preceded us, because in no time at all, he's laughing his ass off and describing our getaway to whomever is on the other end of the receiver. "Great then," he says. "We'll see you there tomorrow morning at nine. . . . Yeah, I've got the records right here in my truck."

He hangs up, immensely pleased with himself.

"Got it," he says. "Car, company apartment, and $400 a week. And all I gotta do is sit in a broadcast booth and open my mouth."

And do what? I wonder.

The station and studios in Colorado Springs are Big Time. Fifty thousand watts of clear channel broadcasting from the Rocky Mountains all the way across the Great Plains into the foothills of the Appalachians. It's a hokey Top-40 format, but by golly it's got an audience of millions and has the national advertisers to prove it.

National advertisers mean national money, and the station, Leroy assures me, is well appointed and well run. The studios have up-to-date equipment and plenty of supplies, which he says we won't even have to pay for out of our own pocket! Best of all, when we're issued a paycheck—and every two weeks, we *will* be issued a paycheck—we won't have to run, *literally run*, down the street to the bank to cash it before all the funds have been withdrawn. "It's a cushy setup," he tells me.

The studios are everything Leroy's made them out to be—spacious, clean, and nicely furnished. There are bathrooms. With toilet paper, even! The office employees and the traffic girl are all well groomed, polite, and professional. There's even an officious office manager bustling about to make sure things run ship-shape. A union shop—we've hit the Broadcast Bigtime!

Then I meet Tweedledee and Tweedledum. They're so aptly named that when I first see these fabled business partners it's all I can do to keep from cracking up. Between the two of them, they must weigh close to a half a ton. Huge doesn't even begin to describe them . . . and *round*. They look like monstrous, redheaded babies who might enjoy a good cigar—constantly. I can hear them wheezing before we even enter the room. Leroy greets them effusively, introduces me, and before they even say hello, they're bickering and finishing each other's sentences. I fully expect to see one of them pull out a bat and bop the other on the head with it. All they're missing are the beanies. They even share the same first name.

"Told you she'd be a blonde," says Tweedledee.

"Bullshit! You said she'd be—" says Tweedledum.

"Cajun? You're full of crap," says Tweedledee.

"Shut the fuck up and gimme my—" says Tweedledum.

"Fifty bucks? Fat chance. Fuck you," says Tweedledee.

"Nice to meet you," I venture.

"C'mere and—" says Tweedledee.

"Give Papa a hug," they say together.

Firstly, I know that hugging's not a great way to start a business relationship. Secondly, I wouldn't know what part of them I might get my arms around to hug even if I wanted to. I look to Leroy for help and he just winks. *They're just funnin' with you. Sit down.* I do.

"We don't believe in hiring females for on-the-air slots," says

Tweedledee.

"But we're thinking of using a woman's voice for commercials," finishes his partner. "You got a—"

"Demo reel?"

"Yes, sir. I do."

"You—"

"Know production?"

I dig into my purse and pull out the tape of advertising spots I'd produced under Leroy's tutelage. I'm rather proud of it, actually.

Tweedledee and Tweedledum thread it through the reel-to-reel tape player behind their desks and listen approvingly as my voice touts bookstores and flower shops, concerts and supermarket sales. Pretty sedate stuff, competent and professional.

"You'll do great," they say. "You're hired."

Just like that? I'm a little perplexed until I realize that these guys really *do* want Leroy in their stable of talent, and they're willing to front me some spare equipment and an unused storage room in order to keep him here.

Now, I know that I would never have gotten through the front door had I not been with Leroy, but I'm still feeling pretty flush that I've landed the gig. I'd once dreamed of working on Madison Avenue as a copywriter-producer, and here is my chance to make it happen! Not only will I be writing and producing the spots, I'll be in charge of setting up the production studio and managing the operation. Expenses will be minimal—after all, I have a huge new library of music snippets I can use as background, and one of the best voices in the country available to me free of charge. The Tweeds will split the profits with us fifty-fifty, and we'll provide exclusive advertising content to their radio and TV stations—that they can distribute and sell as they see fit. *What's not to like?*

Studio D Productions is hooked up and running commercials within the week. Leroy settles into his morning-drive and Saturday-night time slots; I'm bringing in new advertisers, writing copy for their spots, and doing the production in our new digs. We're using state-of-the-art eight-track Teak tape recorders with a couple of turntables, multiple microphones, and an engineering board. I'm learning mixing, dubbing, splicing, and engineering—all the guts that go into making a good, listenable commercial that flows into the programming without offending listeners with the "SundaySUNDAY*SUNDAY!*" screaming and reverb typical of mid-century American radio advertising. Our mellow, low-key new "sound" is so appealing to a younger, hipper class of entrepreneurs that we're soon asked to do regional campaigns for clothing outlets and fast-food eateries. I discover I have a real knack for composing jingles and turning them into background tracks.

We even start doing in-studio interviews with musicians and celebrities passing through Colorado Springs on tour, and I get to ask impertinent questions of everyone from Stevie Wonder to Captain Kirk. People are inviting Leroy and me to do benefits and emcee events. We're included on guest lists. I've finally gone, dare I say it, *legit*.

After the chaos and amateurish nature of our previous gigs, this life is so refreshingly professional, I feel it's what I was *made* to do. Granted, the mandated Top-40 playlist is boring as all hell (how many times can you play Silly Love Songs without running amok and strangling someone?), but Studio D is humming. I can't wait to get up in the mornings and get to work.

But while I have a great deal of creative leeway, Leroy is chaffing under the heavy bit of Tweedledee and Tweedledum's tedious Top-40 format and by-the-book management style. A style which means there is *no* room for improvisation, *no* room for new and tasty product, and definitely *no* tolerance for all those amusing little quirks of character that Leroy is so rightly known for—like not showing up for work. Or showing up for work shitfaced. Or worse, getting into creative arguments with the management and reiterating his point by putting on his backpack and boogying. My real job here, it is soon apparent, is to prevent this from happening—and it's proving to be more difficult than I would wish.

Leroy is one of those guys who has what I call a "gestational attention span"—he's gung-ho for nine months while the project is coming together, but he loses interest as soon as there are dirty diapers to be changed. I nurse no illusions that our cushy little setup will one day be endangered by his irresponsible antics, but I'm not expecting it to come so soon.

We've been in Colorado Springs for six months. Today, the station is holding a grand Open House to celebrate their tenth anniversary and the early success of our new production studio. Even my parents have flown out from California to see what we're doing and wish us well. There are local celebrities, autograph-seekers, and potential clients milling about just waiting to be schmoozed up for new business—and Leroy is nowhere to be seen . . . and *hasn't* been seen for the last three days.

I came home Tuesday evening to find the apartment empty and his backpack missing. Tweedledee and Tweedledum are beside themselves; I've failed them miserably, they tell me. It's all my fault. I *knew* they'd had this event planned for months and I still let him get away—like he always does.

I'm in despair. How could I *not* have known this would happen? My suspicions fall on the sweet blond nurse who lives in the apartment below us, the one who Leroy and I invite to dinner pretty much every weekend. *She's* been missing these last few days, too. I call the hospital to see if she's heard from him, and no, they haven't seen her all week. I am such an idiot!

Leroy finally shows up late in the evening, dressed in a velvet tux he's rented especially for the occasion. I am so angry I can scarcely look at him, but he's all smiles and bonhomie. We pose for pictures together, introduce each other to the guests, try to pretend there isn't an elephant standing between us taking a gigantic elephant-sized dump on our well-polished shoes, but I know that this time it's truly over for us.

I've not told anyone about the phone call I got from Chicago yesterday. The one from Murray Fisher. The one in which he told me that the book he's been editing off and on for the last twenty years for a writer named Alex Haley is finally finished and about to be published.

The book is called *Roots: The Saga of an American Family*, and it's about to become one of the best-selling works in the history of publishing.

CHOMP CHOMP CHOMP

Just excerpted in *Playboy* magazine to enormous acclaim, the film adaptation is slated to become the first TV mini-series next month. He and Barbara have split up, he tells me, and he's moving back to Los Angeles. He wants me there with him, will I *please* consider moving into his Mulholland house? "The city lights will be even lovelier with you basking in them, Lit-tle Swee-tie. . . ."

I'm going.

THE MULLION OF MULHOLLAND

Murray arrives at the Stapleton terminal wearing a long black leather trench coat, black jeans, black leather boots, and a black Borsalino fedora with a black leather hatband. He's carrying one perfect yellow rose that seemingly glows against the supple leather. As he strides across the concourse, working it, *owning* it, every eye in the place is on him. I can hear people whispering—*who is that?* At six-foot-five and dashingly handsome, he's impossible *not* to notice. The whole concourse seems to be vibrating with his awesomeness.

Now, this is a man who knows how to make an entrance, I think, and I can't believe that he's here for *me*. Smiling at *me*. That he's here to take *me* back to Los Angeles to start a new life with him. And what a life it promises to be! *This is like something out of a fairy tale*, I tell myself. *Only it's for real!* I have to be the luckiest girl on the whole planet.

It's all I can do to make my feet move toward him, fall into his arms, just hold him there immobile for a long, *looooong* minute breathing in the leather, the rose, his musk. I'm too afraid to move for fear I'll break the spell and come crashing back into reality. But he's not letting me loose. We could stand here for hours like this, just clinging for dear life as the world moves on around us, not caring what a single one of them might think of this odd pairing. *I can exist on this plane in this dimension, right here, forever!* His arms tell me he's thinking the exact same thing.

And so we hug, rooted, immobile, oblivious. Five, six, ten minutes go by and reluctantly we break apart, take a long look into each other's eyes. It's been almost three years since we last saw each other—just that one time at his party, though he's edited my stuff and we've been writing to each other as friends ever since. But we both knew even then that at some point, *later on*, we'd be exactly where we are right now, taking up where we had to leave off there in his living room, thwarted by our previous commitments. Timing, as they say, is everything.

Suddenly he's dropped his arms and is shaking himself like a big hairy dog after a long walk in the rain, *Brrrrph Bph, Bph,* he goes, then, of our newly interrupted clinch, a jaunty, "Well! Now that *that's* out of the way . . ."

Some men might have gone to mush after such a romantic reunion. And some might have backed away in embarrassed silence, humbled by the intensity. But leave it to Murray to break the spell with such a refreshing combination of pretense and absurdity. I burst into hysterical laughter. *Ohh, yeeessssss.* After endless months living amongst the plainspoken and un-ironic, it's *so* good to be back with someone who has a sense of *playful* drama about him instead of the depressive, self-involved diva kind that Leroy dishes up.

"I've sent all my things on ahead of me, and we'll go get your stuff from your place then drive to LA," he says. "But first," he pauses for effect, "we'll have to buy a car. Is there a Volvo dealership around here?"

We're driving over the Continental Divide through the recently opened Eisenhower Tunnel after first stopping for provisions in Vail. Our new Volvo is handling like a champ—even up here in the rarified air—and the smell of new car and pâté and fresh-baked bread has been tormenting me for the last forty-five minutes. It's time for a picnic, and that's all there is to it.

"Murph m'love," I say, "tunnels always make me horny. Can we stop somewhere and enjoy our lunch?" It takes him about five seconds to reach behind the seat and fish a bottle of '66 Chateau Margaux from out of his carry-on bag. *Nice.*

"There's a corkscrew in there somewhere, too," he says. The urgency

THE MULLION OF MULHOLLAND

in his voice bids me hurry up and find it—which I do. I marvel that this single bottle of wine we're so cavalierly tossing about probably cost more than I make in a week, and I'm still reeling from the fact that he's bought this car, brand new off the lot, with nary a blink, and paid for it with a credit card. I've never dated a man with a credit card. It was only in the last few years that my *parents* finally got a credit card. *Truly*, I think, *I've hit the mating jackpot.*

I uncork the bottle and take a long, unceremonious pull. *There must be a law against this over and above having an open container in a moving vehicle. We've not even bothered to let it breathe. What would Roddewig say?*

Even in its un-oxidated state, the wine is ambrosial. I feel it first in my knees, then a soft heaviness warms my chest, my arms, my head. As we exit the tunnel, all I can think about is getting this man into a grassy meadow and having hot monkey sex with him in sight of the gods, the forest creatures, and probably the freeway. "Pull over. Now." I don't have to ask twice.

It's our first time together, and his roar echoes off the mountainsides, bounces down the walls of the canyons, rolls across the plains of eastern Colorado, and likely sets off seismic detectors from Denver to Wichita. I probably lose more of my hearing in this one interlude than in all the rock concerts I've attended before or since. It briefly occurs to me that maybe I've bitten off more than I can chew, but I'm so buzzed on the wine and the company that my doubts are fleeting. Spent, I entwine a chain of meadow daisies in his starting-to-gray hairs. He reciprocates by producing an exquisite gold and jade necklace from a pouch he's been carrying around in the inner pocket of his jacket. "This was given to my mother by the Empress of Japan," he says solemnly, "back at the turn of the century when she was a little girl, living in the palace court." Murray's grandparents had been Methodist missionaries in service to the royal family. He's looking off down the mountain now, and his eyes are welling with tears.

He lifts my hair from the back of my neck and in fastening the clasp, claims me. "Here's to the first day of the rest of our lives together," he says. Only, when he says it, it doesn't sound trite or overused. Unlike me, he's not being ironic; he means it.

It's been a long time since I wanted to belong to someone, let him own my heart and my body. It's been a long time since I've even *thought* about trusting anyone with my feelings, secrets, and longings. But the "rightness" of this moment is overwhelming, and I can't imagine a finer choice for me than this man. *My* man. My *Murph*. "Thank you," I murmur as he traces the chain along my throat with his finger. It's more a prayer than a whisper.

Alex Haley's masterpiece isn't just an international best seller; the mini-series has propelled *Roots* to the realm of literary and social phenomenon—an instant classic destined to be read by school children for generations to come. Within a few months of its release, the book has already sold a million copies and Alex and Murray are euphoric. They've literally spent the last twenty years coaxing out the story of Kunta Kinte, Alex's distant African relative, tracing the ancestral narrative from the boy's capture by African slavers in 1600s Gambia all the way up through the generations to Alex himself. With Murray shepherding and Alex slogging through the content, they've kept the project going on little more than the funding the two of them can cadge and cobble together and an unshakable belief in the righteousness of their efforts.

Now, finally, after all those years of struggle and frustration, Alex's epic saga has given historical voice to an entire people—and elevated all of America along with it.

But poor Alex! Never a gregarious sort to begin with, he has spent the last months doing book signings across the country, and day after day, week after week, lines of people bearing his book stretch out the door and down the street, and around the block of the stores and lecture halls and shopping centers where he appears. Many of them are holding multiple copies. "For him," says one woman, patting her hugely pregnant belly. Alex has a kind word and an inscription for each of them, and refuses to

THE MULLION OF MULHOLLAND

leave the venue until everyone in line has been seen. Next week he leaves for Japan to start a tour through Asia; after that, Europe; then, a triumphant visit to Africa.

Amid the excitement and exhaustion, it all feels a bit surreal. After so many years of penury and insecurity, Alex expresses a profound bewilderment at his "overnight" success. He's more than a sensation; it seems he's become almost a religious figure, with strangers reaching out to touch him wherever he goes, often bursting into tears upon meeting him, begging him to bless this child or offer prayers for that elderly grandfather. Talk shows, state invitations, celebrities of all stripes and nationalities are calling for him, jockeying for an audience. There is no way to process the experience of picking up the telephone while you're brushing your teeth one morning and having the voice in your ear say, "This is the White House calling for Mr. Haley, please hold for the President."

He's been staying with us while he gets his life organized in Los Angeles—buying a house, shopping for a wardrobe befitting his new celebrity. His fashion preferences up until this point can most charitably be described as "rumpled." When you're dining with kings and movie stars, the typical writer's attire would be considered a bit too *too*—even for the most gracious among them—and Alex is representing something far larger than himself.

"Are pants *supposed* to be shiny?" he asks one day while the tailor is assembling bolts of fabric for his approval. "Sometimes all we can do is entrust our lives to the experts," I say. "Such matters are beyond the scope of the common man...."

The crowds, the trappings, are an indignity he must endure—and that's what he's doing, *enduring*. So today, I'm in the kitchen fixing the three of us Thanksgiving dinner. Alex has been invited to share the table of pretty much everyone in America, but this weekend he's just holing up in our house. Hiding.

I've gone all out; Virginia ham—which I've been soaking in a tub for the last two days to desalt—turkey and trimmings, side dishes and relishes. It's the first formal Thanksgiving meal I've prepared in several years, and I'm totally impressed with myself. *This will be a feast to remember.*

CHOMP CHOMP CHOMP

Alex is so drained by the last months that he's almost ashen. He's not what one might call athletic to begin with, and when I look at his weary face, I'm truly worried that he's heading for a heart attack. Murray and I have been living on the periphery of Alex's experience, but up until the moment he shuffles into the kitchen, I've not truly realized the toll all this has taken on him. He looks at the mountains of food I've prepared over the last days, walks over to the big floor-to-ceiling windows and stares out over Los Angeles, spread before him as if in tribute. He closes his eyes, and I can see that he is weeping.

"It's all I've ever wanted," he says quietly, "and it's all out there waiting for me to take it." His voice is as furrowed as his face, and suddenly he seems like an old, old man with a too-tired soul.

He looks up again, shakes his head slowly. "And now that it's here, what I want more than anything in the world," he sweeps his arm across the window, more exasperated than disdainful of the acclaim, the celebrity, the glittering audiences, and the fawning sycophants, "is a plain. Baked. Sweet potato . . ." His voice trails off.

I'm stunned, maybe even a little bit disappointed. But I know that I've just been granted another life lesson—from the mouth of a man who speaks with authority: *Be careful what you wish for; you just might get it.*

ALL AN ACT

Picture this: A tall, well-dressed, and vaguely sinister-looking middle-aged man holds the door of his Volvo open for the diminutive little blonde. She looks to be about half his age, and seems quite hesitant to get in, trapped between the door and this large threatening male. The tension between the two of them is palpable, even to the casual passerby on the street. We can't hear what he's saying, but *she's* shaking her head no. Emphatic.

The man is getting impatient; his neck muscles tense, his fists begin to ball. "Get in the car," he hisses as she tries to shrink back away from him—but there's nowhere she can go except into passenger seat.

"No. I don't want to," she says in a small yet defiant voice.

"I said, GET IN THE CAR! NOW!" Heads turn as this plays out at the curbside, but the guy is undeterred. Angry. He's so big, who's going to try to stop him?

"No." She shakes her head, scared now, looking for an escape route. But he looms over her, blocking her way. Slowly, with great deliberation, the man looks first to the right, then to the left. Then he draws back his fist and lets fly, hard, right into her stomach. As she doubles over, coughing and retching, he knees her in the face, sending her flying backwards into the car, slamming the door behind her.

Then, satisfied, he looks around again—right, left—brushes his hands together and shakes them as if to rid them of dirt, calmly walks around to the driver's side of the car and gets in. Starts it, drives away leaving a stunned crowd of onlookers tittering among themselves.

We rehearse this until we get it perfectly—the timing, as I pretend to fold over his fist, the inflections as I gasp and choke, even his animal grunt as he punches me in the gut. You can't *imagine* how well it goes over at parties and in front of fancy restaurants. By the time he fake knees me to the chin, whoever is watching is usually running back inside to telephone the cops and we're collapsed in a fit of giggles halfway down the block. It should be a total hoot to perform our little charade when we leave the Playboy Mansion tonight.

I've been there as a guest, but this is the first time I'm going as an invitee of the house—which means that the unspoken expectation that I make myself available sexually has been trumped by the fact that I'm here by virtue of my status as Murray and Alex's friend.

This splendid home, set on five extraordinary acres of sensual delight, is a wonderland for sybarites. From the legendary rock grotto to the blue- and red-lit bed chambers off the game room, from the orchid greenhouse to the rare-book porn collection in the paneled library, it truly is, as then-named Lew Alcindor first described it to me, "the middle-class Valhalla."

Women of unspeakable beauty and men of unwholesome fortune vie to prey upon each other amidst the literal gardens of pleasure publisher, Hugh Hefner, created to set the stage in the magnificent old Bel Air Tudor, a house just dark-wood gothic enough to add a pinch of decadence to the whole proceedings.

For reasons not entirely unknown to me, I've been dubbed the "token intellectual bimbo" of the group gathered here tonight, probably because I've hosted most of them in our home up on the hill, and found that sometimes we all prefer a good dinner conversation to the mindless couplings available at the mansion over on Charing Cross. Murray and I are a couple in spirit as well as in name, and despite the many invitations we get to modify our self-designation, we're steadfast in our monogamy. There's simply no one better suited to either of us to be found in the city.

Despite the august company seated around the baronial banquet table, at this moment on the world stage, Alex is The Big Deal, a Bigger Deal than even Hef Himself, and it's disorienting to see our fabled host fawning over the man who up until recently was his employee—and not a particularly vaunted one at that.

We've just been served drinks by a member of the house staff. Alex is obviously reveling in the attentions being heaped upon him by people who

ALL AN ACT

would have surely scourged him on the street had he dared to approach them only a few short months ago. Writers and editors, though essential to the publication arm of the *Playboy* enterprise, are generally segregated from the social torso unless one of them has achieved recent celebrity. It's not a snub so much as a function of the antithetical mindset separating nerd from nincompoop. I have to hand it to Hef's social secretary, Mary, for keeping the mix lively yet under control.

Alex is doing his best to fit into his newfound role as assistant moral compass and spiritual guru of the *Playboy* operation. There is a sense that *Roots* and the ethos of rectitude and reconciliation it evokes may seriously influence the upcoming national elections and help to put Southern Christian evangelical and social progressive Jimmy Carter into the White House. That's *legacy* stuff for a publisher who's spent much of his considerable fortune advocating on behalf of racial equality and the socially marginalized. I'm actually wondering if Hef is going to use this occasion to come out and inform us all that he's found Jesus. But no, he's simply praising Alex for his vision and his stellar contribution to *Playboy*'s mission, hailing him as the new Gandhi, the social conscience of our generation.

Murray squeezes my arm. As Alex's long-time editor and champion, Murray is basking in this acclaim every bit as much as his celebrated writer. He's been on the outs with Hef ever since he left the magazine to help Alex finish up the massive task of bringing the book to fruition. At the time, everyone at the magazine thought this brilliant editor, who had guided the magazine almost since its inception and brought it to its current prominence in the publishing world, had lost his mind.

"Why would you want to leave a six-figure job (this in the early 1970s) to write a book on genealogy?" he's asked time and time again. "You've won Pulitzers. You've invented a *literary form* for God's sake." Indeed, the *Playboy* interview is now standard format for magazine interviews, and Murray is justly proud of his contribution. He's also morally committed to bringing the story of African America to the country at large, and no amount of money or acclaim is going to deter him in that cause.

When I'd first come to his home, I took a peek at the Rolodex of contacts on his office desk. The very first name I'd flipped to was Malcolm Little, Malcolm X, whose autobiography Murray had ghost-edited in the 1960s. That it had been written at a time when the black separatist movement forbade intermingling among the races bespoke the trust its leader must have had in this privileged white Eastern elite. I know that this moment here at Hef's table is more than a triumph of vision for Murray; it's a personal vindication as well, and I'm thrilled to be here to share it with him. I squeeze his thigh under the table, beaming right along with him.

Then Alex offers a toast in return. "To our gracious host," he says, "and to my friend and brother. Here's to you, Fisher. 'Tween you and me we make one *hell* of a good writer."

WE ALL COME DOWN

Roots was supposed to make our fortune; indeed, the book has sold millions and millions of copies around the world and Alex has become the best-selling African-American author of all time. But Haley's attorney, Lou Blau, has other plans for Murray's 10 percent. Somehow during all the celebration and international hoopla, his gentleman's contract got morphed into a lump-sum payment—in the mid-five figures—not even enough to cover Murray's expenses over the long years from inception to publication.

Alex, godfather to Murray's kids and longtime houseguest of Murray's mother (at whose Tarrrytown, New York, home Alex had lived while writing much of the text—"my white mother," as he describes her in his fund-raising lectures), is suddenly *incommunicado*, unavailable except to those of significant enough import to merit his newly stellar attentions. And that, apparently, no longer includes Murray Fisher.

I urge Murray to seek his own legal counsel—he has, in effect, co-written the book, just as he has the autobiography of Malcolm X. But he is adamant that the public perception of *Roots*'s authorship remain Alex's alone, its moral power undiluted by scandal or tainted by internal discord. Murray's stance is noble, and he never speaks of this betrayal, but I think something dies inside of him the day he gets the registered letter from Blau's offices. All his happily-ever-after dreams, the ones that brought him the acclaim he'd so quietly sought on behalf of others, the ones that brought him to *me,* have vanished in the stark, black engraving on the creamy white paper. "With this check, accept final payment. Thank you for your services."

Yes, we're still impassioned with each other, we still entertain a fascinating guest list, and in public at least, Murray is still effusive about Alex's successes, but slowly his enthusiasm for life in Los Angeles is subsumed in bindles then baggies of cocaine, and his literary friends are replaced by hangers-on and the sort of women who describe themselves in the personal ads as "discreet." I never know whom I'm going to run into at the breakfast table or find sleeping in the guestroom, in the living room, or sprawled out on the office sofa. The house begins to smell of other people's sweat and stale liquor.

One night I awaken to find him in convulsions, a froth of white spittle bubbling from his nose and mouth. His lips are blue and he's hardly breathing. An empty vodka bottle has tipped over into the mound of white powder he keeps on his bed stand. Apparently he has taken one too many of his new sleeping pills. I know that he'll be livid at any public hint of impropriety to "The Brand," but I also know that I don't want my friend and lover dead in my arms. His body shudders itself off the bed and onto the floor, and my efforts at CPR are having minimal effect.

His spit and snot are all over my face, and the taste of his vomit is making me retch by the time the paramedics get here, get him on oxygen, and roll him onto a stretcher.

I follow the ambulance down Beverly Glen to the emergency room at UCLA, and sit in the waiting room while he's being resuscitated, dreading the moment they revive him and I'll have to go in and confront him. Lately his rages have been terrifying, and his wrath almost Biblical in its vehemence—his roaring physically painful to my eardrums. When he realizes that his private foibles are now a matter of public record, *I* will become the source of his anger, not his addictions. I know that my decision to save his life is also a decision to end our relationship—if not right now, then very soon.

Surprisingly, when he comes out of his stupor there in the ICU, he's grateful, thankful to me for saving his life. "I'll cut back," he promises, "this is my wake-up call." But we both know his words are just a momentary salve to a greater hurt.

Over the next months, I watch, heartbroken, as this once princely man becomes hollow, brittle, and soulless with Alex's betrayal. He won't even acknowledge that Alex has had anything to do with it. "Blau signed all the contracts while Alex was out of the country," he tells me. "Alex will make right by it."

Meanwhile, he's resumed his binge drinking, snorting up massive amounts of cocaine, and going for days without showering or even bothering to get out of bed. The visitors to our house become sketchier still, and I notice that small objects d'art are missing—my perfumes gone from the bathroom, his Rolex watch nowhere to be found.

The morning I discover a pubic hair—not my own—in my toothbrush, I can no longer deny the reality of our situation. Worse, there's nothing I can do to stop his further descent. Murray adamantly refuses to even consider that he might have a problem. "That night was just a mistake," he insists, and none of his "friends" wants the party to end. "It's better if you don't stay here anymore," is his answer to my suggestion that he check himself into rehab and let me help him get clean and dried out.

"Oh, Murph," I choke, as I try to stifle the keening that's building in my chest, "are you sure you don't want to marry me and have my children?"

My desperate humor is lost on him. Indeed, it's his entrée for The Big Goodbye. "I've never been more sure of anything in my life," he answers.

I let myself out of the house and stumble down our driveway to the entrance just off Mulholland Drive. It's one of those perfect velvet nights in the Hollywood Hills—deceptively calm and lulling. And yet there is a hint of not-so-distant menace on the night breeze. The Santana winds are coming, the seductive about to meet the surreal, and my mind is both numb and spinning at the same time. A sudden gust rustles the eucalyptus and shimmers the stars and the city lights, creating a mirage where they meet. My disorientation turns to hallucination, and my focus becomes like ice: sharp, crystal, frozen in time. It's the perfect night for suicide.

The entrance to our driveway is on a blind curve where street racers have taken to holding nightly competitions out of sight of the city police. As I huddle in the bushes, arms around my knees, bare feet resting on the asphalt of the roadway, I know that all I have to do is stand up and step out from behind this hedge, and I'll be as dead as I'm feeling at this moment.

A car roars by, then a truck. *It would be so easy*, I think, *and this pain will all be over forever.* I think of my failed marriage, my failed career, my failed aspirations, my failed loves, everyone *else* I've ever failed, and my despair grows and presses itself into my brain until it's displaced everything residing in my memory. I *have* no memory—there is nothing to counteract the sour stinging emptiness that has taken me over. I finally understand what it means to *just let go.*

I don't know how long I've been sitting here, but the lights are starting to suffuse with the colors of dawn. Curiously, the very numbness that has invaded my being has also prevented me from directing my physical body to actually *do* anything, so no speeding drunk is now grappling with his civic conscience, and no hit-and-run driver is on the phone with his defense attorney. The city awakens from its heedless night, and I'm still here, besieged and bereaved, but whole and unsplattered.

Today is the first day of the rest of my life, I hear myself say to the small part of me that's left.

PART TWO

TEMPTING FATE

He's coming down the escalator at the Century Plaza Hotel just as I'm starting up. Even without looking at the nametags, it's simple to tell the doctors at a medical convention from the people who are there trying to sell them stuff. The marketing reps are all movie-star handsome, groomed to the teeth, and damned glad to meet you. The doctors look like nebbishes, too socially challenged to make eye contact for fear of being solicited.

At twenty-eight, I've somehow lucked into the best job a single gal could ever hope to snag. As a malpractice insurance rep, I get to dress up every day, drive into town from my little place in Malibu, and take doctors out to lunch—for a living. Once or twice a month, I fly to the fanciest resorts in the country and play tennis and golf with them, ski with them, and take them out to dinner—for a living. Not surprisingly, I get to date a lot of doctors.

The man on the escalator looks like the archetypal Dartmouth professor. He's buttoned-down and tweedy, wearing a sky-blue cashmere vest that matches his eyes. To complete the ensemble he's chosen pleated gabardines and tucked a couple of textbooks under his arm. Too well dressed to be a doctor, but far too self-possessed to be a salesman, we lock eyes as we pass. The next thing I know, he's bounding up the escalator steps behind me trying to catch up.

"Are we having a lovely day?" he asks, just singsong enough to indicate irony. Okay, he's a doctor.

Outside it's one of those breezy, sunny February afternoons where big, puffy clouds traverse a sapphire sky. It's crisp and not quite cool enough to be cold; the kind of day that suggests one's time would be far better spent in the rigging of a 42' sloop sailing the Newport Coast than stuck here inside the stuffy conference rooms of a mid-winter radiology symposium.

"I'd *rather* be sailing," I say, aping a current bumper sticker.

At this, he arches a brow and gives me a second look. He smiles. "Bob," he says. "Mid-winter radiologic."

"Allena," I reply. "Medical malpractice." I know right then and there that I'm going to marry this man and have his babies.

"Look," he says, "I have to give a talk on imaging modalities right now, but would you like to have dinner with me afterward?"

"Yes, I'd love to." (Oh *my*, yes.)

We have an early dinner at Harry's Bar and American Grill, then we have a second dinner down the street at Trader Vic's because we want to keep on talking. And when the kitchen closes there, we go back to Harry's again for a third dinner. Robert (I can't bear to call him "Bob") has to head for Newport in the morning, and I have to be in Mammoth, so this is all the middle ground we're going to get if we're going to hit this off tonight.

By the end of the evening, we've uncorked the better part of the last decade. We've spilled everything we've had bottled up over the common landscape of these crisp linen tablecloths, finally free to let it all gush out and sully, then left it on the table for the busboy to clear away and dump with the night's garbage. Tidy. The sense of inevitability is liberating, and he seems as certain of the possibilities before us as I do.

When it comes time to say goodnight, he seems agitated, almost crestfallen, like he's been given some wonderful gift only to have it snatched away. *This calls for some sort of token.* Normally, that token would be an invitation back to my place in Malibu, or at least a thoughtful quickie here in the hotel parking lot, but tonight is unique in my experience—this has all the earmarks of a real *romance,* and I am loathe to break the spell.

So I untie my silk scarf—my favorite, go-to-conference one—and drape it around his neck. "Here. Keep this for me until I get back?"

When he feels the slight weight of the feathery silk, it's as though a stone has been lifted from his shoulders. "I'm going to worry about you out there on the road alone." he says. "That's a long way to drive by yourself."

My job requires that I live out of a suitcase; I routinely drive a thousand miles a week—and then some. This is the first time anyone has ever expressed the slightest concern for my safety or comfort, and I'm genuinely touched. "I promise I'll be fine," I say.

"I want to give you something," he says. "I want you to keep it in your trunk in case of an emergency." *Signal flares? He's going to give me signal flares? Jumper cables, maybe?* He walks to his car and removes something I can't see, then opens my trunk and puts it inside. "Don't look until you get home, okay?"

Pacific Coast Highway goes by in a blur all the way up to Point Dume. Maybe this is what they mean by destiny. My car feels like a warm blanket cuddling me home, my skin is tight and tingling. There must be enough endorphins coursing through my system to keep me smiling for the next ten years. It's not until I'm out on Highway 395 the next morning, halfway to Mammoth and stopped for gas, that I remember he's stuck something in my trunk "for emergencies." I open the lid expecting a new flashlight or maybe a little love note written on a cocktail napkin. Instead there is a manila envelope tucked into the corner underneath the tire jack. Inside the envelope, I find a note and ten one-hundred-dollar bills. *"For when I can't be here to help you out,"* it reads.

CAUSE FOR PATIENCE

For all his sweetness, it's soon apparent that Robert is single in a world of openly available women for good reason.

For one thing, he's a hoarder. His spacious Newport Beach apartment is packed, literally floor-to-ceiling packed, with plastic trash bags of unopened mail. It's mostly financial statements, advertisements, and grocery store throwaways. One of his bedrooms is filled with texts, pamphlets, circulars, unopened packs of snack foods, cartons of paper goods, unmatched shoes, clothing, used Kleenexes, crumpled wads of currency. It's as though he's undressed and emptied the contents of his pockets into this room every night for years—which, as it turns out, is exactly what he's been doing. No wonder his ex-wife took off for Texas with their baby son. She probably had trouble finding him in all this mess!

Although Robert's lived in this apartment for the better part of a decade, he says he's never once used the kitchen, and I believe him. He has no pots, no pans, no silverware, cups, plates, or glasses. Instead, he has boxes of plastic forks, cartons of Styrofoam cups, and a Dumpster's worth of empty food packaging lining the countertops and poking out of the cupboard shelving. The living room is stacked with books and record albums—along with loose reams of paper, reports, patient files, stacks of x-ray films, CT scans, and dictations. In the middle of the room, like some bizarre avant-garde art installation, stands an enormous and uninhabited fish tank with about a half-inch of scum congealing at the bottom. I'm afraid to look in to see what might be decomposing.

He's left a narrow pathway through the piles of clutter to a big leather easy chair where he dictates his cases, and the folding card table on which he files them—a surface which also, apparently, serves as his dining-room table. The apartment has a commanding view of the back bay—though it is partially blocked by more piles of paper grocery bags—and a sliding glass door reveals a 8' x 20' balcony stacked with boxes of more books, cartons of Ramen noodles and bottled water, a weight machine, a bicycle, a telescope, assorted survival gear, and inexplicably, a case of champagne.

So I'm astounded to see that his clothes closets, by extreme contrast, are impeccable and perfectly organized, his shirts arranged by color and formality, all expertly laundered, pressed, and lightly starched. And there are clean sheets and pillowcases on his bed, which although unmade, is nonetheless sweet-smelling and inviting.

I can work with this.

After cleaning out motel rooms for a living, I can work with anything. Besides, now I can afford to hire a housekeeper to help me clean this hoo-rah's nest of its droppings. By the time his mother comes out from Minneapolis to meet me a few months later, the place is sparkling, organized, and well equipped with kitchen and housewares. The beautiful old mahogany pieces that were hidden behind bags of junk and debris are buffed and gleaming, and the splendid oriental carpets that used to grace his grandparents' summer home are proudly displayed on the newly cleared floors. It's taken a work crew and a whole case of plastic garden bags, but the place is looking like . . . well, home.

In addition to his complete disinterest in housework, Robert has another quirk that quickly becomes apparent. This man has no life outside of his practice, nor does he appear to want one. We do meet several times a week for dinner at the same restaurant—though he's usually at least an hour late—and he orders the exact same thing for months on end. He leaves for work at six in the morning, gets home at midnight or later, works thirty-hour weekends, and refuses to take a vacation or even an evening off. On the few occasions I *do* get him to accompany me somewhere, he is cordial, courtly, even witty and engaging. But after an hour or two at the most, he becomes increasingly agitated and lets me know in no uncertain terms that he "has to get back to work." Always, there is his work "to get back to."

When I remind him that as a radiologist he has the ability to determine his own hours, his location, and as much or as little vacation time as he chooses, he responds that no one else can do his reading—as though he's the only doctor in Orange County qualified to interpret a CT scan.

"Besides," I mention, "you can always hire a *locum tenems* to take over your cases for a few days."

He won't hear of it. "What if they see what a good contract I have and try to underbid me?" he says. I soon learn not to expect any more of him than he is prepared to give.

Some might find this sort of lifestyle stifling. Certainly it's not the sort of thing most women would sign up for when they consider husband material. But I have, and for me, it's a great match. While I'm disappointed that he is unwilling, or more accurately, *unable*, to share all the interesting places and experiences I enjoy and intend to keep on enjoying, I also accept the fact that I'm not going to change his propensity for work any more than he will change mine for sloth.

The sense of security and permanence our odd non-interaction provides us is enough to compensate for the lack of camaraderie; I can find activity friends anywhere, but up until now, a secure lifestyle has been far more elusive. I think back to the years of scrounging for work and having to be ready to move out on a moment's notice, and decide it's a more-than-decent tradeoff.

So when Robert pages himself at family gatherings, at concerts, at the dinner table, anywhere he prefers not to be at the moment, I take it in stride and take a taxi home. If he prefers to repair to a quiet nook and read while I go out on my adventures, well, I grew up around doctors and know how they get. Daddy spent so much of his time worrying about other people that it was simply understood we'd leave him alone when he came home to recuperate.

I still go into my Santa Monica offices, and I still travel around the state lobbying doctors, but my heart just isn't into it anymore. I'm much happier here in our sunny apartment on the Back Bay, with our cat, our cockatoo, and our library full of books and music. In fact, I'm sitting on the sofa enjoying just that when I notice the cramping . . . and this blood.

I've always been scrupulous about birth control, so I'm pretty sure I'm not pregnant—I'm nearly thirty, and have never even had a scare. Maybe my IUD has become dislodged and is sticking into something it shouldn't be sticking into? Or maybe my body has rejected it and I'm having a particularly aggressive period?

Whatever. This hurts too much and there's too much blood running down my legs to be dithering over the cause. I'm down the elevator and into my car without even stopping to grab a towel from the bathroom.

The triage nurse at Hoag Hospital takes one look at me and orders me onto a gurney.

"Are you pregnant?" she asks.

"No." *What a dumb question.*

Fifteen minutes later the doc is pointing to an image of my fallopian tube and telling me it has ruptured because there is a baby growing in it—and now I'm in the process of bleeding to death.

"Ruptured ectopic pregnancy," he's saying. "Emergency surgery." *I didn't even know I was pregnant!* His words go floating past my ears and settle somewhere beyond the examining table where I sit. *This is me he's talking to.* I'm terribly confused.

I hate kids. I used to look out the window of my office high above Wilshire Boulevard and actually get *offended* when I saw a mother walking down the sidewalk with a child in tow during business hours. If someone with a kid is seated next to me on an airplane or in a restaurant, I won't even hesitate before asking to be moved elsewhere. Kids are noisy, fidgety, ill-mannered, and inappropriate—like little dogs yapping through the foyer. I've had enough babysitting and elder-sistering to last a lifetime, and I don't care if I never see another baby as long as I live.

So the idea that there is a little person growing inside of me, one that's destined to die in the next thirty minutes before I even have a chance to meet it, is disconcerting at best. Not that I'd ever expected to have a baby, but I'd always imagined that first pregnancies would be a time of wonder and rejoicing, shared with a loving husband and happy friends. Something to announce at a party or a family dinner, where toasts would be made and congratulations given. Now I'm facing a kill-or-be-killed moment, and it occurs to me that this little being will probably only ever be known as a life-threatening malfunction in my nether apparatus. Moreover, that thought makes me overwhelmingly sad.

Compounding my distress is the fact that I am going in for an emergency surgery, under general anesthesia, without first having a chance to meet with the surgeon or prepare myself for the physical trauma and the emotional aftermath—if there *is* an aftermath. As much as I hate to admit it to myself, I'm not only fighting my terror, I'm fighting horror, too—and a profound sense of maternal protectiveness for this poor doomed fetus. *This isn't the way it's supposed to happen. If only I'd known; maybe I would have thought more kindly of the little buggers.*

"We'll need to notify your next of kin," someone is saying. "Who would you like us to call?" *My next of kin* . . . As morbid as this sounds, it still has a nice ring to it. All these years I've been giving out my parents' number as "next of kin." Now I finally have somebody who cares for me because they've *chosen* to, not because they have to.

I give them Robert's number. At this moment, he's at another hospital across town, perhaps reading some other lady's ultrasound and informing her physician that she has a ruptured ectopic pregnancy. She needs immediate surgery. . . .

"Honey, I really need you to be here with me," I tell him after the nurse has explained the situation to him. "Please come be with me? After all, this is *our* baby . . . what if I don't make it?" I'm trying not to freak out, but it's pretty hard to hold it together by myself. This has all been so sudden.

Robert is kind and reassuring. "Hoag is an excellent hospital," he tells me. "I used to work with these guys, and you're in fine hands." Then he drops it in my bloodied lap—those three little words that subsume all hopes, all entreaties, all commitments—my legacy as a doctor's daughter now come back to haunt me as a doctor's almost-wife. "I can't come until

CAUSE FOR PATIENCE

late tonight," he explains matter-of-factly. "I have patients." Of *course*. He has *patients*. Why didn't I guess that?

I'm not sure what makes me sadder—that he doesn't come, or that I understand why not.

When you're lying alone in a hospital bed awaiting the cutting table, it's hard not to think about death. Surgery is one of the stranger rituals we humans have invented. Even more than religion, it's the ultimate expression of our surrender to faith and unreason. What other species would voluntarily allow another of its kind to rip it open and remove its innards? Then pay a fortune for the privilege?

The anesthesiologist is reciting the informed consent like he's giving me the last rites; *Spiritu sancto . . . Coma. Death. Coma. Death.* This is what I'm reciting to calm myself instead of, *Kill. Robert. Kill. Robert.* My unfortunate embryo is as much his doing as it is my own, but *heeee*'s *busy*. With *patients*! The only bright spot I can see in all of this is that the scare of nearly losing me will be enough to force him off the fence he's been straddling over "setting the date." We've tentatively agreed to marry "at some point," but the timing never seems to be quite right.

First there's this radiology fellowship or that convention, then there is the question of his precocious eight-year-old son, Stevie—who alternately lusts after and detests me. Stevie lives with his mother and stepfather in Texas, and only comes to stay with us on vacations, but I still haven't figured out how to tread a common ground with him. He's wholly uncompromising, and both hugely possessive of his father and dismissive of me. It's a bad combination for all of us. This unnerving child with his genius IQ and his troubled soul exudes some deeply creepy Oedipal overtones, and when he's out here monopolizing our little household, I find it best to simply be out of the country. So *that* needs to be resolved before I can feel comfortable starting a new family with his father.

After the boy's last visit, I confessed to Robert that I can't bear the idea of coming between him and his needy young son. Maybe it would be best for all of us if I recommit myself to my job and move back to Malibu? At this, Robert began to weep. I'd never seen him cry before, or even lose his composure. I'd spoken this, fully expecting a reluctant capitulation, a good-bye full of sweet but knowing regret. Instead he'd dropped to his knees and begged me to stay with him. "Please don't leave me here alone," he pleads. "I can't do this without you."

I felt profoundly torn. I knew that the course of the rest of my life—and probably Stevie's, too—depended on what I said next. A promising career, my autonomy, and a chance to make a real contribution to society lie with my work. Or, I could devote myself to being the best wife and mother I can possibly be, a helpmeet to a man of substance, who will give, and more importantly, *keep* me a family. But I can't do both.

Madre and all her friends have given me an apt example. These women of an earlier generation—a generation borne of the Great Depression and honed by the Second World War—were made of sterner stuff. Madre's cohort was duty-bound and obedient, trapped by circumstance and biology. Not only did these women work full time to put their warrior-husbands through medical school, law school, and post-docs, but the political atmosphere of the time dictated that the educated couples of the post-war decade breed themselves into eugenic frenzy to counteract the explosive population growth of, as Grandmother would delicately put it, "the less fortunate."

Most all of our family friends had four, five, even six children, and the wives *still* worked to help support them all. We kids were generally polite and well behaved, but our moms periodically went unhinged with the pressure. The dads just went missing, and the resulting family dynamics were generally, well, *fractured*.

Oldest siblings like me who were stuck with overseeing the brood in our parents' absences vowed not to fall into the same trap our mothers had. We simply didn't have that much energy—or that much ambition. And I want to *enjoy* motherhood, not just survive it. I know that Stevie, for whatever his reasons, is going to do his best to make sure that I don't.

But I can't tell Robert that—he loves his son and his son loves him. Later that evening, his tears vanquished, my fears of incompatibility shunted into some darker recess of my mind, Robert takes me out to dinner, and in the same parking structure where he first kissed me, asks me to be his wife. "Yes," I say. "Yes, I will." There's not a moment's hesitation in my answer. I'm shocked at how easily the words slip out.

My new fiancé takes me to our neighborhood Neiman's and together we pick out a smallish (by Newport Beach standards, anyway) diamond of exceptional fire and liveliness. The price tag leaves me gasping, but then again so do Robert's monthly billing statements. Although no money is tendered, we both agree it's a perfect ring "for future consideration," and I'm focusing on that reassuring commitment right now, flashing its rainbow facets through my traumatized brain as I lie on this cold steel table; its brilliant promise guiding me toward a better and more refracted light as the Demerol hits my blood-brain barrier and my life begins to fuzz into marshmallow clouds. "You should be feeling very sleepy in a few moments," says the anesthesiologist. I am. But what I'm also feeling is abandoned.

AWAKENING TO REALITY

My pelvis feels like it's been patched together with railroad spikes, but my room is sunlit and cheery, and there's a beautiful view of the marina and harbor just outside the window. Friends and family have sent pretty flowers. The surgery has gone well, and they've managed to salvage one half of my interior lady parts, so "You shouldn't have *too* much trouble getting pregnant again."

"Getting pregnant again" is the *last* thing on my mind at this point. It will be six weeks before I'm recovered enough to go back to the office, let alone travel anywhere. That probably isn't going to work for my bosses, who need me *now*—and who most likely will scurry to replace me as soon as I give them the news. The final vote on a major piece of legislation is coming up in a couple of weeks, and now I won't be there for the crucial push. I see three years of hard work circling the drain.

It would appear I've not only lost my fertility, but along with it my job and my financial independence as well. And amid all this angst is the awful knowledge that there *was* a little person growing inside of me—and my broken body killed it.

Robert still hasn't shown up, though he's left a message that he'll be by this evening—after work—to make sure I'm okay, and he's bringing me a "surprise," he says.

A surprise! My world is singing again. *The ring! My beautiful, fabulous diamond ring!* The one that will tell everyone—especially me—that someone values me enough to throw in his lot with me, entrust me with his future, and mine with his. Suddenly all the pain and terror of the last twenty-four hours evaporate and I forget all the disappointments of my checkered romantic past. That ring is a great big "*fuck you*" to every man who ever betrayed me, and every woman who ever slighted me because I dared to stay single. With this ring, I'll *belong*, and every time it flashes in the sun or glows in the candlelight, it will signal that I'm part of a larger whole; that someone loved me enough to make me his family.

By the time Robert finally makes it to see me, I'm nearly giddy with anticipation. *What a perfect gesture, coming here with an engagement ring after all this.* The melodramatic possibilities here are rife, and my fevered imagination is running with them.

There is a knock on the door, and here's my guy, smiling, tender, dressed like a fashion plate. In my mind's eye, I'm filming this scene for posterity, writing, directing, *willing* it along the script I've already imagined. He's carrying a shopping bag and a picnic basket, and there is an air of conspiracy about him. He shoos the nurse out of the room and locks the door behind her, grinning like a happy idiot. Something's up, something *wonderful*.

"I brought you something," he says, placing the picnic basket on my bed. My heart burns with a little start of adrenaline. Forcing nonchalance, I open the lid, peel back the cover. Maybe he put the ring box in here? Underneath this napkin, maybe?

Something moves, then springs out at me. It's his—now our—Abyssinian cat, Rudyard.

I nearly burst my newly sewn guts laughing. "How did you sneak him up the elevator?" I ask, incredulous. *This is just wonderful! Our whole family is here to witness the happy occasion!*

Rudyard, glad to be free of his wicker prison, settles gingerly into my lap, purring, grooming my thumb with his rough little tongue.

"He's missed you, too" says Robert. "I climbed up the fire escape with him so no one would get suspicious if he meowed."

He pulls up a chair, takes up the napkin, and lays out the feast he's brought for our supper. There's a warm quiche, pâté, crusty bread, a salad, even a bottle of champagne, which he pours into my plastic water glass, and sets to cooling in an ice-filled barf bucket. *This is going to be one for the romance books.* I see myself telling this story to our grandbabies.

CHOMP CHOMP CHOMP

Dinner progresses, we chat, Rudyard explores the room and purrs in my lap, but nothing is said of the ring. Then it's time for Robert to go. He captures our cat from the windowsill, enticing it back into the picnic basket with a bite of pate. "I still have a lot of studies to finish this evening," he tells me. Maybe he's playing coy, waiting for me to bring up the ring so he can "forgetfully" pull the red leather box out of his pocket.

"Honey," I start, "did you get the ring? It would sure help cheer me up when you can't be here to visit. . . ."

He looks at me as though I'm still shaking off the anesthesia, and nonchalantly continues repacking our cat. "I decided that's too much to spend on a ring," he says. "There's other stuff I'd rather do with that money."

Something inside of me grows dim and then extinguishes itself.

He's right, of course. *Any* money is too much money to spend on a diamond ring, but if ever a grand gesture was called for, this was that time. And he's just blown it. Royally.

"I thought you'd appreciate me sneaking Rudyard up," he sniffs, as if the two are conflated and I'm being unreasonable. Perhaps I am. Of *course* I am! I know by now that it's silly to want Cinderella stories and happily-ever-after endings; it's absurd to invest the gravity of a lifelong commitment into a small sparkly stone. And I detest the diamond cartels as much as anyone. But that sparkler and all it represented meant a great deal to me in this sad and troubled tangle—and now he could buy me a rock of ten times the size and brilliance, and it wouldn't rekindle what has just been lost.

I'll still marry this man, and I'll still love him as I've promised, but he'll never ever again have my schoolgirl's heart the way he did up until a few moments ago. "I'll come by tomorrow evening to check on you," he tells me as he lets himself out into the hallway. The heavy door clicks behind him after belching a final little *whoomp* of Lysol-laden air. I'm too depressed to be angry, and too disappointed to cry. Was I disappointed in him for his callousness? Or in myself for my grandiose expectations?

The duty nurse comes by to give me my meds and make sure I'm tucked in for the night. She looks at my chart and asks perfunctorily,

AWAKENING TO REALITY

"And how are we feeling tonight?" I realize that I don't even know how long I've been here. "What day *is* this?" I ask. She looks at her watch, then at me. "It's Saturday, February 14," she replies. "Valentine's Day."

DRIFTWOOD

During the recession of the early 1980s, female middle management, the first in our nation's history, is making a tentative toehold for itself in corporate America. We're still considered something of an experiment if not the butt of late-night comedians' jokes, so when the economy goes south, we're the first to get canned. Not surprisingly, I'm among them. After all, I'm currently of no use to the company's mission and I'm perceived as being insulated from impoverishment by Robert's money. As the jolly VP who "lets me go" tells me over his lunchtime scotch and chicken piccata, "You're too pretty to work, anyway. It's not as though you *have* to have this job, and there are family men here who *need* it."

So, comforted with my unemployment check and my docile new home, I'm trying to heal my mind and body, but can't shake the feeling I'm only taking up skin. After ten years of wondering where the night's dinner is going to come from, or if I'll have a roof over my head by the end of the month, it's frighteningly easy to just kick back and coast. Robert notices my malaise and takes me aside. "Aren't you happy?" he asks me. "You've got everything you ever wanted."

I do. But I don't have a sense of *purpose* anymore. "Maybe I should get another job . . . ," I begin.

Robert takes me by the shoulders, looks into my eyes. He's very deliberate. "Don't worry about the baby," he tells me. "And don't worry about getting a job. I already have one, and I make more than enough for the two of us. You just relax and get well." He's right, of course.

"Do you want me to put you through medical school?" he asks suddenly. "You know I will. I'd be glad to, actually." I consider this for a moment. Getting my MD has always been sort of a preordained conclusion in my life. I've procrastinated as long as I can, throwing out every box-of-tacks diversion I can think of to avoid going back to school, but the inevitability is beginning to catch up with me. I'm running out of excuses.

"I . . . I'll think about it," I mutter. But Robert knows me better. He knows I'm cut of a different cloth—the kind of cloth that doesn't do well with sick people. The kind that unravels when it gets other people's blood on it. It's not that I'm fastidious, or that there's anything squeamish about me. It's just that there's a darker side to me, one that I don't dare to explore as an adult the way I did as a young girl toying with bugs under a lens. I'm *too* analytical, *too* detached. Blood, viscera, suffering, and disease bring out an element of the Nazi doctor in me, one that rather *enjoys* the power trip and justifies it with high-mindedness. Unchecked, it's all too easy to let it become something monstrous, something beyond humanity. Becoming a doctor would both define me and destroy me, and we both know it.

I think Robert feels this way too, which is why he became a radiologist. His interactions, his experimentations, are all on celluloid and in black and white. There's no element of human suffering in them for him—merely the theoretical.

His eyes get kindly. There is a twinkle in them that suggests the fine humor that he doesn't often show—even to me. Although everyone who meets him describes him as "nice," no one would accuse him of being especially compassionate. He hugs me to him, then with a wry little smile he hands me another little lesson. "Look," he says, "why beat your brains out if you don't have to?"

HOUSE UPON THE SAND

We've set the wedding date and bought ourselves two plain gold bands—purposely plain, I might add—to seal our troth. There's something almost perverse about listening to my girlfriends fake-squeal when I show it off. We all know we're just going through the motions; this ring is one step above a cigar band, and if it were up to Robert, we'd not be doing this his-and-hers ring thing at all.

But so many of my friends and coworkers have been teetering on the corporate treadmill, terrified that with the slightest misstep they'll tumble off into the unemployment line, that my escape from cubicle tyranny has given us all something to cheer about. I've grabbed the golden ring; I've married a doctor. There is hope!

The first order of business is to get us out of this singles apartment complex and into something more suitable to our new domestic status. Having finally escaped the dating rat race, I'm only too familiar with the less honorable intentions of our more predatory neighbors—male and female alike.

An ad in the local throwaway paper leads me to a little teardown rental on the nearby bluffs above the sea. This poor old dilapidated summer home is just biding its owner's time until the real-estate market improves enough to bulldoze it and build a multi-gazillion dollar manse in its footprint. Leaky and mice-infested, the roof is warped and pitched at an alarming angle, and the fixtures are straight out of the Sputnik era, but it's on a fabulous lot right over the sand, heavily wooded in a neighborhood bereft of big trees, and located in one of the most exclusive private communities in the country. It's an easy walk to an otherwise inaccessible private beach, park, and trail system, and best of all, the price is right. I sign the lease agreement without even consulting Robert, let alone asking him if he wants to move to Laguna.

I've already got our stuff half-packed into cardboard boxes by the time he comes home from the hospital that night. As usual, his shoes are splattered with barium and his mind is a thousand miles elsewhere. After living in this apartment for ten years without ever meeting a neighbor or lighting the pilot on the stove, he's fine with whatever I want to do.

"Oh-kay . . ." is all he says.

Emerald Bay is everything I'd hoped it would be—a magical kingdom to rival nearby Disneyland. Only *these* fairy castles are real and inhabited by actual princes and princesses—minor royalty, titans of finance, political scions and their trophy wives—all of whom are too busy either making money or off spending it to stay here and enjoy the splendid private beach, the perfect swimming bay, the lovely, landscaped peace of the place.

Down here by the rocky bluffs, it's only me, the occasional lone jogger—"there goes another divorce," as one wag puts it—and the old-timers, those hearty denizens who've owned property here forever. Back in the 1930s and '40s, Emerald Bay was where wealthy Pasadena families stashed the quirky aunts and cousins who had legitimate claim to the family fortune but just weren't "quite right" enough to be seen at public events and social gatherings. Most of these outcasts never left their seaside asylum, inheriting the homes that were too distant or too noisy to contesting heirs who were irritated by the constant sound of the breakers on the shore or annoyed at the effect of the salt air on their orchid gardens.

In the late afternoons, I've taken to swimming the length of the bay with a few of these eccentric geezers, and although they're a good fifty years older, I'm always hard-pressed to keep up with them. As a kid, I never got used to the shock of being thrown off the dock into the chill June waters of Belmont Shore—Madre knew that the only way she'd get any peace during the long months of summer vacation was to douse the five of us in ice water early every morning so the shock to our systems would still some of our rambunctious energy.

True, the "bracing" water hardened us, and I learned to be a strong swimmer, but the only reason I struggle along now is because I love these old ladies and gents with their wonderful stories and their cranky, ribald senses of humor. I know I'll never be one of the beautiful people I see at the other end of the bay, the brittle, gilded ones who sit on the beach glinting thousand-dollar sunglasses and seven-carat diamonds and never so much as get their hair wet in this cold, green water. I never was any good at their catty junior-high games anyway. I just want to enjoy the solitude of this quiet beach and recover from the first thirty years of my life.

Not that I'm unimpressed with the glamour of this place. On summer weekends and holidays the bay erupts in a festival of lavish beach parties—complete with set design, fireworks, grill-masters, and even champagne fountains and ice sculptures emerging from the sand. College kids home from school work the family margarita machines and distribute designer drugs-du-jour from their makeshift kiosks, while private security and the occasional Secret Service details shuffle awkwardly about the sand in their black suits, walkie-talkies, and hard-soled shoes guarding people whose privacy is a matter of national concern. At times like these, the bay becomes a circus of power and show, glitter and excess.

But in the off-season it's almost eerie sitting out here on my rickety little balcony in the mornings, enjoying my coffee while the surf crashes on the deserted sands fifty feet below. The mansions perched along the shoreline are each more splendid than the last, giant ego monuments for the rich and the envied, yet they seem devoid of life, their balconies unused, the interiors still and quiet but for the efficient ministrations of the house staff. Never once do I see another person out here enjoying the morning air alone with their thoughts and their coffee; their castles all but abandoned as they labor in the city to support them—leaving only me to enjoy the irony.

A dog begins to bark just as dawn turns the sand to coral. Not quite dark but not yet light, it's misty out, the air salty and heavy with the scent of eucalyptus and Torrey pine. I wrap my hands around my coffee mug against the chill of the late March air and almost hear Grandmother greeting her morning joe as she loads her cup with fresh cream from a pint bottle. "Good old coffee," she says to no one but the steaming herald in her cup—her friend in her solitude. "Good old coffee."

Today, I know what she means. The morning ritual of grinding, boiling, brewing, easing the transition between dream state and waking, coffee is dependable, unchallenging, a touchstone with which to steel myself for the day's trials to come. "Good old coffee," I hear myself saying, recapitulating an old woman's secret disappointments. Alone in a crumbling house with just myself and my resentments. *Am I all that much different?*

The dog outside is insistent, and I go out to the balcony to see what is setting this one off. The beach below is deserted, yet the dog continues sounding the alarm. I, too, am aware of a presence, but cannot pinpoint what or where it might be, for there is nothing for the barking to triangulate off of but the fog.

And then I see them, no more than thirty feet offshore in the shallow trench between the tide line and the drop-off to the ocean beyond. It's a mother gray whale and her new calf. Barely submerged, lolling, rolling, scraping barnacles in the fine-grained sand, they are playing mama and baby games here by themselves, removed from the pod, enjoying this moment alone on their long journey back up the coast to Alaska. I'm dumbstruck at the sight of them, marveling at their size and proximity. They bump and nuzzle and spin in place, then, slowly, majestically, the mother rolls to her side and the baby begins to nurse her.

I've seen gray whales migrating out in the open sea, and I've watched the smaller pilot whales playing with porpoises in the Catalina Channel. But this is something altogether magnificent and private, something no human was meant to see.

The dog runs along the shoreline, dashing into the surf then scenting the whales and racing back to the safety of the sand. I can smell them from here—warm, mineral, the mingling of placenta and seaweed. And I know without even looking that this spectacle is being played for me and me alone. I resist the urge to shout out to my neighbors, "Wake up, people! Look what you are missing!"

But I know I would break the spell; it's just me and my coffee and this exuberant dog in the early morning light. I'm humbled and honored at the same time, stunned at this gift from an outer world, one beyond my imaginings yet somehow so much my own. I'm not sure what this all means, but I also know it's changed my life—though I've yet to understand how or why.

I have everything a spoiled-rotten girl could want—a house on the beach, and an undemanding husband who gives me pretty much anything I ask for. There's the elegant little convertible, the sailboat, a ski condo, more jewelry than I can comfortably wear at one time, and a passport filled with colorful stamps and visas. Shop girls in snotty boutiques address me by name, and maîtres d'hôtel at trendy restaurants hold my table when I'm fashionably late. And yet . . . I'm unhappy.

BIOLOGICAL IMPERATIVES

It's after midnight, and as is my wont of late, I'm running the length of the bay by moonlight. The community is guarded around the clock, and the mansions along the sand are dark and quiet, so I have this whole sheltered stretch of coastline to myself—carefree and cloistered. The cove is flat, unobstructed, almost an exact kilometer from point to point. I can't imagine a more perfect place to let go of my thoughts and just let my body take me over. Running. Running.

On nights like this, when the moon is out full, the air still, and the sea calm, I can let my mind blend into the cosmos until my feet are no longer touching ground, propelled by only the rhythm of my breathing and the sensation of atonement. Usually when I reach this state of surrealism I'm humming a mantra of sorts, a snippet that links me into the music of the spheres—that high, tinny, thirty-two-cycle tone that permeates everything from household electrical circuits to the sound of the blood coursing through my eardrums. Maybe it's a holdover from all those earaches I suffered as a kid, but now the ringing in my ears is sometimes enough to drive me to distraction unless I counteract it with a melody line.

On this particular night it's the chorus of James Taylor's "Country Road"—which I consider a vast improvement over that god-awful Coke commercial that has been looping through my head of late.

I'm really getting into the syncopation. *Walk on down* (step) . . . *walk on down* (step) . . . *walk on down a country road* . . . when the music in my head abruptly stops and I'm nearly overcome with a sense of nothingness. It's so startling and stark, so thorough and immediate that at first I think I've become enraptured—or have suffered a stroke. But no, my feet are still setting down one after the other, my legs are still pumping.

I hear that annoying little voice again and it's poking my complacency: *You're running down a beach at two-thirty in the morning! What do you think you're doing, you idiot?*

Comes the response: *I've done everything I set out to do. I have everything I've ever wanted. Where am I supposed to go from here?*

Presumably, I've another fifty or sixty years of life left on this planet and I've nary a goal, a passion, or a heart's desire to fulfill. *So what now? Hmmmm? What the hell am I supposed to be doing now?*

I'm quite serious in this little debate; there has to be more to life than simply consuming and expiring. One supposes this is the spiritual crossroads that so many of our great thinkers and theologians discuss in their texts. Maybe it's the "bottom" that alcoholics and druggies hit. Or maybe it's Huxley's doors of perception that I never quite managed to kick open during my youthful psychedelic revels.

No matter, it's become incarnate here on this deserted beach as a literal voice on high. Call it God speaking to a lost soul, or call it auditory hallucination brought on by rhythmic disorientation. Whatever it is, the voice in the darkness has a message for me, and that message is loud and clear. And it says:

You're. Going. To be. Knocked. Up.

"Yeah, right," I go. One ectopic pregnancy is enough for me.

The voice on high just snickers. *So you say*, it says.

A month later, I'm pregnant. The little blue cotton swab tells me so, and the ultrasound has confirmed. When I tell Robert that it's for real this time, seeded in my womb and not my tubing, there is rejoicing; I've not seen him so puffed up since our first days together. Suddenly he is home for dinner again. "All I ever wanted," he confesses, "is two boys and a house by the ocean." No mention of a wife to go with them, but that's assumed. I'm feeling pretty good about my contribution so far.

Our bookshelves groan under the weight of all the child-rearing books, pregnancy guides, and developmental charts I've bought. I pour over epidemiological studies on risk factors and nutritional requirements.

BIOLOGICAL IMPERATIVES

There are bottles of supplements in our refrigerator and special "pregnancy pillows" on our bed. I'm so conscientious about this fetus's health that I even hold my breath when I drive past the oil refinery on the way up the hill to visit my parents—though I worry that the temporary hypoxia might starve its developing brain.

My newfound sense of protectiveness extends beyond my growing belly; suddenly the world demands my interaction, I feel connected to the whole human family—the good of it and the not so good. I'm out to dinner with Robert when an oily fellow with gold chains and matted chest hairs lights up a cigarette. As he's only sitting a few inches away, I politely ask him to put it out. "I'm pregnant, you see . . ."

It feels so good to be able to say this—not just because it bothers *me*, but because I'm finally looking out for someone besides myself. However, instead of smiling in happy recognition and snuffing his smoke, the man glowers at me, takes a defiant puff, and blows it into my face. "I *own* this piece of real estate, lady," he snarls. "Go fuck yourself."

"Looks like someone's already beat me to it," I note, glancing down at the rising moon of my belly, "but I'd still appreciate it if you'd put that cigarette out so I don't projectile vomit all over your '*Poo-Poo platter.*'"

At this he bristles and half-rises, leaning across the table into Robert's face, not mine. Robert's seen me stand my ground before, and right now he's cringing at what he rightly suspects is coming. Like a turtle drawing into its shell, his head scrunches into his shoulders as he looks around furtively, searching for the exit door.

"You wanna go outside?" growls the guy, now fully engaged in his umbrage. "You wanna go outside right now?" Robert's not having any of it. He slumps down into his chair, mumbling apology. The drunk is undeterred. "I'm talking to you, buddy. You want a piece of me?" Robert doesn't.

I, however, am on a roll. Flush with maternal hormones, I'm feeling protective of not only my fetus but of my sweet feckless husband as well.

"Excuse me, sir," I say, trying to distract the guy's ire, "but my husband obviously doesn't want any part of this. If you want to pick a fight, I'm afraid it's going to have to be with me. If you'd like to go outside, *I'll* go outside with you." It's not just a statement of fact, it's an invitation.

I look him full in the face, then I stand up and step back from the table, prompting Robert to sink even farther into his chair. It may not be possible for a six-footer to disappear into a place setting but he's doing a good job of trying. I feel the same surge of righteousness I did on the day I came to the defense of that sweet little redheaded fat girl on the schoolyard. Bullying only encourages me.

Besides, this guy is not only drunk, he's sloppy drunk. If I learned anything from Leroy, it's that a sloppy drunk makes an easy target. You just let him swing first, then bop him on the nose while he's trying to regain his balance.

Now, *I* know it's all bluster, and I've not the slightest intention of getting myself into a knockdown drag-out with some surly lout, but the lout doesn't know that, and now his pride is trapped by his own testosterone. The poor man is actually considering my offer. He seems confused, as if he knows *something's* not quite right, but he can't figure out just what.

The waterfront restaurant is semi-upscale, and although I'm sure it's seen its share of bar fights, they probably haven't involved the owner of the place and a tiny pregnant lady in a twinset and pearls. Patrons around us begin to whisper, then jeer and call out their disapproval from around the room. At first I think they're mad at me, then I realize they're rooting me on. I notice a couple of guys at the bar elbowing each other in the ribs and laughing, thoroughly enjoying the spectacle we're creating down here in the dining room. It's Friday night, and a little bit of drama is just the thing to add some excitement to the evening. I've got this crowd in the palm of my hand, and I'm in just the mood to slap it upside this bully's shoe-polish black toupee.

The guy at the table next to him grabs his arm. "Hey buddy," he warns, "calm down. The lady's pregnant." Despite this irrefutably good suggestion, the drunk twirls and takes a clumsy swing at him, connecting only with smoke-laden air. With one quick pop to the temple, my newfound friend sends him flying into his appetizer plate.

Robert has had enough. "I'm not leaving a tip," he announces curtly as he buttons up his jacket and ushers me out of the restaurant. "I don't

BIOLOGICAL IMPERATIVES

know why you do this sort of thing. . . ." He's trying to sound offended, but I can tell he's smiling. He'll never admit it but he's *proud* of me.

Some men might have leapt to defend my honor, or thrown a punch in defense of theirs. Some might be shaking with rage, or trembling with disaster averted. But mine is simply concerned for propriety. His, not mine.

Humans are strange and dangerous beasts, and Robert is relieved to be leaving their midst—back to the dark of his hospital lair where they're nowhere around and he's safe. He knows I'll be happy and fine on my own as long as he's there at my back. Far from appalling, I find this endearing. He knows that our lives will go on despite all our foibles and all of our fears; he's content just to let me be me. And that's what I love about this man.

PRODUCTS OF CONCEPTION

We're on our way to a dinner party in Westwood when I feel the first twinges. After four months of blissful gestation, my body knows without knowing that this doesn't bode well. They're not painful tugs, but they're not the usual gripping and stretching I've come to welcome as "growing pains" either. My conscious mind hasn't yet grasped that I've suffered a miscarriage, yet somehow knows this is something dank and moist and primal—and awful. A crushing sensation plasters me into the passenger seat and I try not to breathe for fear of dislodging this thing that my body already knows is gone.

Whoever was trying to become human here inside of me has decided that it's just not worth the effort. It's given up the ghost and hung up its little baby jersey, and what's left of it is now in the process of leaving the building. Me.

I don't mention this to Robert, but our hostess is a retired RN, and she's seen the signs all too often. She takes me aside and tactfully asks if I might need to "talk." I've yet to admit to myself that this is happening, and so much of me is invested in my new identity as a mother-to-be that the possibility doesn't even enter my mind, but as the cramping increases and the gathering damp becomes a trickle then a steady expulsion, it's no longer possible to ignore the obvious.

As her other guests enjoy the bounteous Christmas feast she's spread out on her table, I sit on Mrs. Bennet's toilet, the POC, the "products of conception," as the clinical notes put it, weeping from between my legs in a grotesque mockery of the tears seeping from my eyes. This is a labor, but it's no labor of love. It's a labor of abject failure. I begin to truly understand the verb, the modifier, the absolute truth of the word "empty." Void,

PRODUCTS OF CONCEPTION

hungry, meaningless, discharge.

I know that the little creature has already begun to take human form. When amidst the cramping and the terror it finally plops out into the blood-sodden bowl, I cannot bear to look. Can any woman? Has any woman *ever*? There is something unholy about this. Something so dark and so evil that the common sewers are the only place to hide the offal.

But this is your baby! Your baby. MY baby. This isn't happening isn't happening isn't happening . . .

There is only denial and horror, not even the benediction of numbness to bring me back to sanity. I feel as though I am about to dis-integrate—and in a sense that's precisely what I'm doing. Dis-integrating. The compulsion to turn and look is nearly overwhelming, but the horror prevents me from moving. Maybe if I just sit here quietly, I'll wake up and be able to go back downstairs and enjoy the party.

The minutes pass as the placenta drops and the bleeding slows while I'm trying, unsuccessfully, to return to my wits. My body is here on this commode, in this suburban bathroom, in mid-1980s USA; my mind is watching the scene play out from elsewhere, somewhere beyond time and human history. Somewhere that only thwarted mothers know about and cannot bear to acknowledge—a place where they eat their unfit own, and devour the leavings of their presence.

Older women never speak of miscarriage to the newly pregnant. Out of compassion? For fear of hex? But this ritual has come to *me*, rather than I to it. The compulsion is born of survival instinct evolved to hide the evidence of genetic failure . . . *my* genetic failure.

I drop to my knees in front of the toilet and reach into the gore for my child. The lump of gel surrounding it washes off in the sink to reveal a tiny glistening creature that looks like nothing so much as a cocktail shrimp. Ludicrous, magnificent, beginning to slime. *So this is what my body has created and rejected—so this is the little being who has rejected* me. *I hold it in my palm, roll it gently between my thumb and my finger, learning its tiny contours and heft as though my delicate compressions might somehow urge it back to life—or forward it into the beyond. Anywhere but here in this terrible place between my hopes and my reality.*

I press my lips to the bloody mass and ever-so-softly kiss it hello. Hello my little One. It smells like the whales I saw in the cove; warm, fishy, essential. Then I wrap it in a toilet paper shroud and gently return it to the toilet. I press the handle goodbye. Like an interrupted daydream, and to all but me, as inconsequential as a floater goldfish, it is gone.

"Robert. *Robert!*" I call from the bathroom, beseeching. "Robert, please come here? I need you."

Home from the hospital, I never knew such sounds could come out of a human being; disconsolate, wailing, *keening* until my voice is hoarse and the muscles of my chest exhausted. I grieve not for the little life that never was, but for my loss, my failure, my utter humiliation. In grief my resentments turn ugly, unworthy. *Even illiterate peasants can pop out babies*, I rage. *Even meth-addled trailer-trash breed more than they can feed. Why the hell can't I?*

Um, because you're the kind of person who thinks loathsome thoughts like these, comes the quiet voice of my conscience. *When you're more deserving of motherhood, maybe you'll become a mother—you sniveling yuppie scum!*

I'm beginning to realize that there's more to this mom thing than just having children. There is a grace to the whole process of *becoming* a mother that has eluded me, a part of the human family that I've cut myself off from, and until I can smile when I see little kids, or cherish the wonder of a newly born life, I will remain barren and toxic—whether I ever have children or not.

THIRD TIME'S A CHARM

I can't tell if Robert is heartbroken or simply disgusted, but he's more distant than ever, lost in his work, and when only two months later I tell him that I'm pregnant again, he announces that he's taking a preceptorship in San Francisco, and that I'm here on my own for the duration. He doesn't even offer to take me with him. "I'll be staying in a hotel room while I'm there," he says. "You wouldn't like it."

He's right, I wouldn't. But neither do I want to face this third pregnancy alone. The grief after losing the last two nearly destroyed me, yet here I am again, elated and with child. The whole thing just seems too paradoxical. I'm not sure if I should be celebrating or slitting my throat for comic relief, but whatever is coming, I'm scared to death. *What cruelty and mercy be, bounded in our tyrannies . . .*

Robert has left to pursue his studies, and I'm wandering the aisles of the ranch market trying to divert myself from all this pointless worrying. *Look! They have an entire aisle devoted to granola, three dozen different kinds of cheese, and fresh fish from New Zealand,* I'm telling myself. *Why, the poorest American of today eats better than the kings of only a hundred years ago. Don't worry about this baby; at least it won't be hemophilic . . . SHUT UP YOU FOOL! DON'T JINX IT! Six kinds of fresh mushrooms, a row of bottled hot sauce . . .* When over the top of the soup aisle, his head just visible above the canned chowders, appears the most excellent man-child in the whole of Orange County, California.

They're only half-kidding when they say that Newport Beach has a face code, but this boy is absolutely jaw dropping—one of those people you chance upon every once in a great while and feel privileged just to be in the presence of. He has long, thick, surfer-blond hair and a tan so glowing you could read by it. He's even wearing the puka-shell necklace that matches his perfect white teeth. All I can do is stare and give silent thanks for my eyeballs.

Maneuvering around the water crackers to get a better look at him, I bang my shopping cart into the kombucha display—completely blowing my feigned nonchalance. "May I help you?" he asks.

"*May I help you?*" is one of those leading questions that fairly begs a smartass answer, sort of like, "*Is there anything else I can do for you today?*" The answer, obviously, is "Yes. *Please.*" The degree and extent of that "yes," however, is grist for all kinds of mischief. In this case it's all I can do to refrain from jumping up and down and clapping my hands like an afternoon game-show contestant.

As it turns out, Weegl, as I come to call him, is not only gorgeous, he's a sweet and gentle soul as well. Shy but observant and brilliantly funny, he's recently transplanted from a small southern town and is studying to be a filmmaker. He's just finished his shift as a volunteer lifeguard and coach at the Special Olympics pool, and is as desperately lonely as I am for someone creative to talk to and laugh with. He's thrilled when I invite him home to dinner, and a few weeks later, when I ask if he'd like to move into our spare room as a companion and helper, he's quick to take me up on it. Is there room in the garage for his bicycle? Of course. Would I mind if his girlfriend comes to visit? Not at all, she's darling, and I'd welcome the company.

Thus does the bay get its first male nanny, and while the womenfolk come to further resent the nubile Swedish au pairs their husbands have hired to keep an eye on them, and the men quietly shrivel in outrage, Weegl and I spend the next seven months having an absolute blast joshing, exploring the town, and watching my body bloat, all while titillating our gossipy neighbors.

I'm convinced that the constant flood of endorphins coursing through my system are building the happiest, healthiest baby any woman has ever produced, and I don't care if I scandalize every socialite in the county—I'm having the time of my life, and *no one* is going to spoil it for me.

As my belly grows, so does my dependence on Weegl. By the time I'm ready to pop, I've gained nearly 50 percent of my starting weight and the only relief I can get from gravity is in the ocean. Every day, Weegl lugs me down to the beach, guides me through the surf to the calmer waters beyond the shore break, then after I'm wrinkled and soggy, he drags me out and pushes me back up the hill—like Sisyphus's rock, hands braced against my ample butt—as my legs propel my Humpty Dumpty torso up the incline.

As excited about the impending birth of "our" baby as I am, he readily agrees to be my labor coach, Robert having demurred with, "I had enough of ladies in labor when I was in medical school." So Weegl and I read the books and manuals, we do the Lamaze course together and practice it diligently, and by the time late October comes around, I'm feeling much like the Halloween pumpkin I've come to resemble. My obstetrician is delighted with my progress and my heart is full of joy. What could possibly go wrong?

ALL HELL'S EVENING

The hallway is freezing, the gurney is icy, and my body feels bloodless. Nurses bustle and jabber around me. Orderlies jockey their wheelchairs and stretchers, bumping me out of the way. The world has gone on in this bright Halloween morning, but I, newly "delivered," have not. There is a disquieting finality to the cold that has settled over me, and though my hearing is fine-tuned, I cannot move a muscle except for my eyelids—and even that's a struggle just to manage a blink.

Curare-tipped darts are what Amazonian tribesmen use in their blowguns to paralyze their prey—and their enemies. It works by blocking the nerve-to-muscle impulses of the brain, and I'm here to tell you, the stuff is very effective—and terrible. Though I'm acutely aware of everything that's going on around me, try as I might, I cannot utter a sound, not even a grunt or a moan, let alone move a hand or an extremity to signal for a nurse. I'm bundled like a mummy, strapped to this gurney, and have no way to call out or even indicate my distress—I am, for all purposes, a living corpse. Locked in. Conscious and cognizant, but gone to the rest of the world.

It occurs to me that my reality has caught up to my self-delusion; I'm here in this world, but no longer a part of it, perhaps stuck like this for the rest of my days on this earth. No one has bothered to tell me what's going on, or what they've done to me, so I have no idea if this is permanent or just a side effect of some medication they gave me after everything went south. . . .

I remember: the baby presented breach and sideways, his little hip where his head should have been. After twenty-four hours of unproductive labor they finally decide to cut him out of my body, then after they have taken him away for a moment to clean him, a nurse brings him back up to my face to show me, and the doctor says, "Kiss your baby."

Kiss him? I haven't even met him yet! What a presumptuous thing to say. All of you people, GO AWAY!

All I want to do is hold this new little person—he seems so familiar—examine his little body, touch him, and contemplate our first meeting, but instead he's whisked away as the chipper voices in the operating room suddenly turn to urgent whispers and the mood turns from celebratory to somber. Something has gone terribly wrong. "I just can't get the bleeding stopped," says my doctor. "Hit her with the Pitocin again."

The heave of nausea is intense and immediate. This is the sixth time it's wracked me in the last five minutes. Every time they shoot another dose into the IV, my whole body convulses. From what I can gather, my extended labor has so weakened my system that all the drugs they shot into me to "help it along" have interacted with the ones they're now giving me to make it stop. Worse, in attempting to free the breach, the doctor has sliced into my uterine artery and I'm bleeding uncontrollably—but still fully awake, paralyzed, terrified of choking, unable to turn or twist my head to avoid aspirating whatever comes up. I'm afraid I'll die right here on the table and never get to see my baby again. The doctor sounds angry now. "It's always the doctors' wives. Push the goddamned Pitocin," he's saying.

That's all I remember until this moment. Whatever happened afterward, what's happened to me in the interim, I don't know. Did the baby make it? I've no idea, and at this moment, I honestly don't care. My struggle right now is with me, and I'm not all that sure I care to continue. It's just. Too. Damned. Cold. And why can't I move?

This is a nightmare beyond nightmares. Am I dying? Does anybody know I'm in here? What if I never come out of this and they shunt me off to a ward somewhere and stick feeding tubes into me and make me listen to Fox TV and ads for mesothelioma lawyers twenty-four hours a day? I can't imagine a hell that would compete.

Two nurses are chattering in the doorway, excited about tonight's big Halloween party. "I hope he doesn't show up with her," one of them is saying.

A hint! My brain goes into gear. So I've been lying here two days now.

I struggle and fail to get the nurse's attention. If this is what freezing to death feels like, I think I'd prefer being burned at the stake. Seized by violent shivering, my abdomen clenches, and something inside of me moves—I feel it leave my body. "Oops," says the nurse, finally alerted to my presence by the sudden stink. "Let's get you cleaned up." She rolls me to my side and changes out the sheet in one practiced move. *Well! That's one way to get their attention.* "Oh, honey," she says, "You're trembling. Are you cold? Do you need some more warm blankets?"

I want to cry out at this kindness, but all my energy is focused on moaning in the affirmative so she'll know I'm alive and conscious. I can't get control of my chest muscles, or my throat, but somehow manage to tighten them just enough to make my breath audible. She's heard me! Alerted, she finally looks into my eyes and that ineffable spark of recognition is exchanged. *I'm back!*

Is this how my baby is feeling right now? Trying to learn how to breathe, to make the terror of his new circumstances known to someone who will understand and comfort him? Maybe we're both figuring this "life" thing out together? I hear Robert's footsteps coming up the hallway, recognize the scent of leather and wool and cashmere before I can see him standing next to me. All I can do is blink and hope he knows I'm aware.

"The baby's fine," he says. "I just spent a few hours with him in the nursery, then held him while he slept. Do you want to see him?"

"gNnnnnnghooo . . ." It's all I can do to gurgle out, but at least I've made myself understood. I really *don't* want to see him right now. What a first impression this would make on the poor little thing. Your mama's a vegetable, little boy. Welcome to the world.

"That's okay," says Robert. He understands what my body's been through. For once I'm grateful that his medical training has removed his emotionality from the moment. "You just get some rest, and I'll be back tomorrow." I'm too exhausted to do anything else.

When I awake the next morning, I'm propped up in bed in a bright, cheery day room. A nurse is giving me a sponge bath. I'm holding her hand as she washes me, and I can move my fingers, my legs, and my toes. An IV bag of blood drips into my arm, and my tummy is swathed in pads and bandages.

"You're back! Good morning!" she says, welcoming, matter-of-fact.

"Good morning," comes my voice back to her. It's as though I was never gone. But there is nothing in this room, none of these pretty flower arrangements, no stream of morning sunlight playing off the walls that catches my attention so much as the insistent new sensation tingling away on my chest; this gargantuan pair of gazongas where my breasts used to be, and the warm little mouth that isn't yet attached to them. "I want my baby now."

"He's on his way," says the nurse.

When she places baby Alec in my arms, I know with every cell of my being that *no one* is ever going to pry this baby out of them again—and no one does.

They try, though. When the duty nurse comes to return him to the nursery, saying, "You've lost a lot of blood, dear. You need your rest," I nearly fly from the tangle of tubes into her face, fangs bared, nails unsheathed, fully intending to draw blood. She shrinks back behind the safety of her clipboard and calls for my doctor, alarmed and affronted. He just rolls his eyes and shakes his head. "I know this one," he tells her. "Best to just leave her alone; she'll be fine."

On the cutesy little sign with the teddy bear that hangs outside the door to my room, I cross out the "Hi, my name is:" part and scrawl, "CAUTION—churlish mother. Knock before entering!" They do.

Even the roving photographers and life-insurance salesmen trolling the hallways for business are cowed. But I figure these craven idiots damned near killed me *and* my baby. Now that we're finally together, I'm not going to give them another chance to finish us off.

For the next week, I eat holding this baby, take my bath holding this baby, and when the attendant comes to strap him into the car seat upon my release from the hospital, I climb in next to him and order the driver to gun it, leaving the astonished young woman agape in a cloud of rubber and molten asphalt.

My delivery was botched from beginning to end, from the moment my OB-GYN purposely scratched my amniotic sac a week early to coincide with his vacation plans, to the clueless student nurse who permanently collapsed my vein, to the jabbering, tubercular immigrant family who end up camping out and coughing their lungs up in my private (and insanely expensive out-of-pocket) hospital room ("overflow" from the Medicaid wards they tell me). With all of my heart, I hope I'll never set foot in this accursed place again.

Alec turns out to be one of those fabled babies who sleeps through the night, never fusses, and rarely cries or gives me a moment's trouble. There's no need for him to, really, because Weegl and I are at his side constantly. He's more an appendage than a separate person, and when he's not in our arms or at arm's length, he's in his baby backpack strapped to one or the other of us on the beach, shopping, attending classes, out to dinner. There's always a flower in his hair and a smile on his face. The child only stops laughing to eat and sleep, and even then, he laughs while he's dreaming. I love the sound of that throaty baby chuckle more than anything else on this earth.

Even Robert is charmed; I catch him changing the occasional diaper, singing an off-key lullaby. Our household is so full of love it seems it will burst, and one early morning before Robert leaves for the office, it does.

It's his ex-mother-in-law calling from Texas. I'm fixing breakfast for everyone, so I'm not really listening, but when the house goes deadly quiet and Robert hangs up, I know something terrible is about to happen. When he comes to me he's ashen, almost puzzled, it seems.

"Jodie was murdered last night," he says of his ex-wife. "Stabbed to death in their living room by her new husband. They've got him in custody, and Stevie is safe, but he saw the whole thing. I have to go back there and get him now." He leaves the room shaking his head and muttering, "I *told* you she was mean," he says.

I just make it to the bathroom before I vomit. I've only spoken

ALL HELL'S EVENING

to Robert's ex-wife a few times, but in spite of Robert's insistence to the contrary, she's been just lovely to me—and Steven absolutely adores her. This news is so horrifying that it doesn't even sink in that it's for real, just that there are now steps to be taken. Precisely *what* we're going to do, how we can possibly *begin* to go about making things right for this shattered child, will have to be dealt with later. When Robert calls from Texas to tell me that Steven wants to finish out the school year with his grandma in Houston, I'm ashamed to admit I'm relieved.

MRS. PALMER'S ROSES

Once, back in another lifetime, I'd been a mountain mama, but now I'm pretending to be one of these respectable ladies-who-lunch in Chanel and Armani instead of dancing the night away in leather fringe and love beads. I sit on a couple of civic boards and associations, help put on fundraisers, and own an overpriced tract house by the sea, so I guess that makes me pretty hot stuff in some people's eyes. But one day when a neighborhood real-estate maven asks me why we don't buy a bigger house, and I jokingly tell her that my husband is "only a doctor," she smiles at me, pitying, and tells me she "understands."

The social hierarchy of this town is based on money, not merit or breeding or civic accomplishment. The only person who knows what a sham I'm really living here is my baby son, and mercifully, he's not talking. It's *hard* keeping up appearances, especially in a place where thirteen-year-old boys get golf courses when they *Bar Mitzvah* and women wear emerald jewelry "suites" to their aerobics classes. Keeping up is not only exhausting, it's impossible—and I'm getting sick of it. While I'm running myself ragged trying to get Steven enrolled in a good school and get his new room ready for him when he comes out to live with us, Robert is spending more and more time at the office, and Weegl is making final plans to go off to university overseas, so it's just me and little Alec and my mounting anxieties.

I'm crazy about my baby, yes, but know that our world is about to change in a big way—and not in a way I would like. Who wants to raise a child in a place where women feel naked without fingernail polish and daytime diamonds? I want to make all these entitled rich people vanish from this pretty neighborhood, and turn it into a nice strawberry field.

MRS. PALMER'S ROSES

Then I'll plant an orchard, and onions and cabbages and keep a flock of industrious little hens out where the community tennis courts are now. My inner Danish farmwife is screaming at the pseudo-socialite who's keeping her kitchen garden at bay, and the psychic disconnect is driving me nuts.

For therapy, I've been planting dwarf fruit trees in the narrow strips of dirt that delineate the borders of our miniscule lot. Along the south wall of the house, I've strung up rows of rain guttering which I've filled with potting soil and planted with lettuces and herbs. I water these from out of the bathroom window with a hose I've rigged up to the showerhead and threaded through the screen. I've even built raised beds for corn and root vegetables and installed them on the roof—an admittedly ill-conceived project that's done nothing to improve relations with our posh urban neighbors. Nor has the timber wolf puppy named Ginnie Wolf who now lives in the Disneyesque dog-cave of granite boulders I've had built on the back patio, and who I walk with along the beach and back in the hills behind the coast highway late every afternoon, baby on my back, poop bag in hand.

I've managed to grow some apples and oranges, but my real enthusiasm is reserved for my tea roses.

Chosen with an eye to color coordination and coaxed along with a combination of threat and gentle flattery, the tea roses are thriving in the stone planter that's centered on the tiny patch of manicured grass that comprises our front yard. It's just large enough for five bushes, and I've nurtured them all into perfection. Every leaf is manicured, every thorn symmetrical. I fertilize them with kitchen compost and home-brewed earthworms that by my calculations have amortized out at about thirteen dollars apiece. The resulting blooms, which last throughout the year in the Laguna climate, are spectacular in their profusion and velvet purity. Here, at last, is my sanctuary from the pretense that surrounds me.

After a time, I begin to notice that every Sunday morning when I come out the courtyard gate to fetch the weekend newspapers, there is a gaping hole in the fabric of my floral tapestry—usually a bud, perfect, pristine, and full of promise—gone with only a severed stump to mark its passing.

As the weeks go by, the sense of violation drives me to the brink of madness. Even the Dog-Chow-red droppings of the neighbor's rheumy-eyed little Shih Tzu lay benign on the grass, environmentally neutral by comparison. (And how I detest that rotten beast.) Those are *my* flowers, damn it! Who could be doing such a senseless, selfish thing?

Finally pushed to the limit of my neighborly endurance, I crouch one Saturday evening behind the wall abutting the rose planter. I've fixed a hamper of cold herbed chicken and chilled a bottle of chardonnay to keep me company, and I'll lie in wait here all night if I have to. I'm determined to catch this vandal in the act and have it out with them.

Sure enough, just after sunset, old Mr. and Mrs. Palmer, the reclusive couple who live in a little house on the point—the biggest, most desirable property in the entire bay—come doddering down the sidewalk and stop in front of my roses. Slowly, painfully, they loose each other's arm and bend over the blooms, inhaling as deeply as their frail old lungs will allow, their eyes closed, lost in some distant reminisce. Then Mr. Palmer takes an ancient penknife out of the pocket of his equally ancient cardigan, and with a measured little swipe, severs a bud from bush. With a creaky bow, he shyly presents it to his plump and bent little wife.

Something about the way they're looking at each other leaves me embarrassed and ashamed—as though I'll never fathom, let alone hope to find such depth of feeling for another soul. Chagrined, I watch them shuffle slowly down the sidewalk, past the immaculate display gardens of the far-too-rich, and around the corner path that leads down to the sea.

At the end of that summer, I hear that old Mr. Palmer has died and Mrs. Palmer has successfully resisted her children's attempts to move her out of the decaying old beachfront and into a suitably exclusive "retirement" home. But on Saturday evenings while her neighbors sit down to their catered lobster fests on the beach or prepare for gala events at glittering venues in town, Mrs. Palmer still makes her torturous way down the sidewalk to my rose planter. And every Sunday morning I find one of my plants partially but carefully denuded.

The next week I decide to intercept her. I've vowed to confront her about respecting my property and not destroying the beautiful roses I've worked so hard to grow and share with the neighborhood. Although I've

MRS. PALMER'S ROSES

worked myself up into a lather and practiced my speech in front of the bathroom mirror to get the tone just right, I doubt I'll actually say anything to her, but I'm so frustrated, I feel that I should at least make the effort.

So as Mrs. Palmer makes her way toward my roses, I step out from behind the courtyard gate and sit down on the stone planter in front of my house—my baby on my lap as a prop. Mrs. Palmer comes up to me. "How lovely your roses this evening," she says in her thick German accent. "And the little one, such a blessing!" My infant son flashes her a beatific grin. I say nothing. She knows I know. "Others?" she asks indicating my child with a bristled eyebrow. I think of Steven and all of our previous well-intentioned encounters that have ended in abject failure. Summer is over and he's about to move in for good.

I'm on my own here. Robert is married to his practice, Weegl has left to make movies in Europe, and my long-awaited baby's needs are soon to be usurped by the demands of a brilliant, disturbed, horrifically traumatized addition to my household. Tears sting my eyelids and the essential unfairness of the cosmos overwhelms me.

"My stepson is coming to live with us next week," I sniff as Mrs. Palmer nods sympathetically. "His mother just died, and he hates me with a passion. I've got my new son—who I'm just getting to know, and now . . ."

"Honey," she says seizing my wrist in her arthritic grasp. In her faraway and ageless gaze I see the eyes of my baby as he suckles my breast—and my tears spill over.

"Honey, you never know where love is gonna come from."

I look down at her wizened arm, and for the first time see the tattooed numbers. She kisses my baby on top of his golden head and reaches over to the roses. With that ancient old penknife she cuts a perfect blossom and hands it to me with a little bow. Then she waddles off down the sidewalk and out of sight.

STRANGE BREW

Alec has just turned two, and twelve-year-old Steven is struggling to adapt to his strange new world of surfer cool and California blonds. When he first arrived here in Laguna Beach, he begged me not to tell anyone about his circumstances. "I don't want people to look at me and think, *There goes the poor little kid whose mother got killed*," he says.

I'm taken aback. Amid all the horror, he clings to the mundane, the practical. *How will it look? How will I fit in?* My heart aches for this preternaturally composed "little kid."

He tells me he herded his younger stepbrother and sister into a bedroom during the attack and instructed them to barricade the door with toys and furniture to protect them from the raging just outside. He tells how he watched through the window as his stepfather chased his mortally wounded mother onto the front lawn of their fine home, stabbed her six times more with a kitchen knife, then followed her across the street into a neighbor's living room where he finally finished her off.

Then he tells me that he and his mom always had a clairvoyant relationship and that just after she died he'd gone up into his grandmother's attic to be alone and cry. There in the stuffy, windowless room, he tells me, a piece of cellophane began to rattle, then wave as though it were a flag in the wind. He moved his hand around it but felt no stream of air.

192

It continued to rattle. "Mom?" he asked. "Is that you?" The paper rattled some more. "Mom, are you okay?" Nothing, absolute quiet. "Mom, are you *not* okay?" It rattled, then was still.

The poltergeist accompanies him to California. He's taking a shower one morning when a shampoo bottle comes flying out of the bathroom and narrowly misses striking baby Alec in the head. I instinctively hurl myself toward the bathroom door. Steven is just staring out of the glass enclosure, white as the suds in his hair. "Did you see *that*?" he asks, his eyes huge. The shower stall is at a far right angle from the door and there is no physical way it could have flown from his hand around the corner then made another ninety-degree angle turn into the living room.

Halloween at our house is a nightmare. Glasses fall off countertops of their own volition. Dinner plates end up on the floor when there is no one near the table. I'm standing in my bathroom when the wall-length plate-glass mirror shudders and then cracks—completely, from top to bottom. At my wit's end, I stand there screeching to the heavens, "Damn it, Jodie, *I* didn't kill you. I'm trying my best to raise your son the way you would want me to. Now GO AWAY AND LEAVE US ALONE!"

I feel like a fool, but the mischief finally stops.

Steven's grandmother buys him one of the first Apple computers—a far more elegant machine than the primitive Compaq I battle with—and he spends much of his time alone in his room programming violent video games and reading books far beyond his years—*Moby Dick*, *Shogun*, and *Lord of Darkness*, tales of mortality and revenge.

It's in this atmosphere of foreboding detent that we've all just filled our plates and sat down around the house and patio tables for Thanksgiving dinner. Both sides of the family have gathered here this year to celebrate the holiday and enjoy the fine beach weather, so I've gone all out to make this a feast to remember—with an entire countertop of roasts, breads, grains, vegetables, salads, fruit dressings, wines, and dainties. There's truly something for everyone here—from the most traditional meat-and-potatoes for the purists to the Indian curries and chutneys I made for my sister's medical-school classmates who are here to share a little slice of Americana over the break.

The November sun is warm and the patio flowers are out in full, so we're eating buffet-style wherever anyone chooses. Steven is in his element, holding court with his grandmothers in the library off the kitchen. The doctors talk shop at the main table just inside the house. In his "low-chair," the hose-able desk-like affair he favors for outside dining, little Alec gnaws happily on a drumstick, Ginnie Wolf, our young timber wolf pup, ever faithful by his side. He laughs as he tosses her an occasional Brussels sprout to augment her feast of roasted guts and gizzards with scrambled eggs and gravy.

I'm just biting into a smoked-turkey enchilada when the telephone rings—probably my brother calling from his girlfriend's house in Minneapolis. But no, it's my ex-obstetrician, and this isn't a social call. "I'm so sorry to have to tell you this," he begins. No doctor calls his ex-patients on Thanksgiving—especially not out of the blue—unless there is something dire afoot. I brace myself for whatever is coming, but what he says next comes as a complete shock. "We were just informed by the CDC that some of the blood you were transfused with may have come from a tainted supply. We're going to need you to come in for an HIV test as soon as possible." Then comes the *real* kicker. "And I'm sorry, but we'll have to test your baby, too."

After I'd "come to" following the Caesarian section, I'd fought tooth and nail against getting any more of anyone else's blood, but Robert had gently convinced me that there was a better-than-even chance I'd die without it, and only a miniscule one that it would be contaminated with the newly identified immunovirus.

The world is just now hearing about this "gay plague," and although no one I know has been diagnosed, my friends in the Laguna Beach community are growing increasingly edgy about the possibility of contracting it. No one dares speak of what we all know is out there waiting, and the tension is putting a damper on everyone's social life—waiting for the stiletto to drop and taking bets as to who will be the first to succumb. "At least that's one thing you don't have to worry about," says my hair guy

Barry, as he snips away at my bangs. "If *I* caught it, I think I'd just *die*."

It was only last week that I'd been telling him how lucky I was to have come of age in a time when all we had to worry about was a dose of the clap. "How sad," I say, "that kids in their teens and twenties today will never get to know that openness, the *fun* we had in the sixties. Sex, drugs, rock 'n' roll is over, replaced by pop, Prozac, and *Morning in America*." Yeech.

Now, it appears, I've finally gotten my comeuppance for all the exuberant frolicking of my youth. But what clutches my heart and drags it down into my stomach is the thought of the little boy there in the baby chair out on the patio, the one with the golden hair and the laughing eyes who clapped his hands in delight as I handed him a turkey leg. "Oh, lucky boy," he said.

RECKONING

The first blood draw goes badly. "I don't have any pediatric needles," the doctor tells me, "but I'm using the smallest gauge I have."

Let's see: You knew I was bringing a baby in, but you couldn't take the time to requisition a child-sized needle? This is the same doctor who induced labor a week early without telling me? Nice.

Not surprisingly, the needle he's using is too big for Alec's little veins, and the doctor pokes him again and again, like some great crazed mosquito stabbing for blood. My baby is trying so hard to be brave, but his little eyes are welling with tears and his chin is trembling, and I can see that this is not only very painful for him but terrifying, too. "Sing the ABCs with me," I tell him, barely able to contain my rage, my desire to pound into a bloody pulp this man whose incompetence and greed have already caused me such angst. I thought I was rid of this quack forever, and now he's back in our lives in the most horrifying way possible—as the bearer of dread tidings. Finally, the needle finds a productive vein and the doctor draws an alarming number of syringes full of blood from my child.

"I'm so sorry about this," he says again as I hustle my son and myself out of his office. The last time I was here, the man had tried to seduce me. *Great way to head off a malpractice suit,* I remember thinking. I won't sue him, of course, for the same reason policemen never testify against brother policemen, but I'm hoping that one of his patients has the courage to run his ass out of town. In the meantime, all I can do is wait for the results of the HIV test.

They're not long in coming. "This is the hardest phone call I've ever had to make," says the doctor. "Your ELISA panel came back positive"—he lets that hang there—"but your baby is fine," he adds, hopefully. "You'll

RECKONING

need to go get a Western Blot Assay to confirm. Again, I'm so sorry."

Yeah, asshole. Me too.

I've dealt with impending death before, but it's always been in the abstract, one of those "what ifs." Even my unborn babies, as traumatic and heartbreaking as their loss had been, were still not yet sentient beings, and certainly not *my* sentient being. Was I supposed to be freaking out for what would become of my children—especially Steven, now *doubly* traumatized—or could I just kick back and panic all for myself?

I'm not sick, I tell myself over and over, *the lab made a mistake. Just like when they told me I wasn't pregnant with Alec—but I knew I was, and I WAS. And I have my baby to prove it.*

The next two weeks pass in a daze as my poisoned blood samples are subjected to a more stringent diagnostic review. Whatever the conclusion, I've decided coastal Orange County is not where I want to spend the last months of my life. The stress and the politically insular, snarly attitudes of our neighbors are eating at my soul. It's just not a good place to raise my children, and now I may not even get a chance to do that. Worse, it has me trapped. My stepson is in school here, and I won't uproot him again. My husband has his practice here, and he won't leave it. My house and home are here and if I'm to survive HIV, or AIDS, I'll have to get treatment here. I'm effectively stymied.

On top of all this, Robert utterly refuses to deal with Steven's emotional trauma, spending more and more time at work and less and less time at home with us. We meet him at restaurants three or four times a week for dinner—and he's always late—but increasingly we all get the impression he's living somewhere else, like a trucker who maintains a secret family in Dubuque and only comes home on the weekends.

Sitting around the dinner table one night we wonder aloud what Robert is *really* doing at the office. Weegl, back from London, remarks on the fine meals he's missing, but twelve-year-old Steven sums up our thoughts perfectly. "Don't worry about Dad," he says. "He's out doing what he wants to be doing." Then he comes up with the zinger: "I like to think of Dad as just a good friend of the family."

CHOMP CHOMP CHOMP

It's true. Our little crew is floating along in a ship without a rudder, and we're only going through the motions because it's convenient for us. Steven would rather be elsewhere, far away from me, and Robert actually *is*. Weegl is about to set off on his career, and I'm just living here with my baby like a glorified housekeeper. There is no home here, because no one wants there to be one. I might as well be running a boarding house.

By the time the lab calls back to tell me that the ELISA test was a false positive, that I'm healthy as a horse and they're sorry for my distress, the news is almost anti-climactic. I already feel deadened, my spirit sapped, like a butterfly in a killing jar.

It's not all that easy to abandon a lifestyle, pick up a baby, and move out in the middle of the night, and there is no graceful way to explain why it is suddenly necessary, but after discussing the situation with Robert, we both decide that it might be best for all of us if I take some of my things and find another place to stay until our domestic situation can stabilize. In my heart, I've never left Malibu, so it only seems right to take a little place on the beach there and let the rhythms of the sea reset the amphetamine buzz of this toxic city.

It takes me all of one day to find and rent the little place on a seawall at Big Rock, move in some minimal furnishings for Alec and me, and go about repairing the damages I'd done to my soul by living a life I knew I wasn't meant for. Our circumstances may be vastly reduced, but at least they feel authentic again. That night, as I listen to the same ocean lapping along the same timeless shore, I couldn't be further from the gilded prison that had trapped us all in our senseless charade. I'm half consumed with guilt, and half elated to be free of it.

GOLDEN VANITY

Shortly after Alec was born, I began sublimating my mental frustrations into physical exertion—*working out,* as it's more grandly described—and four years later, my body is back in semi-competitive shape again. I'm bicycling two hundred miles a week, running thirty or forty, swimming four or five—not quite obsessively, but certainly more than is required for good health. Through a friend I hear that the Ironman Triathlon has just started to accept women participants, and I'm thinking about wrangling an invitation to give it a try; if nothing else, I'll add an interesting bounce to the race's competitive mix.

Hearing of my folly, another friend has invited me to Molokai to train along the designated routes—and I've decided to take her up on it. A little R&R along with my S&M might be just the thing to jolt my brain back into productivity.

I think of all the time and calories being squandered in this endeavor—time and calories that could be used for the good of mankind instead of to power my selfish pursuits. There's no good excuse for what I'm doing, but I rationalize the expenditure by telling myself that it will make me stronger in the long run—that maybe all this training to *endure* will have a payoff somewhere down the road.

The mindless rhythm of my feet slapping the pavement, the *click-ka-chick* of the derailleurs as I pedal my way up and down the bike paths between Santa Monica and Laguna, and the muted *whoosh* of the salty sea waters meeting the slight resistance of my eardrum—that tiny sliver of skin that separates us from the primordial soup that spawned us—makes me feel a little bit better about what I'm doing, numbing my mind to my mounting failures.

Sammy's ranch in Molokai is a humble affair on the Kalaupapa Peninsula, close by the perpendicular bluffs overlooking the last remnants of Father Damien's leper colony. *Hansen's disease*, I'd learned as a youngster, is where your nerves all die and your flesh rots off from infection. Some kids might delight in sharing their last name with a sports legend or a movie star, but it tells us something that I'm secretly pleased to have a dread disease—a Biblical curse, in fact—associated with mine. *Be nice to me or I'll touch you,* I used to say to my gullible classmates as they scattered in fear. Although the affliction is now easily treatable, it still retains an aura of quarantine, of "the other"—and thus a rarified *inclusion* of the few so afflicted. On some strange level, this appeals to me, too. I'd always intended to visit the colony; it calls to me with the same primal intensity that prompts Muslims to the *haj* or the Mormons to Mountain Meadows. I will go to where the lepers once lived and reclaim my lost sense of exile.

My plan is to ride horseback through the forest reserve on the northeastern end of the island, and I'm up with the dawn to catch my mount. Horses run free on this part of Molokai, forming a loose herd within the main road encircling the island. These are simpler days, before the condos came—and charming ones, free and poor and rural.

My mount, Goldie, is an aptly named palomino thoroughbred with a coat the color of summer wheat. He has an honest gaze, a steady gait, and a propensity to trot with his tongue hanging out, like a golden retriever flying its head out of a passenger seat window. Obviously not racetrack material, and no one wants a show horse who can't keep his tongue in its proper place, so Goldie is here on Sammy's ranch learning to work the trails.

GOLDEN VANITY

Thoroughbreds are not my favorite breed as they have a tendency to get stuck in overdrive—especially when caution is called for—like when they're tearing along a hairpin mountain switchback or through a field strewn with barbed wire. Once they get it in their mind to run, it takes the forearms and shoulders of a body-builder to convince them that they're on a collision course with their own stupidity.

But this guy seems amenable to a good, long ride today, and ultimately that's all I'm looking for. He lets me catch and saddle him with nary a hitch, and off we go into the forest, Goldie trotting along like a big happy dog, tongue wagging slaver in the sweet morning breeze.

We spend a few idyllic hours wending our way up through the rainforest, pausing for breakfast in a raspberry thicket where the fruits grow the size of Ping-Pong balls. I'm pretty sure that Goldie is as clueless about the terrain around here as I am, but we're having a fine time and I know that there's a road down there *somewhere*. There's only that one, and it circles the perimeter of the island, so if we *do* get lost, it's just a matter of pointing the horse downhill. We're bound to run into pavement eventually.

The magic in this place is almost palpable. I'm well aware that the *menehunes*—the island spirits, if such things exist—are likely tracking our progress, maybe taking bets as to whether or not we'll make it out of here before nightfall. They're probably laughing at our naive adventurism right now. As we make our way out of the forest and into a clearing, Goldie catches sight of the long, grassy slope beyond.

Now, a long, grassy slope is to a racehorse as red meat is to a hungry lion—especially after our long, technically demanding trek through a forest. Goldie takes the bit in his teeth and tears off across the meadow and up the slope like a crazy horse, with me alternately yanking on the reins and sawing them until I'm afraid the leather will snap off in my hands. This beast is like a freight train on a runaway track, and it's likely that nothing is going to stop him until he either snaps a leg or drops from exhaustion.

I give up trying to slow or steer him, and lean forward in the stirrups to cover his eyes with the palms of my hands. This usually works on nutcase runaways, but with him? Nothing. He just keeps on running. He's a horse on a mission and it soon becomes clear just what that mission might be. I notice that just beyond the rim of my own limited point of view, the ground appears to stop—as in, *there is no ground*. A quick mental calculation puts us on the east bluffs of the island, famed for the highest natural palisades on the planet. It's a sixteen-hundred-foot drop straight down, and we'll be there in about three . . . two . . .

Time for an emergency dismount!

I click my heels back and push myself off his rump just as he goes flying over the edge. As I fall, I can hear him screaming and screaming and screaming. . . .

Then there is a dull *thumphhh* as my body collides with the ground. I roll, come to a halt, take a deep breath as I try to gather my senses. *The grass smells so sweet and clean here.* I open my eyes, which mercifully are still working. I try wiggling my toes. *Yep, them too.* My fingers are still all intact and I don't appear to be bleeding anywhere. *Whew, that was a close one.* I've been in horse wrecks before, but usually *I'm* the one who comes out the worse for the wear. This is the first time that the horse has been injured. No, wait a minute; it's not injured. It's splattered. What am I going to tell Sammy?

I'm mulling over this awful reality when another one hits. I'm in the middle of nowhere, four hours from my starting point by *horseback*, and I'm not quite sure where that even was. It's going to be a long walk back home, so I'd best get started. I can think about how I'm going to break the news to my hostess along the way.

I put my elbow to the ground to hoist myself up and—my body explodes in burning, stabbing, stinging pain. It feels like my torso is being ripped from my hips. *HOLY FUCKING SHIT!* I must have broken a rib. Okay, I'll try getting up on the other side. The pain, if anything, is even worse. *What have I done to myself?*

No matter how I attempt to right my body, I'm thwarted by its violent and uncooperative reaction. I simply cannot move my center without being driven back by the pain.

GOLDEN VANITY

I know I can't stay here—there's not a soul around for miles—and I've obviously done something pretty dire to myself or it wouldn't be hurting like this. Slowly, gingerly, I manage to roll onto my side, curl up in the fetal position, maneuver my knees until they're facing downhill. Then with great deliberation, I push, then balance myself up onto my shins. If I keep my back and hips absolutely still and straight, maybe I can slide on my knees like a supplicant approaching the chapel at Lourdes. I'll use gravity to get me down the hill.

It's a long way down to the road, but I can see it off in the distance, and there's a mule path, or something resembling one, down the side of the palisades. All I can hope is that someone is hiking up today, and I'll meet them on the way down; otherwise it promises to be a long, unpleasant afternoon.

It's nearly twilight when I finally reach the road, but I only have to sprawl there for a few minutes before a couple of local kids come driving by in an old pickup truck, stop and stuff me into the back, and drive me to the island's only infirmary. By miracle of circumstance or federal subsidy, there is a technician on duty, and I'm disrobed and cut out of my custom riding boots before I can even beg the guy not to slice them up.

The x-ray tech is jovial, professional, cute as hell, and speaks with that lulling soft Polynesian accent particular to Hawaiian natives.

"So tale meh, dahlin', whare is yo ridin'?"

I describe the enchanted forest, the lush glens, the giant raspberries, the meadow clearing. I tell him about Goldie's last romp and his hellbent suicide run. As I do so, the man's face grows dark and he begins *tch*-ing and wagging his finger at me. "Th' menehunes don like da *haoles* messin' up dere foress," he says with finality. "Gerl, ya lucky ya be alife. Ya be'd in da spirit jumpin'-off point."

This, he explains, is the magical garden where the ancient gods and goddesses went to hurl themselves into the ether in the wake of unfortunate love affairs. He holds the x-ray film to the lightbox. "Looks t'me like ya got off wid only a bwoken back."

Oh, great.

CHOMP CHOMP CHOMP

Here in this little pre-war island clinic with the green tile walls and the stained linoleum flooring, my life takes another left turn. I'm not going to be competing in the Ironman anytime soon. From the looks of the squished vertebra on the x-rays, it appears I'm not going to be doing much of *anything* anytime soon.

I'm airlifted to Honolulu and stuck on a gurney in the holding room at Queens Hospital, my ruined riding boots and my daypack under my arm. And here I wait, and wait, and wait for a doctor to see me. The place is full of methadone addicts and crazy mutterers, and eighteen hours later I still haven't been given anything for the pain—let alone been seen by a doctor. Making a public scene goes against my stuffy WASP sensibilities, but I begin screaming profanity along with the rest of the good people waiting to be treated. An orderly, then a security person, come over and urge me to shut up. They're used to this sort of behavior, I guess. But I'm not.

Island mentality or no, I know that if I'm not stabilized and the swelling stopped soon, there's a very good chance I'll end up paralyzed. But for lack of routine medical attention, my life will effectively be ruined. Any thoughts I once may have nursed about cashing it in and retiring to Hawaii evaporate then and there.

So I scream and keep on screaming, raw and loud and long. I'm embarrassing myself, but it just seems like the right thing to do given the circumstances.

When a doctor, weary and bloodshot, finally appears, I calmly tell him I've been lying here for eighteen hours with a 32 percent compression fracture of the L1 vertebra, the films are under the gurney, and can I PLEASE get something for the pain? And oh yes, I'm a private payer with my own insurance policy . . . my card is in my purse and what the holy hell is wrong with this place, don't you have plantiff's attorneys in Hawaii?

When he looks at the films, I think the poor man is going to split a gut. "GET HER A FUCKING ROOM RIGHT NOW! AND GET HER SOME MEDS!" He storms out after the triage nurse with two orderlies fighting their way toward my bed in his wake. An IV cart appears, along with a syringe full of Demerol.

GOLDEN VANITY

Now *this* is much more to my liking. I float for a while in a hallway until they wheel me into a nice, airy room. The obese lady in the bed next to me is going through withdrawals and pauses every few minutes to puke into a bucket on the floor.

"Hi, nice white lady," she says to me between heaves. "Welcome to Hawaii."

When I finally get her on the phone, Sammy is relieved to hear that I'm still alive, if more than a little bit worse for the wear. When I tell her the story, far from being angry, she is conciliatory, apologetic even. "I should have warned you not to ride there," she tells me. "And I never much liked that horse anyway. He's been squirrely since the day I rescued him from the knacker—which is probably why someone sent him there in the first place."

I'm taken aback at this. The idea of such a magnificent, if profoundly stupid, creature ending up as dog food is heartbreaking. Maybe he knew the only reason anyone wanted him was because he was gorgeous. Maybe he really did do himself in on purpose. "I hope the folks down on the beach make a nice luau out of him," she says. "At least I can take a deduction for the inventory loss."

I remind her that I'd *chosen* to ride the horse and that she'd lent me her Hermes saddle, which unfortunately has gone down with the ship. When I offer to buy her a new one, she gratefully accepts. "That saddle was worth ten times what I paid for the horse." This admission makes me even sadder.

I'd come here to brood and feel guilty about my failures as a wife and mother. Now I can brood over life's crappy unfairness as well. Am I really all that different from that poor, dumb animal? I don't know what I'd been hoping to prove to myself by coming here. Maybe it was just to catch a break from all my self-flagellation. But once again, I've managed to snatch defeat from the jaws of victory and screw my life over a good one. Worse, this time my ineptitude has cost an innocent creature his life. After all, he was only doing what he had been bred and born to do—run. Running as I had been running, blindly and up a hill over the edge to forever. The only difference between him and me was that he had had the good sense to keep on going.

"Again, I'm so sorry about Goldie," I say as I tell Sammy goodbye.

"Oh," she says ruefully, "Goldie was just his barn name. His registered name was "Golden Opportunity.""

RECOUP AND REGROUP

Newly fitted with a back brace that does more for my posture in thirty seconds than Grandmother's admonitions did in twenty years, I make my way back to the mainland. It's necessary to purchase two first-class airline seats and the services of a small fleet of town cars to do it, but I manage to get myself to UCLA Medical Center without damaging my spinal cord any further than it already is.

When I call Robert to let him know I'll be a little bit late in coming down to pick up Alec, and give him the news of my latest mishap, his answer is entirely predictable. "I suppose you're going to want me to pay for this?" he says.

My father's reaction is similar; "God damn it, why do you *do* this to me?"

Their responses show why I've never quite trusted men in an emergency. It's always about *them*. I've never much trusted women either, as they're generally pretty clueless in times of true urgency, but when the chips are down, at least you can always count on your girlfriends for sympathy and comfort.

"Oh my god, you're there all alone with Alec, what can I bring you?" says my neighbor Andrea.

"Do you need me to come up and stay with you guys?" says my girlfriend Linda.

"Oh no! Honey, that's *awful*," says Madre. "Do you have enough clean sheets?"

Alec is more practical than all of them. He's only four years old but he's got his priorities straight and he's not in the least bit worried about my injuries. "Should I make you a sandwich, Mummy?" he asks when he first sees me immobilized in my new steel contraption. I know what he's really asking is, *Can I make myself a sandwich, Mummy?*

"Go for it, kid," I tell him. Over the next few months, he's going to get really good at it.

The child helps me set up camp on the bathroom floor of our tiny little apartment. This seems the most practical solution—it hurts too much to move, and everything I need is right here; the cool tiles that dissipate the summer heat, a sturdy towel bar to help me raise myself into sitting position, and a nearby toilet which also doubles as a prop to help me brace myself when I need to stand.

Alec brings me fruit and sandwiches, and dozens of books to read to him. His stuffed animals become playmates and cast members in the intricate ongoing melodrama he stages in the hallway just outside the bathroom door. The animals, it seems, enjoy flying into the walls and ceilings as projectiles, pummeling each other senseless, and waging war on the "invisible bad knights" who live just outside our house—but who are conveniently repulsed by the sea at our back door.

Consequently, he spends a lot of time out on the balcony over the seawall, reading his dinosaur books, casting spells and the occasional stuffed animal that's fallen from his good graces into the churning waves below. Our reality is pretty whacky, so I don't try to dissuade him from having an active fantasy life to counterbalance it.

Trussed up in my back brace, I look more like a cyborg than a onetime trophy wife, but slowly I teach myself to walk again, then shuffle-jog along the beach, and finally to start running the dirt trails of the Malibu hills behind my house with Ginnie Wolf—the two of us bolting across the Coast Highway from our front door into the rugged coastal mountain range just beyond. Together we run up Las Flores to Stunt Road and down into the Cold Creek preserve with its remains of old Chumash villages, then along the twisted trails of chaparral into Topanga, and back down to the beach—back to our little place on the seawall.

We're rounding a bend toward home one day when Ginnie Wolf begins to bristle and whine. In a cloud of dust comes a fine lady on horseback surrounded by a pack of six enormous mastiffs. I feel like a peasant

RECOUP AND REGROUP

woman confronting a royal entourage, afraid my little wolf and I will be torn to pieces by her retainers if I make a wrong move or accidentally make eye contact. "Down," I hiss to Ginnie Wolf, grateful for all those years I've spent training her.

She drops in an instant, head to the ground in a position of abject submission, and I turn away and cover my face against the dust and the dogs. They pass us without a word of acknowledgment. The rider and I both know it's best that way. The big dogs would have fought Ginnie Wolf to the death if we'd paused to exchange pleasantries, and with the odd metallic contraption encasing my neck and my torso, who knows what they would have made of *me*?

We return home unscathed, but this little scene has upset the natural order of my world. The wolf has sensed my intimidation, and more to the point, so have I. Until I can get back on a horse, and ride through these mountains alone, I'll never be fully recovered—and neither will my pack.

BACK IN THE SADDLE

The moment I see Dalsenda running at liberty in an open field, I know she will be the horse of a lifetime. A dappled Arabian mare, her flowing mane and tail catch the morning sunlight as she dances across the meadow, floating like a fairytale unicorn. I half expect to see candy and rainbows spewing from under her tail in her wake. When she notices me watching her from atop the three-rail fence, she slows and trots over, looks me up and down, then sticks her head right into my face and begins snuffling my cheek and ears with her muzzle.

We're hooked. For the rest of the morning, she won't let any of the other horses in the pasture come near; she menaces them, chasing them off with flattened ears and a snake of her neck when they approach to see what she's got cornered. I've been looking at potential mounts for several months, and seen dozens I like, but this is the first one who's claimed *me*.

Dalsenda, the owner tells me, has never been ridden; in fact, she's barely been broken to halter, but even with my messed-up back to consider, I sense that this horse is both honest and good. I know that she'll give me her best.

Alec and I move out of our little beachfront and into the guesthouse on a ranch estate farther up the coast; the nearby stables and training rings—and easy access to the Malibu trail system—will be perfect for my plans for Dalsenda. Alec is thrilled with the little brown pony who lives on the ranch, and Ginnie Wolf is glad to have room to run where the neighbors won't freak out when they see a wolf frolicking in the surf in their front yards.

After Dal and I spend a couple of weeks on groundwork—enhanced

BACK IN THE SADDLE

by a fifty-pound bag of carrots for bribes—we're both confident enough to go under saddle for the first time. In my mind's eye, the two of us are already poking our way along the backbone of the Malibu trail system.

Dal's learned her basic voice commands—"walk," "trot," "canter," "ho," and "back"—and can perform them off lead in the ring. Soon, she's comfortable carrying the light English tack I've chosen for her and learned to accept the leather straps, reins, and dangling metal stirrups. So with no small trepidation, I bring her to the railing and take a deep breath. I'm about to get back on the literal and proverbial horse and I'm praying this doesn't turn into a rodeo. Dal has been kindly and willing so far, but if she decides to go ballistic at this unfamiliar new weight on her back, I'm not sure what the result might be to my own. I've just spent two hard years relearning how to walk, how to bend, how to lift and flex again, and I'm more aware than most of the possible consequences if I've misjudged Dal's good intents. Breaking another set of bones just isn't an option for me at this point.

Sometimes you just have to chuck your common sense and go for it—the first time you drive a car, the first time you make love, the first time you eat sushi—and this is one of those times. But this one stands out because it's the first time I've had to trust a non-human being I care about not to kill me. *You don't have to do this*, comes the little voice of rationality that lives in the front of my brain. *Oh yes you do*, says my conscience. *This is what we call "integrity."*

My right leg is hovering over Dalsenda's smooth white back. She stands there quietly while I try to even out my breathing and relax my knees. If she senses my nervousness, it will make *her* nervous, too. *Oh who are you kidding*, comes the voice, *you're scared shitless.*

I've been working toward this for a long time, and the moment of truth has finally arrived. My plan is to let my leg down slowly, settle my weight onto her back one little bit at a time, and let her get accustomed to the new sensation gradually. But at the last moment, I just say *to hell with it* and let gravity make the decision for me. I plop onto her back and wait for her to freak and bolt at the sudden weight.

Dal just stands there, quietly and calmly crunching the last of the carrot I bribed her with. Then she turns around and looks at me in that wise and patient way horses have about them. There's something almost motherly in her eyes. *You okay up there?* she's asking. *Can we get going now?*

Dalsenda turns out to be a most enthusiastic "go-er." It's almost as if she's as driven as I am, and there's such an intuitive understanding between us that I don't even need to tell her what I want her to do, she just does it—and lets me know what she needs *me* to do to help her do it. Any lingering concerns about skittishness are allayed the day we come onto an open field just as a twin Huey helicopter lands and disgorges fourteen firefighters dressed in full-duty attire—complete with face masks and air tanks. Dalsenda just stands there watching, fascinated, while they set and extinguish a practice brush fire no more than thirty yards in front of us. This mount is bombproof!

Over the coming months Dalsenda and I explore the myriad trails and canyons of the Malibu, the hidden places, the waterfalls and orchid grottos. In our wanderings we come across steelhead trout and illegal pot plantations, old Chumash Indian sites and rock formations so steep and craggy I'm astonished she can even climb them—but she does, and does so without any urging. Best of all, being mounted on the back of an epically gorgeous white Arabian mare allows me to peek in the backyards of the rich and famous along the trail sides without having to worry about being shot as an intruder. More than once we're hailed by some fabled face and complimented on what a striking sight we make. I think Dal enjoys the attention even more than I do—though all she ever gets out of it is a handful of baby carrots, while I snag more than a few dinner invitations.

The privilege of friendship with a horse—a true partnership in which each member of the team trusts and teaches the other—is perhaps the most gratifying human/animal interaction our species has ever developed. The freedom of space, the sense of power over environment and constraint, and most importantly, the zen of becoming at one with the

BACK IN THE SADDLE

ineffable, all combine to heal our psychic hurts in a way best appreciated only by those who have actually experienced its magic. In loving this splendid animal, I too am healed and come to truly understand what's meant by the old cowboy saw, "There's nothing better for the inside of a man than the outside of a horse." In her company, I am fearless.

A TRIP TO BEYOND

Alec is an enthusiastic stall-mucker ("Let's go shovel shit, Mummy!") and he loves both acrobatic vaulting and riding the little brown pony the stables keep around as a companion horse for the big hunter-jumpers, but we've yet to get out on the trail together. When one of my editors approaches me about writing a feature on parent-child horse-camping, I jump at the chance to share my obsession with him.

With this assignment, Alec and I can combine a fishing trip with a horse trek, ride into the backcountry, and let the magazine pay for it! "Sounds perfect," I tell my editor. "Where are we going and what's the deadline?"

"Up to you," she says. "Make it somewhere you can get the whole 'horse packing experience.'"

The old-timers in Mammoth Lakes used to rave about the fine golden trout lurking in the icy water of Lake Hortense, but when I lived there I never had the time to get back in and see for myself. Here is our chance. On horseback, we can get far enough in to avoid the day campers while still remaining within an easy afternoon's ride back out—and the horses can do all the heavy lifting. So I arrange for a guide and three horses to pack us in the first week after Labor Day—when all but the most die-hard of summer tourists have left the High Sierras for the flatlands, and the hunters have yet to begin shooting at dark moving objects. With any luck, we'll

214

have the whole lake to ourselves. I pack relatively light with a small but adequate three-season tent, our warm down sleeping bags, and Polar Tec clothing for the cool summer nights. The meadow greens, piñon nuts, and wild berries will be plentiful this time of year and I've packed plenty of dried fruit, nuts, jerky, cornmeal, and seasonings for the fish that will comprise the majority of our meals. I've even thrown in a couple of lemons to garnish our catch, and some crystallized maple syrup candies for a treat after our hard day's ride into camp. Now *this* is what I call luxury camping.

Eager to be under way, we show up at the assigned hour to meet with our guide at the pack station. It's early in the morning and I'm dismayed to discover this guy is not only an hour-and-a-half late, but when he finally shows up, he's not even from the outfit I've contracted. "We trade off our stock and employees, lady," he tells me. "I come with these here horses."

He looks down, adjusts himself, and spits. Surly, hung over, stinking of stale beer, and not at all thrilled about having to spend his day taking some city lady and her kid up into a crater lake, he's apparently not too sure how to get to it, either. As I go over the topographical map with him, he's vague and uncertain about how we'll approach the drop over the final ridge. "Let's call your boss for directions," I suggest. "Or would you rather someone else comes to guide us instead? Alec and I can wait."

"Nah, they all left for Bishop," he snarls. "I'm stuck with ya."

We reserved the services of a guide and horses weeks ago. More to the point, Alec and I have prepared, packed, and driven seven hours to get here on time. I'm not about to be dissuaded by some drunken cowboy with a rotten disposition.

Just to be sure we're in the right place, I call the pack station and the owner answers on the first ring. I guess he's not in Bishop after all. I reconfirm our reservations, explain my concern, and ask him for another guide who might be a bit more amenable to actually doing the job he is being paid (handsomely) to do.

The owner tells me to put the fellow on the line. I do, and after a few rude remarks and snide comments, the guy hangs up and gestures for

CHOMP CHOMP CHOMP

us to saddle up. He haphazardly loads our gear into the packhorse's panniers, kicks his skinny little mare in the ribs, and takes off up the trailhead before Alec and I are even mounted.

It's a good ten-to twelve-mile ride in, so we keep up a brisk pace to get into camp while there's still time to set up and catch our evening meal. I am generally familiar with our route, having hiked the area back when I lived here, but around noon, our guide stops and dismounts on a ledge about one hundred feet above a steep rock talus that leads down to a small stream. "We're here, lady," he announces.

Well, no, we're *not* "here." I pull out the topographical map and politely explain that our agreed-upon destination is a good three miles up a mountainside from "here," and suggest that he remount and get us and our gear to the site while there's still time for him to ride back out. He responds by pulling a snub nose .38 out of his saddle pack and making a nasty reference to my anatomy.

Well! This ain't my first rodeo, and I'm not your typical city slicker. It's going to take at least a Colt .45 to intimidate *me*. "Knock it off, you idiot!" I tell him.

"Your boss is aware of both our written contract and your crappy attitude. More to the point, I'm here on a publicity assignment for my magazine and I'll be writing about the experience. Are you sure you want me telling our readership you just pulled a gun on me?"

He considers this for a moment, then spits out a wad of chaw–which splats into a muddled glob at my feet.

Without risking an honest response, he remounts, cursing under his breath and whipping on his poor horse, and takes off up a narrow granite outcropping instead of the longer—but less treacherous route—around the minarets.

Alec and I are trying gamely to keep up with the string, riding close behind—after all, the fellow does have our gear and our food—when the lead mare slips and falls onto the rocky trail. The packer gives her a vicious kick in the side and yanks her back up onto her feet. Then, in the same spot a few seconds later, the pack mule follows suit, slipping on the rocks and going down onto the trail. Before I can stop him from going any farther, Alec's gelding, too, loses his footing and falls down on top of Alec, stepping on his hand and crushing it into the rocks as the horse struggles to rise. I'm off my horse and at his side in an instant, torn between maternal terror and homicidal rage at this rapidly sobering packer.

Alec is dazed, hurt, and scared, but mercifully appears only to have suffered a broken finger. By now it's late into the afternoon—too late to turn around—and I know that the lake is just over the ridge. That's enough for today. We'll hike the last few hundred yards down to the lake and set up camp. I can splint Alec's finger and we'll pack out first thing in the morning rather than risk trying to ride back in the dark when he can't see what's there on the trail ahead of him.

Beside myself at this predicament and our feckless guide's part in leading us to it, I grab the bridle of his horse.

"Listen, you incompetent jerk," I tell him, my face perilously close to his boot level, "I want a fresh pack team here by sunrise to get us out or I'll be pressing charges against *you* for pulling a deadly weapon on a woman and child, and on your *outfit* for gross negligence in hiring you. And if you're thinking of leaving us here and taking off for parts unknown, let me remind you that the pack station has your employee records, and the LA County Sheriff's Department has a *very* long arm." Then, just to reiterate I add, "Also, the way you treat your stock is unconscionable! You ought to be ashamed of yourself!"

There! That ought to show him! I can't believe I've just unloaded this tirade on a man who five minutes previously threatened to shoot me, but I'm righteously indignant and I'm on a roll.

Cursing up a storm, he dismounts and throws our gear out of the panniers onto the ground, then grabs his pack string and takes off down the rock talus in a hail of profanity. Meanwhile, I carry Alec down to the lake, splint his finger with a twig and some tape, and give him half of a crash-and-burn pill—that should take care of the pain. Then I set up our tent and head back up the rock pile for the rest of our stuff. By sunset, our camp is all set, a small cook fire is crackling, and in spite of his wounded digit, Alec has caught us four good-sized German browns to grill on a spit. He's tired and hurting, but delighted by our camp, our tent, and especially all the fish he's managed to catch since we got here. Soon after sundown, we're snug in our sleeping bags, disappointed we'll have to leave early, but still determined to enjoy the night we have left before they come to get us in the morning. We fall asleep to the sound of the night owls and the water lapping on the shore of the remote mountain lake.

Around two in the morning, I awake to something cold and wet covering my face—something freezing and suffocating. For a moment I struggle with disorientation. Am I dreaming? Is some wet wild beast sleeping against the outside of the tent? I flip on the flashlight and see that the roof of the tent is nearly collapsed onto us, and the wet rip-stop nylon is what has awakened me. It's snowing! Heavily.

In those days before Gore-Tex, a three-season backpacking tent and down sleeping bags in a blizzard do not bode well. I know that if we get wet, we're doomed, so all night long I'm up banging snow off the top and sides of our tent to keep it from collapsing and soaking our bags. At first light I look out to see a foot and a half of snow blanketing our world—our gear, our foodstuffs, the trail—and fat drifting snowflakes obscuring everything beyond ten feet.

Not surprisingly, the pack team never materializes. Alec's hand, though taped, is black and blue and badly swollen, but he tries not to complain. When I tell him that it looks like we may have to spend the day and another night in our tent, he just says, "Okay. Let's sing some nursery rhymes." So we do.

For that day and night and all the next day it continues to snow, and we go through every nursery rhyme and fairy tale we can think of. When we run out of these, Alec tells me ancient Greek and Roman myths. And when our tent finally succumbs to the snow and begins to leak, he helps me hold the drips off our bags and tells me stories about his imaginary playmate, who he's named "the little medieval boy," and what *he* would do in a storm.

With his little plush rabbit, Binny Bunny, and me as audience, the child recites verbatim the entire plot line and dialogue from every episode

A TRIP TO BEYOND

of *The Simpsons* aired to date. And when, in spite of myself, I began to panic over my stupidity and our predicament, he kisses me and tells me about a Discovery Channel episode on making snow caves.

When the second night falls, it's still snowing. Our down bags are now wet and practically useless, so we've used them to form a barrier mop around the inside of the tent. To stay warm we just hold each other and sing "The Itsy Bitsy Spider" until I want to throw up. Alec asks me if we're going to die and I tell him I honestly don't know, but I'm going to do my best to make sure we don't. I'm reassured that he seems to accept this as fact. *Mummy will take care of me, there's no need to worry.* That night he learns how to sing rounds.

To my huge relief, the sun comes out on the third morning. Within a couple of hours, the weather climbs back into its typical September mid-seventies, and I am able to dig out our food stash for some jerky. Presently, rescuers come trudging into our camp with dry sweaters and candy bars. They wrap us in the spare slickers they've brought, and we abandon our camp as they lead us up the snowy mountainside to the horses they have waiting above on the ridge. The only thing we bring out with us is what we've been wearing and the wet, beleaguered Binny Bunny.

Once Alec knows we're going to be okay, my little boy breaks down sobbing, telling me how afraid he's been that we were going to die. Terrified to get back on the rescue horse for fear of it falling on him again, he tells me how badly his hand hurts, but he knows it's the only way to get out and get to a doctor. He takes a deep breath and I lift him onto his mount. Mercifully, it's surefooted and stable.

As we make our way off the mountain and back to the trailhead, I curse myself for my shortsightedness—I, of all people, should have known this could happen. *What kind of idiot takes a six-year-old out into the backcountry alone?* It may still be summer, but the Sierras are famous for their treacherous weather. It's hard not to think of the Donner Party, stuck in an early blizzard a hundred or so miles up the range . . . I want to scourge myself and keep on scourging for being such a rotten mother to such a great little kid.

It is only now that we're safe that I realize that my son hasn't been oblivious to either our danger or to my distress; he was just being brave for Mummy. By the time we get to the doctor back in town, I'm sobbing like a baby, and I don't stop until the man takes me aside, gives *me* a pill, and tells me it's a simple break; Alec's hand will be fine. But my conscience won't be still for a long time to come. *I don't deserve the gift of this child. I don't deserve the gift of this child,* is what it tells me all the long drive home to Malibu.

EVIL ELVES

Why is the screen off my window? And why is my front door unlocked? Finger to my lips, I gesture Alec back to the car and tell him to wait and be quiet. Teaching him to respond to the same whistle and hand and voice commands I taught the wolf was an excellent idea—and also a practical one. Right now, he's crouched down in the passenger seat guarding our groceries, eyes barely grazing the bottom of the window, waiting to see what trouble we're in this time.

The front door of our house is slightly ajar, and I'm certain I locked it before we left; we've been getting a lot of mysterious hang-up telephone calls lately and I'm becoming progressively more paranoid because I've no idea who might be making them or why. Our guest cottage is in an oak grove on an estate not far from the entrance to Malibu Creek State Park—the place where they filmed M.A.S.H., as the tourist brochures never fail to mention. It's not exactly remote, but we're still set back from any neighbors—and most of them are gone during the day. If someone wants to break in and do mischief, this is the perfect place to do it. I listen for a long moment for any unusual noises or anything further amiss; hearing nothing, I cautiously poke my head inside the open door. My kitchen is in shambles. Cereal boxes are dumped on the floors and countertops, condiments are splattered all over the walls and ceiling, and a dusting of flour covers the whole mess. Whoever did this must have had a grand old time of it; the enthusiasm with which our home has been vandalized is

striking. My glassware is piled in a corner, every last piece of it shattered to bits—obviously thrown with gleeful (or vengeful?) abandon. The birdcage in the window is open, and in the sink, our two Lady Gouldian Finches lie dead, floating in the water, their brilliant gold and purple feathers still vivid in the soupy mess.

These dear little birds have been our friends for nearly two years, brightening our mornings and sunsets with their sweet twittering to each other. In the evening, they love to fly over and perch on Alec's head, grooming his hair while he's reading, a habit that never fails to make him giggle in delight. And since last month, the female has been sitting on two tiny eggs in the little nest her mate has so carefully constructed from the dried grasses Alec gathered for them. We've both been carefully solicitous of her privacy, as thrilled for her incipient motherhood as her mate seems to be.

Their cage reeks of ant spray and chlorine bleach. Whatever sicko committed this atrocity first gassed and burned them while they were trapped in their cage. I feel my blood running cold through my stomach—gripped with a combination of nausea and rage—grateful I've made Alec wait in the car.

Reeling, I check the rest of the house for damage. Nothing else appears to have been disturbed, but in the hallway, the enlargement of my favorite photograph of Alec, the one of him standing in the tidewaters of New Zealand with a trumpet flower upside down on his head like an elf's hat, is missing. Looking around, I find it carefully centered on the pillow on my bed. The glass covering the frame has been shattered, and there is a hole ripped from the photo where his laughing young face used to be.

Whoever has been trying to terrorize me is doing an excellent job of it—and I've no idea whom it might be . . . or worse, why.

Several weekends earlier, I returned from picking Alec up at his dad's to find a total of fifty-three hang-up telephone calls on my answering machine. No message on any of them, just ten to thirty seconds of someone breathing. I played them over and over, listening for any background noises that might give me a clue as to who was making them or where they were calling from, but could discern nothing.

EVIL ELVES

The telephone company had taken a report and instructed me to start writing down the times the calls were made so they could trace them. I'd dutifully recorded a dozen more in the last week, but they'd come up empty-handed. "Whoever is doing this must be using one of those new mobile cellular telephones," the detective tells me. "There's no way to trace those through the phone company. They could be coming from anywhere."

Totally spooked, I applied for a gun permit, took the gun-owners' safety course, and purchased a small caliber pistol—more to reassure myself than for any protection it might offer. But this latest invasion has taken the harassment to a whole new level. I lock up the house, get back in the car, and drive us straight to the Lost Hills Sheriff's Substation.

The detective who takes the report is initially sympathetic, but when I give him my name and address he suddenly turns cold. "You've got a lot of nerve coming in here," he tells me, "after all you've done to that poor woman. Hasn't she suffered enough without you harassing her like this?"

What? What woman? What are you talking about?

I sit there with my jaw on the floor trying to make some sense of this.

"We know about the hang-up calls you keep making, the vandalized car, the broken windows, and lady, believe me, we're watching you. Melinda has been a friend of this station for years. Her father is a personal friend of mine."

Who the fuck is Melinda? What hang-up calls? What broken windows?

I feel like I'm in the middle of a Kafka novel. I haven't been doing this to this Melinda person; she apparently is the one who has been doing it to me!

I vaguely remember a mousey little woman at the feed store where I buy grain for Dal. Whenever I go in there she eyes me suspiciously, like I'm going to steal a fifty-pound salt block from her or something. Her name is Melinda, I think, but why on earth would she have it in for *me*? Could that be the person he's talking about?

"Sir," I begin. "Who is Melinda? And what has she been telling you about me? The only person I can think of named Melinda is the girl who helps out at the feed store, and I can't imagine why she'd be saying these things about me. I don't even *know* her."

I show him my volunteer's LA County Sheriff's card. I've been working on arson watch patrol for the last year, and have gone through their extensive background checks to get this picture ID. He takes it from me and runs the personnel number through a database on his computer. It must check out because when he hands it back to me his manner has changed considerably. Maybe there's something to this brother-in-arms thing after all.

"I'm sorry Ms. Hansen, I seem to have been mistaken." He leans back in his chair, and his voice becomes folksy. "This lady has had some 'persecution' issues with us before," he confides. "She came in a couple of weeks ago and filed a complaint against *you*. Said you'd been harassing her and her boyfriend."

"Her boyfriend?" I'm floored. I can't imagine anyone wanting to date this person, let alone wanting to harass them for doing so. "Who is her boyfriend?" I ask.

"Greg Von Skinner, the publisher guy."

Now I'm *really* floored. Greg Von Skinner is my neighbor, and a rather attractive one at that. His reputation as a swordsman is well known around town. Ever since I'd moved to the oak grove at the end of the little country lane, I'd watched a steady parade of gorgeous actress/model/whatever types park their Jaguars and Mercedes behind his wrought-iron gates. It was impossible not to overhear their amplified cavorting in his swimming pool just below our balcony—generally late into the night, and generally *every* night. There was not a snowball's chance in hell I was going to get romantically involved with a professional cad like this. But I was equally certain that there was no way in the selfsame hell he and this homely little Melinda person were an item.

Once at his invitation, I'd had Sunday brunch with him, enjoyed his company immensely, and sized up his intentions within milliseconds. *Uh-uh, not gonna happen.* But as a conversationalist, this guy was a hoot: witty, traveled, observant, and quirky. We hit it off immediately and stopped for occasional friendly chats whenever our trips down the drive to our respective mailboxes coincided. Even though we just live across the road from each other, we found we prefer writing to talking face to face, and had exchanged letters on a wide variety of esoteric topics over the last two years. But we'd never had the slightest romantic inclinations—not even a friendly kiss. Why would this woman, if indeed we were talking about the same person, be threatened by *that*?

"She's an odd one," the detective continues. "Had me convinced you were trying to break up her relationship and scare her out of town. He came in and corroborated her complaint, you know."

No. I didn't know. He's dating HER? Maybe they get off on this weirdness?

"They've been going around town telling anyone who will listen that you're crazy, that you're a danger to the community." He takes a long, steady look at me, evidently discerns that he's been hoodwinked, and his eyes turn sympathetic. He knows how hard it is to undo gossip once it's been unleashed in a small community.

"Maybe you should come see what she did to our home," I say. "Killing pets and smashing photographs isn't just criminal, it's psychotic; what happens when she comes after my son? Am I supposed to shoot her?" He looks at his desk a long moment and nods his head. He knows I'm right.

When the sheriff sees the mess in our home, he turns solicitous. "I'm so sorry," he tells me. "I really had her mispegged." He sees my gun on the bed stand and asks me to remove the magazine and empty the chamber. I do so and he asks, "May I use your telephone please?"

"Of course."

He sits on my bed and dials a number. "Hello, Melinda?" he says. "I sure hope you look good wearing orange, because if I ever see anything like this again, you're going straight to County." Then he hangs up. I don't even ask how he knows her telephone number by heart, or why he didn't identify himself to her. But as I clean up the mess that had once been our home, it's painfully clear to me. Alec and I have lived here in the Malibu for the last six years, made our friends here, made it our home. But the time has come to move on. Again.

CROSSING THE RUBICON

Turning forty does something to a woman's soul. The change is nothing overt; nothing galvanizes me to action or contacts me with an urgent message from beyond. There's no jarring physical transformation; I've always had gray hair and an aversion to noisy children. I still look about the same; people still call me "Miss" and card me for wine in the checkout line. Nor is there anything special about the actual birthday itself—the sun rises, food is procured, prepared, and ingested, the sun sets. It's just that on that one day I wake up and realize that I'm a grownup, and time, as Grandmother used to say, is a-wastin'.

At forty, I'm already making excuses to putter instead of acting purposefully. Never one to shirk an opportunity to procrastinate, it's now become something of a fetish with me. I not only stop to smell the roses, I'll sit down next to them, pour myself a glass of wine, and pull out the latest tabloid. I studiously avoid pruning them in the wintertime or deadheading them in the summer. The fragrance of their blooms is carried away on other people's breezes, and their blossoms drop on other people's patios.

More than anything, I'm sick of having to move eighty-pound planters every time my lease is up. I've been lugging roses, metaphorical and literal, around for fifteen years now, and *I* want to root as badly as they do. Learn how they adapt to the seasons in *one* microclimate not consecutive ones, have the chance to compare blossoming and dormancy over the years and not just here—and just this once. Always motivated by a longing for permanence, now I'm becoming obsessed with it. I'm forty years old, and have moved with my household forty-two separate times in that span—pots, pans, books, and shoes. That's enough. If I don't get my butt in gear and get on with my dreams of setting down roots soon, there's no way my energy level will hold out long enough to let me pull my Grand Plan off—I'll be lost in my own entropy, stuck in my excuses forever.

So I take a vow; not out of desperation like Scarlett O'Hara cursing the barren fields of Tara, or sullied by the vagaries of hope like a schoolgirl intent upon securing the affections of an oblivious pop idol, but simply as an acknowledgement of fact. I have no job, no savings, certainly no useful work experience to guide me through the myriad details of what I'm about to undertake, but come hell or high water, I'm going to get myself some land—some real land with acreage—and build myself a ranch that I can finally call my own!

The morning I ride Dalsenda into the oak grove to find that urban gangs have tagged all the trees with graffiti over the weekend, I know I can't postpone our move any longer. Granted, spray paint is preferable to carving one's initials into the bark, but in between the Kentucky Fried Detritus littering the roads and park grounds every Monday morning and the used baby diapers balled up on the picnic tables, my tolerance for city lowlifes has worn thin.

Accordingly, I've been looking all over the English-speaking world for a place where the rents aren't exorbitant and the price of property isn't absurdly inflated by untoward development. I'd love to stay in Malibu, of course, but there's no place I'd care to live here that I can afford to buy anymore. Even in the early 1990s, a livable little house on an acre of land is approaching a million dollars, and the interest rates are nearly 12 percent.

I know there must be *some* place where the people aren't crazed with their own ambition, where traffic is an option rather than a lifestyle, and where the land is respected, not raped for profit. A place where the water doesn't stink with the taint of chlorine, and where horse "lovers" don't confine their captive range animals in twelve-by-twelve metal pipe stalls.

I love New Zealand, especially the lake country around Wanaka and Mount Aspiring, but moving there would pretty much mean that Alec grows up without having his dad around for comic relief. Any place I'd care to raise him on the east coast of America is muggy and full of New Yorkers. And the ideological underpinnings of the heartland are enough to bring a girl to tears. As a single mom with no visible means of support, I'm going to have to choose my environs carefully if I'm not to be beset by suspicious women, and their carnally minded husbands.

I've nearly given up hope when I come across a double-page ad in a throwaway newspaper I've picked up at the feed store. "Where Freedom Is Affordable," says the big banner headline, and judging by the asking prices they've listed here, they're not kidding. For what I'm paying to board my two horses in these worm-eaten stables in Malibu, I could buy myself a whole *ranch* in Piute Springs—and I'd not be vexed with the owner's lecherous advances and mercurial temperament every time I run into him.

The full-color photo ad shows the reader rolling green meadows awash in spring wildflowers. In the near distance, four riders canter through the field on their way into some fantasy world full of ponies and picnic baskets. The woman's long blond hair blows free behind her and her head is turned *just so*, laughing. This real-estate outfit may not know Los Angeles price structure, but they sure know *evocative*. "Call for our free video," invites the trailer on the bottom of the page.

So I do.

The cheerful land salesman on the video tells us about the endless oak-studded hillsides, the pine forests, the warm springs, the wildlife, the open meadows and pastures where our horses can "run free." From astride his roping saddle he tells us, "The Pacific Crest Trail is right outside your back door," then he gallops off into the horizon, presumably toward Mexico—or Canada, along its fabled route. Other neighborly types rave about the excellent local school, the friendly community, the area's rich history. Although it's only a three-hour drive from Los Angeles, it might as well be 150 years away. A nice little house on twenty acres can be had for the price of a well-equipped Mercedes sedan. How can I *not* make an appointment to go see this place?

The moment I drop down into the basin from Highway 58, my blood pressure decreases by twenty points. I open all the car windows, downshift into third, and take a deep breath. The sense of relief that comes washing over me is like a summer rain shower tamping down a dusty road on a hot afternoon. Without even having seen Caliente, I know I've come home.

By the time I get to the railroad tracks three miles into the valley, I'm making mental calculations about how long it will take Alec to get to Robert's house on the train. And by the time I hit the box canyon with its perpendicular cathedral walls and fiery magenta redbuds anchoring the cliff sides, I'm figuring out how much the mortgage payments will be on the fifteen-year-loan I have no idea how I'll manage to procure.

The real estate guy has told me to meet him at the General Store at high noon. It's hard not to be charmed as I pull into the dirt parking lot. The store once served as the community's little red schoolhouse, then as its post office, and since then, variously a bar and grill, a saloon, and greasy-spoon breakfast joint. I can smell the cigarette smoke twenty feet from the door, and through a window I can see the cook flipping burgers with a cig clenched between his teeth. *So much for the state-wide anti-smoking ordinances.*

Four or five pickup trucks block the front entrance, so I go around to the screen door in the back. There between two pickup trucks, their doors opened as if to mark the field of battle and shield onlookers from errant swings, are two grizzled old cowboys—duking it out. They're in their seventies if they're a day old, and I sidle past them, trying to make myself as inconspicuous as possible. I've never seen two old coots slugging it out in public before, but I'm determined to hang around and watch—if only for the novelty.

From what I can make out, they're throwing a lot more punches than they're landing, but there is blood visible on the taller guy's face. And the little guy is deadly serious. "You keep your goddamned hands to yourself, Frank," he says, swinging and missing. "I watched you tryin' to feel her up last night, and I don't like it one little bit!" He swings again, misses, and stumbles forward into his opponent, who takes this opportunity to land an uppercut to the little guy's jaw. It connects with the flat *thud* of hollow bone striking withered flesh and false teeth.

"FUCK YOU, Peewee!" he yells. "She shore as hell weren't fightin' me off too hard." Frank swings again as Peewee staggers back, and connects instead with the door of his truck. A gash opens up across the knuckles of his hand. "Aw, fuck ME! Aw *SHIT!*"

With this introduction to Caliente, actually finding and buying a house seems like an afterthought to a foregone conclusion. I was looking for colorful? Looks like I've got colorful.

Less than a month later, Alec and I have fallen asleep in our new home, listening to the bullfrogs and the hoot owls. *A testimony to determination,* I think as the Milky Way beams down into my bedroom windows. I suspect that in its time it's looked down upon greater follies.

"Is all this ours?" asks Alec, trying to sight our car from the upper border of the property.

I have to admit that it's an impressive expanse. The 360-degree view of the surrounding peaks and valley is breathtaking, and our snap-together modular house far below looks like the oversized matchbox it actually is. At the lower end of the property is an oak grove with a creek bed running through it, and behind us are sculptural granite outcroppings and forty acres of pasture where the horses, scarcely able to contain their delight after years in their steel cages, have shunned the barn and set up shop in the juniper thicket. Beyond all this lies the Sequoia National Forest and ultimately the Great Mojave Desert. The chances of a stalker approaching us from above or behind are insignificant. And the asphalt road below is far enough away that only the most committed are likely to tackle the dirt drive up the mountainside to our house. After decades of the gangbangers and social oddities of outer Malibu, it's a huge relief to feel safe again—if only by virtue of our isolation.

My parents have made the trip down to visit us, curious no doubt as to what sort of predicament I've gotten myself into this time. As they stand on the prim grassy lawn in front of our little plastic Barbie dollhouse and look out over the vast uninhabited expanse of dry scrub and piñon pine, I can't help but feel a bristling of pride. *Yes! All this is mine!*

Madre takes one look at our new place and promptly bursts into tears. Daddy, ever tactful, clears his throat and offers, "Well, it certainly has a lot of potential." It's not much of a benediction, but I'll take any blessing I can get.

TIME TO GET CRACKING

Alec learns to use the post-hole diggers. At the age of ten, he's already taller than I am—as are most people past the age of ten—so the honors go to him, for heavens know we have holes to dig. I've ordered several hundred fruit and nut tree graftings from a commercial nursery, and we need to get them into the ground before our first winter sets in. After that, we've gardens to prepare and plant, irrigation lines to dig and set, fencing to keep the horses in, cross fencing to keep them out, and much more.

Fortunately for us both, the child has become adept at managing the long twin shovel blades, and has figured out just the right mix of mud and water to nudge malleable soil out of the decomposed granite of our hillsides. This is not to say he's entirely thrilled with his new assignments; digging through rock in the heat of late summer can get discouraging.

Many years ago, when I'd lamented my lack of sales progress to my boss Norm, he'd taken me aside and said, "You know, toots, when you dig a hole and you leave for the day, then you come back again the next day? That hole's still there. It may have crumbled in a bit, but there's still a hole in your backyard. Keep digging." When Alec grumbles something about child slavery, it gives me great satisfaction to pass on this trite platitude, knowing that Norm's legacy lives on.

I didn't realize when I bought this place that it came with its own built-in gym and aerobics parlor. I figured there would be a lot of physical labor, but I've never been in such good shape—and Alec's baby fat is turning into a young boy's muscle. Moreover, we're becoming a team, a working one, and I begin to understand why farm families have so many kids; there are *always* chores to be done, and never enough hands around to finish them all. But we make a good stab at it, and slowly our little homestead comes together.

That next summer we have apples, peaches, nectarines, and blackberries on our evening table, and fresh salads every night. Our hens are laying, the horses graze down the brush so we don't have to clear it, and there's even a little waterfall trickling into the makeshift birdbath. My vision is finally coming to be.

Our period of self-congratulation is brief. The range cattle, deer, and raccoons take one look at our newly productive orchards and gardens and go, "Hey, everybody! PICNIC HERE!" I might as well have put up a sign and left a trail of breadcrumbs leading to the ranch. The deer, I've found, can be dissuaded by our wolfhound and a few neoprene wet suits I purchased used from the Goodwill and hung from clothes hangers in the trees. I guess their flapping looks enough like beheaded human torsos to dissuade the deer, but the range cattle are different beasts entirely—as I learn when a ton of longhorn bull discovers that my flimsy three-strand barbed wire fencing is no match to his appetite for sapling fruit trees and fresh garden vegetables.

I suppose every girl entertains fantasies of running into a long laconic cowboy someday, but ever since my fiasco with Leroy I've been steadfast to my motto, "Don't date the locals"—and so far it's served me well. A variety of tradesmen and laborers have come and gone, and although the ranch is shipshape, my love life is nonexistent.

I know the neighbors all wonder what I'm doing up here alone, raising my son by myself and riding horses up in the backcountry, but they also know that I don't hang out at the town bar and I don't entertain gentleman callers. Nor do I consort with the local meth freaks or stoners—although lacking viable options, I've hired more than a few as temporary help, to my regret.

I don't go to church either, which perplexes the good people of the community to no end. Worse, Alec is a sterling student, which annoys more than a few of them, especially those who pride the firepower of their armaments over intellect of their offspring, and who probably suspect that we're a couple of those liberals they keep hearing about on the talk-radio shows.

I may be a model citizen—industrious, generous, and quiet—but damn it, I want a boyfriend. I've worked hard to build this place into something I can be proud of, and now I want to share it with someone who can appreciate it—and help me out.

But here's the problem: While I'd thought that moving here would pre-select for a like-minded individual, its geographic undesirability being a plus rather than a minus, it's that self-same isolation that prevents it from being a good place for anyone who has to work to make a living—which leaves out a good many potential suitors.

"Tru$tfundians" living on their ancestors' beneficence generally gravitate to places like Malibu or Aspen, where social options are myriad and the isolation is more asylum than hermitage. And on the commitment side of the equation, I've discovered that inviting folks up from the city to visit requires they have a constitution of steel and an adventurous streak a mile long—and steel-constituted adventurers aren't the sorts of fellows who are particularly interested in monogamy. So I'm at something of a loss for appropriate male companionship.

The Internet, with its near-limitless dating pools, is not yet widespread—and certainly not into the hinterlands such as this—so unless some early retired bonds broker or burnt-out physician decides to move here on a whim, I'm pretty much stuck with the local pickings. And they're . . . well, *localized*.

In an effort to expand my romantic options, I begin sending along a questionnaire to those few brave souls who answer the personal ads I've placed in such diverse publications as *The Nation*, *Los Angeles Magazine*, and the *New York Review of Literature*.

TIME TO GET CRACKING

DO I BELONG IN THE COUNTRY?

1. What is the largest thing you've ever killed single-handedly?
    (a) A bug, with a zapper.
    (b) A bird, with my patio window.
    (c) A rodent, with my vehicle.
    (d) I refuse to answer on the grounds it might incriminate me.

2. I think a thick layer of dust in the home is:
    (a) An abomination.
    (b) Why they invented household help.
    (c) A tolerable evil.
    (d) An artistic medium.

3. If I saw a seventy-pound lynx in my backyard, I would grab:
    (a) The phone and call 911.
    (b) A gun and shoot.
    (c) A Valium and swallow.
    (d) The kid and tell him to go play with his new puppy.

4. Rattlesnakes make me:
    (a) Scream.
    (b) Cautious.
    (c) Curious.
    (d) Salivate.

5. I generally go to the mall:
    (a) For fun and socializing.
    (b) To stock up on sale items.
    (c) To see Santa Claus.
    (d) At gunpoint.

6. Which best describes your religious orientation?
    (a) None/I pray by myself.
    (b) I pray with other people.
    (c) Other people pray for me.
    (d) Other people pray TO me.

7. How many firearms do you own?
   (a) None, they are barbaric tools of a more savage age.
   (b) Just a rifle, and a handgun by my bedside.
   (c) And a bazooka.
   (d) It depends on how many they're holding in the evidence room.

8. Vicious gossip makes me:
   (a) Nervous.
   (b) Smug.
   (c) Gleeful.
   (d) Wanton.

9. I am thinking of moving away from the city:
   (a) To get away from all the crazies.
   (b) To join all the crazies.
   (c) To save money and collect scrap metal.
   (d) To avoid scrutiny from law enforcement.

10. I lock my door:
    (a) As a matter of course.
    (b) When I remember.
    (c) I have no key.
    (d) I have no door.

11. High-wattage outdoor lighting is:
    (a) Necessary in case I have to go outside at night.
    (b) Necessary to guide the weary traveler to my door.
    (c) Necessary to guide the strung-out meth freak to my apothecary.
    (d) Necessary to guide the space aliens into my bedroom.

12. My proudest moment was:
    (a) The birth of my first child.
    (b) When my bio was published in the alumni review.
    (c) When my bio was published in *TIME* magazine.
    (d) When my bio was published on Megan's List.

TIME TO GET CRACKING

13. How many Guinea fowl are too many?
    (a) One.
    (b) One.
    (c) One.
    (d) One.

14. My children aspire to:
    (a) Med school.
    (b) Ag school.
    (c) Boot camp.
    (d) Getting through eighth grade before making me a grandparent.

15. Which do you like LEAST in your water supply?
    (a) Chlorine.
    (b) Sulfur.
    (c) Giardia.
    (d) The family pig.

16. Rolling blackouts are:
    (a) A scam by the power companies.
    (b) An unfortunate necessity.
    (c) An excuse to play around with my generator.
    (d) What you get after a long Saturday night out drinking with the locals.

Your score doesn't matter, you'll fit in fine.

BYOB

Charlie is a longtime resident and local character who loves his Jack Daniels as fervently and certainly more loyally than he ever has any of his five wives.

The narrow canyon road up here can be tricky—especially at night and *especially* when one has been seeking solace in the comforts of the bottle. Returning from a provision run to Costco one snowy evening, Charlie mismanages a turn in the box canyon and ends up sixty feet below in the creek, his beloved '63 Corvette a now-unrecognizable twist of Detroit steel and red polyethylene smoldering upside down in the rushing water and threatening to explode. He's made his way up the muddy slope and is wandering the road dazed and torn in the December chill, until who should drive by but our local sheriff, Sonny, home from his shift in town.

Charlie, as they say, is three sheets to the wind, bleeding from a nasty head wound, and agitated as all hell. Sonny takes one look at him and orders him into the squad car—he's taking him straight to Bakersfield Memorial. Charlie is in tears.

"I'm damned sorry about the 'vette, man," says Sonny, with genuine regret. "I know how you loved that car."

"No. NO!" screams Charlie, gesturing like a wild man. "You don't *understand*! There's a case of JACK in the back! We've gotta *save* it!"

Now, most officers would simply arrest the guy, book him into county jail, and chalk it up to overtime. Sonny, however, being a child of the ranchland, *does* understand the urgency of Charlie's concerns. So the two of them take off, slipping and stumbling down through the mud and slush to the creek bed below. After a cursory attempt to splash some water on the still-hissing engine block, and finding the doors crumpled into immobility, Sonny pulls out his .357 magnum and shoots off a few rounds at what he estimates to be the rear window, and together he and Charlie rescue the whiskey, drag the case back up the slope, and crack a bottle to celebrate. Sonny drives Charlie home to his wife, who's so glad to see him alive that she doesn't even rag on him for being drunk, let alone notice that Sonny has quietly stashed the remaining eleven bottles on the far side of the house for Charlie to deal with tomorrow. Then, in the true spirit of "To Preserve and Protect," Sonny writes him a ticket for littering and heads back up the canyon toward home.

KILLER PIE

Our little K–8 school is holding a Halloween pie auction to raise money, and since Alec will be graduating next year, I've made a special effort to participate. Among the many other social niceties we lack in these parts is a school library, so the ladies of the PTA have temporarily put aside their long-standing jealousies and personal animosities in the interest of bringing a few new picture books to the classrooms. The women up here may not all be literate, but when their men weigh the ability to read and write against the ability to make a killer pumpkin pie, there is no doubt a contingent of those who would opt for the latter.

    The products of our labors are displayed on a long cafeteria table in the local bar and grill, the patrons of which are currently being serenaded by a country-fusion combo of studio musicians from town. Surveying the auction table, I have to admit that my pie-making skills are modest compared to some of the offerings on display today. I made a mousse out of a big heritage pumpkin from my garden with fresh eggs from my hens, sweetened it with maple sugar, spiced it subtly with ginger and cayenne, and topped it with a geometric design of toasted pumpkin seeds and sugared pecans. I even tracked down some real *manteca* from the Mexican ranch market in Arvin to lard the crust.

    But such invention is shamed by the confection of bulbous marshmallow jack-o-lanterns, cinnamon sprinkles, plastic witches and alley cats, and mounds and mounds of jelly-bean-studded Cool Whip that bedeck the competition. It's as though each participant has tried to outdo the next by dumping the biggest bag of Halloween candy onto supermarket prefab then covering it with a tub of dessert topping. Those who've gone "homemade" and used canned pumpkin pie filling have a special section of the table devoted to their industriousness.

That's where I've entered mine, in the "original ingredients" category, but it's puny and spare in comparison to its country neighbors. Much like myself, I decide—it's lacking in sugary goodness.

In truth, I don't envy pie judges. Like those who must decide Cowboy Poetry contests, they have to wade through the Scylla of sentimental overindulgence without offending the thin-skinned Charybdis of small-talented ego. The politics get even trickier when the contestants are one's fellow neighbors and blood relatives, for in an armed community, awarding the wrong ribbon to the wrong person is fraught with personal consequences.

So I wasn't expecting to win first prize. And I *really* wasn't expecting the judge—a well trimmed, darkly intriguing stranger in a black leather jacket, Man-With-No-Name hat, and prominent gold watch, to bid five hundred bucks for the thing! A good many folks in this community subsist on a four-figure annual income, so paying twenty bucks for a six-dollar pie is a big deal. Bidding five hundred is not only gauche; it's downright offensive—even if it *is* for a good cause.

I'd been noticing him all evening, not only for his sartorial precision, but for the obvious care with which he presents himself. Perfect posture, very proper, almost old British in his reserve. His long, tapered mustache telegraphs a sinister vibe; occult, dangerous, sexy as all get-out. But what most attracts me to him is his *vividness*. He simply inhabits the character he is playing. I know without even making eye contact that this is my man, and I'm not the least bit surprised when he calls me the next morning and invites me to his home for dinner. "A menu of your choosing," he says.

"How did you get my number?"

"I asked your girlfriend who you were, and if you . . . entertain." He leaves the interpretation of "entertain" up to me, and I choose to accept it in the refined sense, "to socialize," rather than the implied one, "to put out." The man is quite formal and well spoken, and I can scarcely contain my delight that he noticed me. It's best, I think, not to sully the waters right up front by confronting him on the innuendo, so I take him at face value. I never was much one for idle flirtation anyway.

He had just bought the old Harkin ranch. The last owner built a lovely home on it for his young wife and filled it with romantic flourishes—sunken bath, bedroom fireplace—to make her feel comfortable up here in the sticks, but she'd given it a try and promptly left him and the house to languish. The rejected husband had committed suicide in it, and the place has been on the market for years without an offer—some even claim it to be haunted.

Apparently, my gentleman caller, Andrew, picked it up for a song, and he's quite pleased with himself at the coup.

"Liquor or wine?" he asks as I settle into the sofa off the cook's kitchen on our first date.

"Ummm, wine please," I say.

"Still or sparkling?" Hmmmm . . . now this is different. Most of the folks up here have Budweiser or Jack Daniels in their guest larder. Wine is something for the effete who live off in the cities somewhere. And "sparkling" instead of "champagne"? This fellow knows his stuff.

"Sparkling, please." Oh, why not? Bubbles are always a fun way to break the ice.

"Blush or white?" Damn, this guy is GOOD.

"Okay, white." I'm taking a chance here. If it's Andre Cold Duck, I'm stuck with them both for the evening.

"Foreign or domestic?" Now I'm impressed. Might as well go all in.

"Let's go with domestic."

"Will Schramsburg suffice?"

"It was good enough for Nixon," I say.

Only an insufferable oenophile would know what a brouhaha the president caused when he served domestic "champagne" at a White House State dinner instead of the expected French vintage.

Now it's his turn to smile at me. He goes to his refrigerator where there's a bottle of *brut de brut* already chilled and waiting for me. By the time he serves it in a proper crystal flute, I'm in love with the man.

We talk about our whacky little community and all the local

KILLER PIE

characters. We talk about our passion for obscure endurance sports. He races bicycles, I race Arabian horses. He's traveled the world on business, I've traveled it for pleasure. His book knowledge is extensive and pompous, mine is extensive and presumptuous. We make a perfect pair.

One night early on, he takes me to his favorite nightclub to listen to live music. A Big City hangout for up-and-coming law and business types, it caters to a relatively sophisticated clientele I had no idea lived anywhere near California's Central Valley—a region known more for its hicks and rednecks than its cultural movers and shakers. I dress the part in a slinky little black dress and strappy heels—the first time he's ever seen me "cleaned up for town"—and there is that sort of emotional reserve between us that new couples face when they're first jockeying to see where they stand in each other's affections. The jazz is cool, the drinks are expensive, and when the emcee unexpectedly shouts out, "Everybody here tonight who's in love raise your hand," Andrew jumps to his feet then onto the table—then leads the room in a toast . . . to *me*! I catch the emcee winking at him—he's arranged this. What a way to announce your intentions!

"I do love you," Andrew says, drawing me into him as the club explodes in applause. "I never thought I'd say that to anyone, let alone a classy little broad like you."

He's being flip, of course, but he's also serious. Our upbringings have been as different as any imaginable, with him as a ward of the state and mine as the cosseted daughter of privilege, but at this moment we are bound by mutual relief and profound gratitude for having finally connected—even in our middle age—with a kindred spirit.

And he is so tender. Before we ever make love for the first time, he spends the entire evening acquainting himself with my lady parts—just looking, touching, massaging, learning the contours and pressures of me with his hands and fingers, formally introducing himself and getting to know the "other" me. There is something reverent about the way he treats our sexuality that matches my own sense of wonder—and there's nothing perfunctory about him whatsoever.

Every night before I fix dinner he draws me a hot bubble bath, brings me a glass of wine, sits by the tub, and tells me about his day. On cold rainy nights we build a fire in the big bedroom fireplace and lie in bed singing along with our favorite old record albums, or massaging whatever body part the other has strained over the weekend's competition. In the mornings he's off to work and I head back to my place to work the ranch and care for our horses. He's taken up distance riding under my tutelage and has proved an apt and eager pupil.

Alec adores him too. After dinner, the two of them wrestle on the living room floor like tussling puppies, work on homework together, go off into the garage workshop to do "guy things." More than once they've turned our formal sit-down dinners into a family food fight with even the dogs joining in the mayhem. And they're always kindly and respectful of each other—bonding as only two guys who love the same weird woman can bond.

All my life I've wanted a family I could truly belong to—that belongs to *me*—and with Alec and Andrew I have finally found one. It's been so long since I awoke and gave thanks for the day, for my place in it, for the very gift of it. Every morning I wake to the man sleeping next to me and the first words from my lips are "Good morning, my love."

So who can say when the seeds of romantic disaster are first sown? Is it in that very first flicker of longing when we meet someone and our imagined fantasies begin to guide our reality, blinding us to it? Or is there some inexplicable need for dominion that slowly overpowers us when the petty slights of any partnership begin to accumulate?

No matter, when our wants dare our needs to duel, when revulsion becomes desire and the self becomes fungible, love turns into a battlefield of egos as each is subsumed into the other. And unless there is absolute trust coupled with absolute forgiveness, the crueler soul will emerge the stronger.

And that's what happens to Andrew. Slowly, almost imperceptibly, he begins to separate me from the person I was, to isolate me even further than I already am from my previous world of family and friends, and draw me into *his* life to the exclusion of my own. And I, delighted to be in his company, basking in his attentions and husbandry, eagerly allow him to do so.

It starts with small criticisms and directives. "Buy this, not that." "Here is how you fold the towels." "This is where we will be spending next Saturday." Small concessions to be sure; it's his house, I'll follow his house rules. It's his money, I'll spend it the way he wants it spent. I can do it *my* way with *my* house, *my* money; it's only fair.

But he's made it more seductive—more *convenient*—for me to be with him, under his rules. Then, once he's moved me in, he begins methodically withdrawing his attentions to exact more concessions.

Over the months, I concede, excusing his heavy-handedness as momentary aberrations, chalking them up to stress—or the ghosts he carries with him from a horrific childhood spent in foster homes. I tell myself that Christian forbearance, the grace of turning the other cheek, is a virtue, and that by exhibiting it in the face of his cruelties I am the more virtuous, thus the stronger person. Though not a person of faith, the religious schooling of my childhood is an odd comfort when no other rationale makes sense.

The first time he slaps me, I laugh it off, pretending an outrage I do not feel. I'm more upset by the petty unfairness of the situation that has prompted it. I purchased a set of mixing bowls for his house—after all, I cook for us five or six nights a week, and he has only this one industrial-sized salad bowl for prep work. I'm tired of bringing utensils from my own place, then taking them back to mine when I need them, so it only makes sense to spend the twenty bucks for a decent set of work bowls for his kitchen, too. He's given me five hundred dollars for this month's "comestibles," as he calls grocery items, so it doesn't seem too big a deal to me. Besides, I've used my own money, not his. They're to be a gift.

When he sees them in the bag on his kitchen counter, he explodes. "I gave you money for FOOD!" he bellows. "Why can't I trust you with *anything*?"

The slap is more an afterthought.

CHOMP CHOMP CHOMP

A month or two later, I'm about to start a fifty-mile endurance race through the Tehachapi mountains when he picks a fight, knowing I'll choose placating him over being at the starting line on time. Maybe he's afraid I'll win again and show him up in his own competitive pursuits. Maybe he just wants to see which one I'll choose; him, or my passion for horse racing. As the starting gun goes off, he's physically pinning my arms against the floor of our tent, sitting on top of me, screaming at me about my selfishness. I'm afraid he's going to punch me, so I revert to a woman's oldest defense: seduction. Fifteen minutes go by before I can get to my horse and get underway. By the time I hit the trail, the others have a four-mile lead on me, but six hours later, I still manage to finish in third place. Had I started on time, I would have won handily. Yet I say nothing, and congratulate his own finish in his first twenty-five-miler later that afternoon.

I tell myself that he's so in love with me and with Alec, the first loving family he's ever had, that he's desperately afraid of losing us. The only way to reassure him is to redouble our efforts to please him—to show him how much we love him. And with each capitulation he grows more desperate in his attempts to drive us away. When we leave, he begs us to return, apologizes in the most profuse and public way. And when we come back, he begins his efforts to run us off once more.

It seems he delights in his cruelties, his toying and taunting, knowing I'll not respond in kind, waiting for my tears and avers so he can escalate his anger and start the dance anew. Gradually the belittlement becomes shoving or choking. His verbal outrage begins to manifest in kicking and body slams. He pushes me over a railing down a steep hillside. He throws me bodily across the bedroom into a wall. And then comes the agonized plea for forgiveness.

But to me, there's nothing to forgive; I love the man, I can rationalize anything. I don't even try to fight back, never return his unkind words with retort, never raise a hand to him except to defend myself. "You're like one of those inflatable punching dolls that every time you hit it, it pops right back up," he tells me, admiringly. "There's not a mean bone in your body."

In tears, he begs me to help him overcome his demons, tells me

KILLER PIE

about the awful abuses he was subjected to as a young boy. When he was only ten years old, he'd tried to kill his father and was sent off to live as a ward of the state. He's never spoken of this to anyone, he says.

"I love you, Andrew. I'll do anything I can to help you defeat the monster in you."

And we try. We both try for the very life of us to isolate the evil inside of him and hold it at bay. But the schism between the Good Andy and the Bad Andy continues to grow. I've taken sanctuary in the "menstrual hut," as I've begun calling my own house—the place where I go to isolate myself from the world of men. Andrew is on one of his periodic campaigns of vilification, and each new beep of our fax machine threatens another missive full of accusation and vitriol. Alec brings me his latest diatribe.

"Dear Cunt," it begins. "I've always wanted to begin a letter that way; it just took you to come along and make it magic."

I laugh in spite of myself. Such dry eloquence deserves its own recognition—indeed, it's one of the things I love about this man, perverted as it seems, even as his words sting me like a rawhide lash. In the screed that follows, he accuses me of trying to give him AIDS, of conspiring to set him up for arrest on domestic assault charges, plotting to steal his guns. . . .

"He tries to control everything and everyone," observes young Alec. "But he can't control himself."

I realize my son is right. Over the two years we've been together, Andrew has systematically separated me from my friends, my family, even my own finances, and now he's threatening to take my son away from me too. "I can show evidence that you've abandoned your minor son alone in an isolated rural cabin for days at a time . . . ," he writes.

Well, technically, yes, Alec has indeed spent the night alone in our house while I've been at Andrew's a few miles down the road—as he does several times a week.

"And it's only a matter of time until Child Protective Services is called in to monitor the situation."

"Oh puhleeze," says Alec. "I've been watching the house alone since I was seven. He's left me alone to watch *his* house overnight. It's not like I don't know how to use a telephone."

"Why does he *do* this?" I beseech my father. Maybe there's a medical reason for Andrew's behavior? I simply don't understand how his mind works, let alone what he wants from us.

"There *is* no common denominator with the seriously disturbed," replies Daddy. "This is why we call these people 'psychotic.'"

I know he's right, and it breaks my heart to leave Andrew for good, but for my own survival and that of my son, we must.

And so we do.

"I will destroy you," writes Andrew in a letter he distributes to friends and family alike. He's offered Alec's trustees double the value of our home if they will sell it to him. In a letter to my father, he accuses me of "shrewdly raising" my son "to be a homosexual so future inheritance won't have to be split with any inconvenient issue." Alec just shakes his head and snorts in derision. "Pot, meet kettle," is all he says.

Andrew's not finished. "I will happily spend ten years of my life and a hundred thousand dollars," he writes to the local paper, "to run her out of town." I know he's not kidding, but I guess he hasn't considered the fact that I'm not kidding either. I was here first. And I'm. Not. Leaving.

TAUTOLOGICAL EMERGENCY RESPONSE

You know how you sometimes wake up while you're still in the middle of a disturbing dream and there's a moment of utter disorientation? Like you're dreaming it's the day of finals and you've been taking a different class all semester? Or the curtain is about to go up on opening night and you've memorized the wrong play?

The Back Bay morning is filled with birdsong, the distant bark of sea lions, the rustle of cattails, and the hum of morning traffic. I always sleep well when I'm here in Newport Beach; it reminds me of other times.

I've come down to spend a few days with a girlfriend and fetch Alec home from his summer stay with his dad on my way back up. Robert is very gracious about letting me use his house—he even lets me keep my books and "city" clothes in the back guestroom where I stay when I'm in town. He's rarely there anyway, so I'll spend this last night at his place rather than driving all the way up from San Diego in one day.

The house is dark when I get there—the boys must be out seeing a movie tonight—so I let myself in the back entrance and go straight to bed. It's been a long weekend.

With the morning comes a knock on the bedroom door, and as I rouse, my son and my ex-husband are standing in the doorway, stiff, formal, peering in at me like they've seen a specter. They're uncharacteristically quiet, and up far too early for me to be reassured. "We didn't know you were here," says Robert. "We thought you were dead."

Before I can digest this, Alec adds, "Mrs. Miller just called. She said our house blew up and they thought you were in it and if you're alive you're supposed to call Sonny because it's urgent." He rushes to me in a blur of tears and unwashed sweatpants. "Oh, Mum, oh Mum . . . ," he cries.

"I'm alive . . . ," I say. *I think.* Robert stares at me as though he's not quite sure. For a moment, I think I see a hint of disappointment cross his face. I am, after all, his *ex.*

"Call Sonny. It's urgent," Robert is saying. Our local sheriff, Sonny, is a friend of mine, and in all the years I've known him, he's been wise, fair, and reasonable—altogether worthy of the trust the community has put in him. But "urgent"? *Nuh-uh.* Nothing's *ever* urgent with Sonny. Something's definitely wrong.

When I'd first moved in, Sonny had stopped by to introduce himself. "I'm not here to enforce the law," he told me only half-jokingly, "I'm here to keep the peace." Then he recommended that I buy a shotgun, as he couldn't promise to be around on a moment's notice. "The helping hand you need is at the end of your arm," is the advice he left me with.

He was right, of course. The first time I call emergency 911 to report a motorcycle versus tree incident, I get an answering machine. "You have reached the Walker Basin Substation of the Kern County Sheriff's Department," intones the voice. "If this is an emergency, hang up and call 911."

An archetypal "good ol' boy," Sonny's grown up with—and periodically raised hell with—the majority of the people he's charged with arresting, so he's developed his own brand of community policing. All those years he's spent mediating family shootouts, "urging" transients and drug purveyors to keep moving on up north, and returning errant young 'uns to the wrath of the family matriarch instead of the county jailhouse have given him a sense of nonchalance matched by few others in the law enforcement community.

All this is to say, he'd rather gnaw his arm off than go out on a call—let alone make one just to stir up trouble. As he's nearly ready to retire and has yet to take a bullet, his laid-back approach to police work seems to have served him well. So when he says "urgent," it really *does* impart a note of urgency.

I shake myself awake and reach for the telephone on the nightstand. Sonny answers with his customary skepticism, tinged with just the right amount of reticence to discourage all but the most seriously offended against. "Yeeesss?"

"Hello, Sonny?" I say. "It's Allena. What's up?"

TAUTOLOGICAL EMERGENCY RESPONSE

"It's gone," he says.

"Alec said something about the house . . ."

"Leveled. Burned to cinder last night around midnight."

I'm prepared for a jolt—maybe my horses have escaped and are running loose in the road, maybe one of our neighbors has finally snapped and shot Andy dead, but I wasn't prepared for *this*.

"We were afraid you might have been in it."

"The barn? The playhouse? The tack room?" I'm more shocked than angry.

"Gone. Everything. Captain Persinger said that by the time they got there, it was so involved they didn't even *try* to go up and put it out."

"All my books, my journals, Alec's toys?"

"Everything."

"Damn it, Sonny! What does he have to do before you guys finally arrest him?"

"You better get up here right away," says Sonny. "One of the neighbors has your horses, and the arson guys are on their way out. They'll be able to give you more information than I can."

I don't need any more information. It's entirely obvious what has happened. Bad Andy's struck again, and he just played one hell of a hand. The only problem is, I'd already excused myself from the game months before.

"I suppose I'd better get on up there."

"I suppose so," says Sonny.

The three-hour drive back from the posh showplaces of Newport Beach is mostly spent in silence. As diversion, we listen to NPR on the car radio. Ken Starr is tormenting poor Monica Lewinsky on the witness stand, and Alec wonders aloud why the president hasn't just told him, "Yeah, she blew me, and no, I'm not sorry. So what's it to you, asshole?"

It seems to me that the whole world is full of bullies. Is there no one fed up enough to stand up to them? Am I going to have to do this all by myself? I look over at my young son. On the verge of adolescence, he's gawky and ungainly and many, many moons too wise for his age.

CHOMP CHOMP CHOMP

He's been right here on the front lines with me for the last two years as we alternately tried to adore Andrew and escape from his escalating rages. Like me, he's made his peace with the breakup of our ersatz family, but he's just as heartbroken as I am that it didn't work out for the three of us. Every now and then we look across the seat and ask, "Are you okay?"

"Yes. I'm okay. Are *you* okay?" Not sure if we're trying to reassure ourselves or each other.

By the time we reach the canyon, the tension has become stifling. Neither of us dare say a word for fear of setting off forces we've no idea if we can contain. As we wait for the electric gate at the bottom of the drive, Alec takes my hand. The automatic gate opener is a gift from Andrew, a much-appreciated convenience that saves us from having to get out of the car to open the gate, then get back in the car and drive through it, then get back out to close it. Then get back in the car. We've made it a habit to say, "Thank you, Andrew," as we push the button that does all this for us.

"I wanted to get you guys something that you could really use," Andy had told us when we opened the gift card. After years of slogging through dust and mud in the heat and snow to open and close that infernal gate, his gift reminds us of his thoughtfulness every time we use it. Sitting here watching it swing open, the irony is not lost on either of us as we curse him in one breath and bless him in the next.

The whole hillside up to our house is littered with burned bits of paper; paper we shortly identify as the remains of our once-extensive library. We know without speaking of it that that includes Alec's drawings, our notebooks, all of our journals. We pass the green orchards we've so painstakingly planted and pruned and pampered, now abundant with the ripe fruit of our labors. Then we pass our herb and vegetable gardens, lush and fertile, ready to harvest. *At least the fire didn't spread; maybe this won't be so bad after all*, I think.

We park at the edge of our rose garden, prolific with late-season blooms we've coerced from the reluctant granite. Nothing looks amiss; even the grassy lawn is still green. But we can smell the stench of wet char even before we open the car door. And as we start up the steps toward the house, we both pause and take a deep breath.

TAUTOLOGICAL EMERGENCY RESPONSE

The remnants of the last five years of our life, the better part of my son's remembered childhood, lie smoking and hissing before us, a stinking slurry of memento and memory. Afraid to look at each other, we sink side-by-side onto a blackened railroad tie that up until yesterday had seen service as part of the retaining wall between our garden and the house. The house that is no longer there.

For a silent moment or two, Alec and I stare into the awful mess. Sonny is right. It's not only been leveled, it's been obliterated. It's ground zero of a bomb blast. Nothing remains; neither stuffed animal, nor marble countertop, not one stick of furniture, nor a smidgeon of clothing pokes through the debris. Pans are melted. Alec's Mother's Day cards and clay trivets, our travel photo albums, everything I've ever written, hundreds of feet of first-edition books, all vaporized into carbon dioxide and cinder. Ashes flutter around us like autumn oak leaves. All those words, lost to the winds.

Andrew has indeed destroyed everything that had been "us."

Terrified of Alec's reaction, I turn toward him, aching for all he's lost, ready to burst into tears if he shows the slightest hint of doing likewise.

The child plops his head onto my shoulder then drapes a gangly teenaged arm around them and pulls me close. "Well, Mum . . . ," he says, matter-of-fact, buddy-to-buddy, "you know how you really, *really* hated to clean house?"

We both burst into laughter as we survey the charred wreckage. That's when I know we'll be staying on. Maybe we've lost our house, but we still have our home.

STARTING OVER

"How many people do you know who get a chance to start completely over with their life?" asks my father. And he's entirely right; owning nothing, I feel liberated.

Alec and I are staying at a monastery down the road, and all we have here are some donated clothes, Aunt Sally's Bible, and a sense of possibility. After a lifetime of dealing with "stuff," all the clutter is gone—along with all its implication—*clutter, baggage, a weight lifted from my shoulders*. We are free.

For a few blissful weeks, there is no past, only the future ahead of us. When the insurance company calls and asks for receipts, I have a built-in excuse to ignore them. "Sorry, everything was burned up in the fire." When this or that public entity wants this or that record, or verification, or certification, I tell them the same thing. "Sorry, it got burned up in the fire," becomes my mantra. A legitimate excuse for confounding the officious, postponing the mundane. I'm not ashamed to admit that I revel in it, using it every chance I get.

But then one morning I wake up and think, "Boy, would I ever love a cup of cappuccino," and the damned process of accumulating *stuff* begins again. It's with a certain sense of resignation that I buy myself a coffee maker and start rebuilding my life.

Mrs. Tweet, the crazy lady across the road from our ranch, died in her house during our absence. The place was poorly insulated and falling apart when she bought it from the first owner back in the eighties (an owner, who perhaps not coincidentally, had also died in it), and when she fell and broke her hip and we weren't around to hear her calls for help, she

STARTING OVER

cooked to death in it in the merciless September sun.

Her heirs want nothing to do with the place, so they are thrilled when I offer to rent it—as is—while it goes through probate. Alec and I have decided to stay and rebuild our own home, and this location, a short walk away, is just perfect for us.

As for the crumbling old house itself, we look at our stay here as an extended camping trip—only with walls and a (marginal) roof over our heads. After she died, one of Mrs. Tweet's dozens of cats knocked the toilet tank off its base trying to get to water and flooded the house, adding yet another layer of stench to the place, so Alec moves one of her mattresses out to the tree house and sets up camp there with his Gameboy, his school books, and the family wiener dog.

Our mastiff, too, prefers the airy tree house to the stuffy A-frame, and the huge beast figures out how to climb the wooden ladder up onto the lower platform in the tree where it spends its days guarding its young master like some arboreal Cerberus—a redneck gargoyle on a plyboard cathedral.

To counteract the summer heat, we rig a garden mister through what once was the living room—now a graveyard for desiccated cats; the "flat cats" as Alec calls the mummified remains we find between the cushions of the sofa, behind the television, under the beds. We shun the bathroom in favor of an outside shower, and in the winter we wear four layers of sweaters and huddle by the potbelly stove upon which we defrost our morning coffee. I daren't use the range top or oven because the elements catch fire when I turn them on, and the plumbing is iffy at best.

But we like to call it our home away from our home—which itself is slowly reemerging from the ashes across the road. We've got the new site all laid out, the concrete stem wall poured, and the subflooring well underway. When I can get the money together, the rough framers will come and the house will start to take shape. I'm so excited to finally be building our new little house that I can almost forget the circumstances that brought us here in the first place. When I think of it in the right light, it's almost as though Andy has done us a favor.

CHOMP CHOMP CHOMP

Our new place is coming along at a steady pace. Second only to the blessing of my perfect son is the blessing of having found Earl and Mitchell to build my perfect little house. Two angels, both of them retired from the real world and living here in Caliente, have consented to make the place I've envisioned in these blueprints a reality.

Between the two of them, they own every building implement and woodworking tool known to mankind. Earl even has an old hydraulic crane truck to set the upper story timbers, and what he can't do or find by himself, his son-in-law, an industrial building contractor, can help him procure. In a place where finding even a reliable weed-whacker is something of a miracle, coming upon Earl smacks of providence. And Mitchell, my dear friend Mrs. Miller's husband, is a master woodworker—who better to craft these beautiful hardwoods into an architectural showplace?

During the day, every day, I am on the job site—ferrying tools, getting materials, huffing lumber, and performing unskilled repetitive labor—much to Earl and Mitchell's chagrin. But they teach me how to drive an eight-penny nail straight and true in two swings, how to set headers and measure twice, and how to lay shingles. From sub-flooring to roofing, they give me a two-year tutorial in home building, and when it's all finished, I know I'll end up with a little jewel box of a house. My home, a place where I can live in comfort and safety for the rest of my days if I wish.

I haven't had so much fun since I was pregnant with Alec. Not only do I have a purpose again, but it's coming together daily right in front of my eyes. Every nail, every board, every tiny cut and measurement is right there for me to see, increment upon increment, *building* something of permanence. All my life, I've patched together and tried to make do, but this project, this *house*, is teaching me the value of patience. Of taking my time and doing it exactly right. Of not compromising *anything* in pursuit of a greater whole. With every wrenched muscle, smashed thumb, and bone-tired end to the day I hear my Grandmother's voice reminding me: "A job worth doing is worth doing well."

FIREWORKS

We finally settle into our new house, and Alec's high-school debate squad is selected to go to nationals in Atlanta. To raise some of the money they need to get there, his school is selling Fourth of July fireworks—and all the kids are expected to do their part. As Alec is captain of the team, and the chances of him finding anyone up here to buy his allotment are slim, I buy the whole one hundred dollars' worth of Safe 'n' Sane novelties assigned to him. We'll make a party out of it—even if it's just the two of us.

In preparation for the big night, we clear out the horse arena, rake all the sand of debris, and ready fire buckets and hoses—just in case. I'm not worried; it's been raining off and on all day, and there isn't anything flammable within fifty feet of the ring, but we've just gotten through the aftermath of one fire, and I've not the slightest intention of going through another.

Our physicist neighbor, Augie, and one of Alec's school chums join us for barbeque and cherry cobbler from our orchard, and even our aging mastiff gets into the spirit with a jaunty red, white, and blue bandana around his neck. It's finally dusk and we bring out the fireworks. Two responsible adults, two straight and studious young men. Augie is a distant relative of Benjamin Franklin, so we're all feeling particularly patriotic, imbued with appreciation for what it means to live in America—and for what our ancestors fought and died for so we could.

"Death to tyranny!" shouts Alec as he lights the first Piccolo Pete. We've gotten through the progression of displays up to the Lotus Flower when we notice a cloud of dust racing up our driveway, scattering horses, narrowly missing the pig, seemingly hell-bent on making itself known.

Imagine our surprise to see it's a truck bearing a couple of guys from the local firehouse—certainly they of all people should know better than to come hauling through someone's ranch in such a dangerous manner.

They pull to a halt at the bottom of the drive and begin leaning on the horn. Of course I go down to the gate to see what they want. "What do you think you're doing?" one of them demands of me. He's red-faced and breathing hard, and he smells of beer.

"We're setting off fireworks in the sand arena. Everything is okay, thanks for checking on us." I turn to leave. "Where do you think you're going?" he demands. "Let me see some ID."

What? ID . . . ?

It's me, your closest neighbor? I bring you apples every autumn and get my burn permit every January? The one that always waves at you as I go riding by the station on my way up the mountain road? Me? Allena?

"What seems to be the problem, sir?" I say. *Okay, we'll play this one professional. Like I haven't run into this stringy redneck a dozen times before around the community.*

"It's illegal to possess fireworks in Kern County!" he bellows.

Now I *know* this belligerent jerk-off is drunk. "Um, no, it's *not* illegal to possess fireworks in Kern County, the high school is *selling them*. I've lived here going on ten years and I've never once seen any notice that they're prohibited."

"It's illegal to create a fire hazard" he responds, weakly.

"In case you haven't noticed, the air is completely still and it's been raining all day," I say. "You couldn't start a fire up here today with a bucket of pitch and a gallon of gasoline."

I've about had it with this unwarranted harassment—especially in front of my guests; whatever bug is *really* up his ass, I didn't put it there. "You've got a lot of nerve driving up onto my property like a maniac," I continue, "endangering my livestock, and lecturing *me* about fire hazards, when three years ago you guys let my house burn to the ground and didn't even come up and *try* to put it out—and you're less than a mile away! We're not endangering anything or anyone—and you know it."

Checkmate. Then I soften. I've dated enough firemen in my life to

FIREWORKS

know their male egos are as delicate as eggshells—their fabled bravado to the contrary. "Seriously," I say, "we're fine. You guys have a quiet evening up there, okay?" I wink at him then turn and walk back up to the arena, leaving him standing there with his pudgy little buddy, both sputtering invective. As they drive off—slowly this time—I light one last firework. My little protest against the tyranny of petty authority.

At ten-thirty that night I'm stepping into the shower when the dog begins to bark. It's been a long day; the last of the firework carcasses have been raked and dunked into the steel trash barrel and doused for good measure—I am, after all, a responsible citizen. Alec is tucked into bed and our guests have long since gone home.

Lenny the Mastiff rarely barks at anything, but Fourth of July up here is a time to be wary. In "Angels: The Strange and Terrible Saga of the Outlaw Motorcycle Gangs," Hunter S. Thompson wrote about the Hells Angels who "rally" through our canyon on the Fourth, terrorizing farmers and ranchers along the way. Indeed there have been clubs roaring through all week. It wouldn't take much for one of them to veer off the road and into a tree, or up my driveway to do some mischief.

Lenny's barking is getting more insistent. *This can't be good.* I throw on my flimsy pajamas, grab my varmint rifle, and go outside to investigate.

Sure enough, there's a flicker of flashlights down in the ravine. Maybe someone has crashed on the curve of death just down the road, or there's someone making their way up the hill to my house. Either way, something is wrong. "Who's there?" I call into the darkness. *Silence.* Then the flashlights go out. *Uh oh.*

"WHO'S THERE? I HAVE A GUN," more forcefully this time. There's a rustling in response and muted voices. Finally comes a hesitant voice, "Kern County Sheriff."

Yeah, right. And I'm Goldilocks. Sonny hasn't made it to the brink of retirement by sneaking up onto ranchers' properties in the middle of the night unannounced—or without a damned good reason accompanied by a warrant. If this is something requiring his immediate attention, he would have certainly telephoned me first to let me know he's coming.

More likely he would have asked me to meet him at the substation at some point in the next few days. And at the *very* least, if this *was* Sonny, he'd be shouting, "Allena! *ALLENA!* It's me, Sonny! I need to talk to you!" so he doesn't get his head blown off. This is no "sheriff."

"If you're the sheriff, what are you doing in my ravine? I'm going to need you to show me some ID." Whoever is down there surely must hear me. But I really don't want to see *anything* except them gone. For a long minute or two there is no response. I don't know whether to run into the house and call 911, or stand my ground and scare them off.

Finally someone calls out, "Are you Allena Hansen? We're going to shine the flashlight on the vehicle now." In the dark distance, there's a white car with some sort of decal on the door. It's parked a long way from the house, but it certainly *looks* official—the light glints off what could be a light bar, and I wonder why, if this is such an emergency, they've not turned it on to announce themselves. But what a relief! It really *is* just the sheriff.

"Okay, I'm going to put down the rifle." I do, and walk into the middle of the driveway with my hands in plain view. "Sonny? Is that you?" I'm incredulous.

"Do I LOOK like Sonny?" comes a gruff voice. And suddenly I'm being jumped, kicked to the ground. A knee cracks into my back and my wrists are cuffed. I feel my head slamming up and down into the gravel of the driveway, grinding, and slamming again. The knee turns into a foot in the small of my back and my upper torso is yanked upward, hard by my hair. My back gives way as ligaments tear and muscles rupture, and I begin screaming for someone, anyone to call 911.

At this my assailant wraps my hair around his hand and drags me down the long gravel drive to the gate. "Shoot the dog! Shoot the dog now!" I hear someone else yelling as poor old Lenny barks his indignation. He can hardly walk anymore, let alone attack anyone, but at least he's trying to do his job.

Dazed, numb, I feel myself being stuffed into the back of a squad car, and as I listen in horror, this thug and his three companions gather round to, and I'm quoting here, "get our story straight."

FIREWORKS

As I huddle there in the back of the car, they concoct this bizarre scenario that has me threatening to shoot to kill them, has them all in fear for their lives. Yet there's nary a bullet hole in me. These are *Kern County Sheriff's Deputies; men who are notorious across the country for never hesitating to shoot at anyone for any reason. And they get away with it!* At least I'll be able to prove they are lying. This will all be straightened out at the station house, I'm sure.

By the time they get through with their script revisions, they have me "shouldering and sighting" my empty rifle, "spinning out and lunging for the deputy's weapon," and "holding them in stalemate at gunpoint." Then the arresting officer holds up his little finger, which has apparently sustained a scratch in the melee. Smirking, he asks, "Do you see? Does everyone see that I am bleeding?" he snickers. "I was in fear for my *life*. Were *you* all in fear for your lives?"

"Yes," they all singsong in unison, "I-was-in-fear-for-my-life."

They cart me down to Bakersfield in the middle of the night where, with my nightshirt in tatters and my breasts hanging out, I'm booked and thrown into jail, charged with five felony counts: 1) Assault on a police officer, 2) Assault on a fire captain, 3) Assault with a deadly weapon, 4) Making terrorist threats, and inexplicably, 5) Furnishing a false ID.

Bail is set at $250,000—nearly three times more than the gangbanger in line ahead of me who's just shot and killed a kid in cold blood.

My back has been so badly reinjured that I am unable to stand or feel anything below my waist. I'm stripped naked, and a matron is screaming at me to "get up, get up, GET UP you lousy little actress!" As she bellows, I use my arms and elbows to drag myself along the filthy concrete floor to an isolation cell at the far end of the building. I am fifty years old, five-foot-one, and 107 pounds of *are-you-fucking-kidding-me?*

They leave me in this filthy cell, unattended all night where I lay soaked in my own urine, moaning for a doctor. Finally, the next afternoon, I'm chained and handcuffed and taken by police ambulance to the emergency room. When the attending physician sees me and hears what has happened, he's in tears for me, but the best he can do is shoot me full of painkillers and furtively take down Augie's telephone number, promising to give him a call and tell him where I am.

Over the next four days, I'm shuttled between four different lock-up facilities, thwarting my family and friends' attempts to find me and bail me out. I'm kept in solitary and incommunicado and denied the use of a telephone or the painkillers the doctor has prescribed. *I've been dragged from my bed in the middle of the night by jack-booted thugs. This is what happens in Aleksandr Solzhenitsyn's Gulag Archipelago, not in my America.*

But, alas, it does. It does.

When I'm finally located and bailed out, I'm devastated. Looking at twelve years in federal prison for something that's been fabricated out of whole cloth, I can't sleep or eat. I cry constantly. I begin to doubt my own memories. This simply doesn't make any sense.

Two years of my life and $40,000 worth of defense attorney later, the case against me is finally dropped for "lack of evidence," and the four officers involved are quietly retired with full pensions. I've still not been able to make sense of what's happened, and it still has the air of a Kafka novel about it, but more than anything, I feel betrayed. I've voted in every election—civic, state, and federal—since given the vote at age eighteen. I write letters to my elected officials, have served as a delegate to both the Democratic AND the Republican State Committees, volunteered for years as a polling place official, raised money for police and firefighters' benevolent associations—*and I no longer trust our public institutions.* If four petty yahoos can make this big a mess of *my* good name, imagine what they can do to some poor dumb kid they pick up off the street?

Long after I'm acquitted, I'm standing in line at the County Planning Commission to get a minor building permit, when I'm approached by a pleasant fellow in a navy blue Kern County Fire Fighters sweatshirt. Out of nowhere he asks me to have a cup of coffee with him. "I was on duty that night when the call came in. You need to know what really happened," he tells me.

After swearing me to secrecy—"I'll lose my pension if they find out I'm telling you this"—he explains that, unbeknownst to me, when I'd

FIREWORKS

first moved up here, the guys at the station had seen me riding my horses up the mountain road behind the firehouse and decided I was a MILF worthy of their attentions.

One of them had proposed a $500 bet that he'd be the first to bed me—the stringy drunk one who'd accosted me at my gate. Apparently he'd been driving by my place on his way to his shift that day and seen the fireworks in my arena. After our confrontation, he'd been so miffed that I'd rebuffed him, he raced back to the station, told everyone that a "gang" (that would be me, Ben Franklin's kin, my honor student son, and his friend) were setting off M-80s in an extreme fire-hazard area, and had *threatened to shoot him* when he told us to stop. His buddy backed him up. Then he demanded that the county send a law-enforcement team the seventy miles up here in the middle of the night to arrest me and "teach me a lesson."

This certainly put things in perspective, but it's hardly just compensation for what was taken from me in the process. I used to be the fire department's biggest fan; now I can't even bear to ride by the station anymore.

Their investigation of my formal complaint is a cruel joke—they'd never rat out a brother fireman—but I do find small comfort in learning that this particular "hero" has had a long history of using his small authority to intimidate and coerce women into bed. Eventually, I'm told, he pulled one of his little stunts on a woman who turned out to be an undercover officer for Internal Affairs. Too late for me, but he's gone now. "Drank himself to death from what I hear," says my informant.

PROCESSING

In the aftermath of the trial, I withdraw from the world. Never a terribly sociable sort to begin with, now I'm a full-fledged recluse. I go weeks without a face-to-face conversation, rarely answer my telephone. I'm not even interested in riding my horses anymore. It's partially fear, but there's also a huge element of anger and betrayal inside of me. More than anything, I simply want to be left alone until all the hate drains out of me.

I'm trying with all my might to understand Christ's admonition to forgive those who trespass against us, to understand the truth behind the words, "Love thy neighbor as thyself." I know I'll never be happy until I do, but I'm fighting with all of my heart against doing so. What I want is *revenge*.

The only salvation I have right now, the only clean picture I can draw from my sullied memory, is of something I saw before all this happened; a scene so magical that going there in my mind pulls me out of my funk when I'm brooding in the dark place where I seem to be stuck. I relive it so obsessively and in such minute detail, that it almost becomes real for me again. It's like a watercolor escape in a fairy tale picture book for me, and I try to go there as often as I can—to put myself back in a happier time.

I'd been riding my race mare, Sadie, up on the Pacific Crest Trail when I'd come to a meadow just short of Robin Bird Springs. There in the spring grasses, I saw a mom bear and her two little cubs grazing along with a small herd of maverick cows and their babies. There wasn't a human being but me around for ten miles. The little bear cubs and the baby calves were chasing each other through the wildflowers, tumbling about together as I watched them from the edge of the forest.

PROCESSING

The little calves would nudge the cubs along with their muzzles, and when they did, the bear cubs went rolling onto their furry little backs, their fat baby bellies exposed to the warm sun. Then the little bears went bumbling after the spindly calves like a couple of cocker spaniels pretending to chase the family cat. The mother bear and the mother cows looked like nothing so much as a gaggle of housewives at a kaffeeklatch, hanging out, gossiping, enjoying the sunny day and their darling new babies together.

When the mom bear finally scented Sadie and me, she woofed her babies up a nearby pine tree, *Woof! Woof!* and the calves all went scrambling back behind the cows as we rode through. As I looked behind me, the cubs were tumbling out of the tree and the mom bear and cows were back to chewing their respective cuds. It's like I was never there.

Now, I had always heard that bears are predators who go after cattle—especially the new calves. But here in this alpine meadow all I see is a peaceable kingdom—four species, supposedly at odds with each other, all at one with themselves and this lovely spring morning. And memories like this are what release me from my hateful demons.

REFUGE AMONG THE REFUSE

While all this "processing" is going on, the millennial real estate boom has finally come to Caliente—and the land pirates are out in full force. Like a swarm of biting flies tormenting the mourners at a gravesite memorial service, I catch them tromping across my property at all hours of the day and night, leaving gates ajar so the horses can get out and the longhorns can get in, touting this fragile and ecologically diverse wilderness as "the perfect spot for your motorcycle or gun club."

It seems like every week someone is sneaking a dilapidated old trailer house up onto an undeveloped piece of land and putting it on the market as a "ranchette." And people are buying them!

None of these places have electricity, most have shared water wells, and the new owners are more intent upon getting blisteringly drunk and shooting off their guns all weekend long than planting trees and gardens or assimilating into our quiet, respectful little community. Go-karts and dirt bikes terrorize our livestock, RVs clog our canyon road, and city people who have no business even *coming* to a place like this are suddenly tearing it apart.

On top of it all, the political aftermath of 9-11 has them all up in arms... *literally. This is GW Bush Country, by God, and we've got the firepower to prove it!* My peaceful little mountain hideaway is suddenly overrun with gun nuts, survival nuts, and assorted "patriots" all bent on teaching Osama bin Laden a lesson by blowing lead into innocent oak trees and across the roadways into the occasional riding horse or range cow.

Besieged by barking dogs and rapacious real estate ladies, I can't take another minute of this!

REFUGE AMONG THE REFUSE

A retired neighbor sympathizes and asks me if I want his hunting site farther up the mountain. He's too old to enjoy it now, he says, and hasn't been up there in years—and he'll sell me the title for not much more than what he paid back in the 1950s. I know the place well from my backcountry riding treks and covet its peace and quietude. It would be the perfect place to hide out and lick my wounds. *What a damned sad shame,* I think, *that I've got to leave the middle of effing nowhere to get away from people,* but what choice do I have . . . ?

"There's only one problem," says my friend. "Jef Kastle's people were squatting up there, using it as a pot farm. And they've left their junk all over the mountain." Jef Kastle is a local ne'r-do-well, and "junk all over the mountain" is being charitable.

The serene alpine meadow looks like a warzone after a firefight. After several years of bedeviling drug and immigration authorities, and threatening to "liquidate" any elected official who opposed his enterprise, Jef's trailer encampment was finally raided. In an operation that still draws *oohs* and *ahhs* of admiration from the old-timers, fourteen agencies of the county, state and US government put aside their political turf wars and united in one great cooperative venture. Helicopters and assault dozers, 4WD personnel carriers, and an armed squadron of foot soldiers with belaying equipment and flame throwers ascended, descended, and otherwise overran the compound, trashing it so completely that it was rendered uninhabitable to even the rattlesnakes and coyotes. Trailers were upended and overturned; tools, equipment, and infrastructure were destroyed; belongings were pulled from drawers and flung over the forty-acre headquarters; even the septic tank was uprooted and crushed under the steel treads of the assault tank.

Now, a year later, tatters that might once have been clothing flutter from high limbs of the Jeffrey pines and gym equipment tumbles halfway down the mountainside. Porn magazines flap in the dry wind—their unfettered wares in full display to the wandering spirits. A collection of patent-leather bondage shoes punctuates the dirt pathway to the cliff-side tree house. There, in an ancient oak tree, hangs what appears to be a fraying and extremely uncomfortable-looking sex swing. I cringe to think of those huge rusting metal springs meeting careless flesh in a moment of passion.

Computer parts and bedding, propane tanks and battery packs, abandoned washers and hydroponic grow lights rust in the shallows of the pond. And punctuating the ruins of every place humans once inhabited are huge, stinking piles of petrified rodent droppings. It's a tick-infested mess of epic proportion. And it's all mine.

It takes my crew the whole summer just to clean out the first layers of trash—the tons of junk and refuse the growers left behind. We cut it all up, bundle it onto the back of our trucks, and haul it down the mountain in trip after trip to the local dump. We clear out a path to the spring, too, haul in cement to repair the old spring box, and restore the irrigation lines that feed the pond. In the midst of all this work, I almost forget about the turmoil in the valley below.

Then in late May, the fires come. They rage for the entire month of June, destroying more than 40,000 acres of bone-dry scrub and forest—much of which hasn't burned in nearly a century.

Next come the monsoons. Unseasonal and torrential, they batter what is left of the scarred landscape, now denuded and vulnerable, and wash countless tons of debris—boulders and rocks, trees and root systems, errant jetsam from distant campsites, and long-abandoned vehicle parts—down the mountainsides and into my watershed. Piles of tangled limbs, branches, root strands, and boulders clog my pathways and block my accesses. Gritty clay five feet deep covers my wellheads and clogs my irrigation channels. The spring box is completely full of silt. Lacking a backhoe, let alone a road to bring it in on, I hike up the hill with my shovel and pick axe every morning to dig out the mess. I have a lot of hard work ahead of me.

REFUGE AMONG THE REFUSE

Some might be dismayed at the enormity of the clean-up job, but to me it's just another grand undertaking, a challenge. I don't have lofty goals here, just a desire to turn this place into something lovely once again. A place where I can sit by the pond in my little rocking chair and read and write and watch the hummingbirds and dragonflies play over the sparkling water—without having to deal with any human beings except the ones on the pages I'm reading and writing.

As soon as the rains are over, it's time to start digging out the spring box again, and that is what I am doing as the hot sun filters through the willows and the lacewings dance with the blueflies, yellow jackets skirting the brim of my cap. I am enchanted with the magic of this little wonderland—the birdsong and light play, and icy flowing springs—and totally oblivious to the seminal nightmare that is watching me, quietly waiting just beyond the bend.

PART THREE

THE URSADENT

From transcript, "Interview With Victim"
Report by Regional Field Warden, CA Department of Fish and Game

On 7/25/08, Allena Hansen called my HQ and stated she is now at home and knows where to find the bear which attacked her. I was advised to go to her house and pick up the shoes and hat she was wearing during the attack for the DNA evidence.

At approximately 1800 hours, I went to Allena's and picked up the shoes and her hat. I was invited to stay and I talked with her about the attack. She told me she was working on the spring box and decided to walk upstream to assess the siltation damage done to the upper spring during the recent rains.

Allena said she was about 4 yards north of the spring box when she looked up and saw the bear sitting in the streambed. She stated that bear made no sound but simply charged her and jumped on her head and bit her three times on the skull. Allena stated she heard three separate crunching sounds. The bear then bit down on her face and shook her violently. She stated she heard her teeth break and saw the bear spit them out. The bear then bit her neck, left breast, and groin.

After Allena fell with the bear and was being attacked, she pushed her left thumb into the bear's eye. As she fought with the bear she thought "this is it." And stated she "made her peace." But she decided to try and stand up when she noticed her dog, a mastiff, was fighting with the bear. As the bear was on top of the mastiff she could hear the dog crying, Allena looked around and called out to the other dog, a Wolfhound. She stated this dog was "the more reliable." Allena stepped over the fighting bear and dog and ran down the stream bed toward her car. She told me she couldn't see the trail and had ended up at the pond down the mountain from her car, guided by the wolfhound. Allena stated she couldn't see because she had lost both of her contact lenses in the attack and because of all the blood on her face.

Once she arrived at the pond, Allena stated she was able to reorient herself and walk out of the streambed and hike up the mountain to her car. As she walked to her car she heard her wolfhound make a "death cry." Allena thought her wolfhound was killed by the bear. Allena stated she climbed into her car and the mastiff got into the car with her. As Allena drove down Piute Mountain Road, she encountered a BLM employee and told him to call 911 and notify the fire station she was coming. Allena stated he told her she needed to stand by while he obtained some of her personal information from her. Allena told me she sped off and left him. She stated he looked bewildered and she drove to the Piute Mountain Fire Station where she was airlifted to UCLA.

THE URSADENT

The midsummer heat can get brutal up here, so by midmorning, I've already been at my work for several hours. It's not like I can simply turn on a faucet and expect to have water come pouring out of it, so keeping the spring box clear and full takes a lot of back-breaking shovel work. I've been standing in a pool of icy spring water up to my chest, scooping out rocks and gravel with a cut-off plastic bleach bottle for the better part of two hours, and my legs are starting to go numb. It's time for a break.

I've noticed the bear, of course, although I've never seen it. The occasional whiff of its scat is oddly human, sharp and acrid with a hint of vegetal fermentation. And I've heard something lumbering around occasionally, a cracking branch or small rock-fall dislodged from somewhere up the canyon. I've even seen its footprints in the mudflats near where I've been digging out for the last two weeks. The bear's a youngish one, with forepaws about the size of my open hand—probably stalking one of the whitetail deer that have been ravaging my fruit trees. *Good. Maybe the scent of a bear around here will scare the damned things off.*

There's really nothing to be concerned about. Besides, my new rescue dog, Deke the Mastiff, and faithful retainer, RK the Wolfhound are sleeping nearby—and if nothing else, my Remington twelve-gauge is loaded and handy within easy reach. Bears come poking around the ranch fairly often, and when we see each other, they're unfailing in their efforts to get as far away from me as possible as quickly as their legs will carry them off. Besides, there's not a bear in the whole Sierras stupid enough to hang out anywhere near two ranch dogs as big and aggressive as RK and Deke—between the two of them, they weigh nearly four hundred pounds, and they're both bred for hunting large predators.

As I climb out of the spring box to stretch my legs and warm up, I can hear the dogs snoring in the cool sand just down the creek. The trees are green and the air smells like a summer camp full of pines and oaks and granite. The birds are singing in the trees and brilliant little bugs are flitting about the surface of the water, the sunlight glinting off their lacy wings. I literally feel like I'm in the middle of a Walt Disney movie and start looking around for the singing bluebirds. But what I *get* is a bear. A *BEAR*! About ten feet away and staring straight at me.

CHOMP CHOMP CHOMP

Like he's been *wait*ing for me. . . .

How many people get up in the morning, fix themselves a cup of coffee, take a deep breath of clean mountain air, and think: *Wow. What a GREAT day! I think I'll go out and get myself mauled by a bear!*

This one's not quite full grown; about the size of the mastiff, but a lot stockier and even more solid, and he's haunched down like a dog, tensed and coiled and ready to spring. *This is not good.* Our eyes meet for a mere fraction of a second, but in this moment, I know *exactly* what's coming.

I'm not scared, and there's no time to react or run even if I were. I'm just hit with this overwhelming sense of dismay. There's only enough time for me to murmur, "*Nooooo*"—more a sad admission than a protest, and *BAM,* he's on me. Right in my face.

He goes straight for my eyes. I instinctively turn away as he charges, leaps, rams into me full force, grabs me by the ears and bites into my nose and mouth—and takes me down.

The next thing I'm aware of is lying in the fetal position on the wet sand with this *thing* chewing on my head. It's biting into my scalp and skull, clawing my face with its thick sharp claws—rending my cheeks, my eyes, my nose—trying to tear my face off. I can feel my skin being slashed and ripped. I can *hear* myself being torn apart, the slick crackle of sinew separated from meat and bone as the bear shakes its head like a terrier savaging a chew toy.

It's making the same noises a dog makes when it's playing tug-of-war—sort of a *gnannnnggg,* interspersed with grunts—only instead of tugging on a thick knotted rope, it's tugging on *me.*

Suddenly I know why the Brothers Grimm told little kids not to go out into the woods, why Grandma warned Little Red Riding Hood not to talk to strangers, and why Goldilocks was really, really stupid. I'm not so much shocked as I am analytical. If I'm going to die here on this forest floor, I want to experience it fully, and if by some chance I should make it out alive, I want to remember *everything* so I can tell people the story. But all I can think is: *My fucking insurance policy isn't going to cover this.*

THE URSADENT

I'm trying to decide whether or not I even *want* to survive. I've been through enough battles with Blue Cross to know they won't reimburse a dime without waffling and weaseling—and that's *before* I have to consider the miseries of rehab. Worse, this isn't just some random bone or ligament we're talking about, it's my *face*. This bloody beast is tearing off my *face*. The pain brings me back to the moment. *Damn. This really is happening to me.*

With each CHOMP, CHOMP, CHOMP the creature takes on my head, I find myself categorizing the injuries and tallying up the damages: CHOMP, GRIND... *deep scalp laceration with possible skull fracture—one year to heal, hair loss, scarring, minimal restriction of activity. This isn't so bad....*

I hear its breath woofling; it's working hard at this. The bear is trying to gain a good grip on my scalp, but my metal hair clip is getting in the way. I give silent thanks to the people at the hairclip factory.

It keeps working on the top of my head, growing more and more frustrated in its efforts, and I keep trying to place where I've heard its bellows and grumblings before. They're oddly familiar, but the context is throwing me off. Then out of nowhere it occurs to me; *I'm being eaten by Chewbacca as he rages on the flight deck of the Millennium Falcon!* I swear they sound exactly the same.

CHOMP, CRUNCH... now it's biting off the top of my head. *Ablation, baldness, extensive grafting, possible skull deformity—YIKES—two years in rehab, damn it! So THIS is what it feels like to be killed and eaten by a bear....*

CHOMP, CHOMP, GRIND, CRACK! It's broken my jaw. CREECH... and maybe my neck! *Awww, c'mon!* Its weight is heavy on my shoulders and hips, grinding my thigh into a sharp rock in the sand. I feel the skin burst under the pressure, and the wet of my blood underneath.

GRIIITCH... ENOUGH ALREADY! Shit, it's got a hold on my face again. Now I'm gonna need facial reconstruction, too! Two more years... it's grunting hard now, and growling while it savages me. Inside my head it sounds like when I bite into a stalk of celery, only infinitely

CHOMP CHOMP CHOMP

more resonant.

At this, I open my eyes and look at the sand in front of my nose. Little red and white chiclets are falling from above. *It's spitting out my teeth?!* Now that's just *rude. Entire mouth reconstruction with prosthetic teeth.*

Here my heart sinks. Blue Cross doesn't cover dental. There's no way I can afford to fix *this*. Now I really *do* just feel like giving up and dying. Dr. Bae is going to be *so* upset; he worked for *months* to get my smile perfect. The bear comes at me again and I feel my neck wrenched in earnest. *Just break it, already; at least I'll suffocate quickly.*

CHOMP, SQUISH! Oops, there goes my eye. . . . *Oh man, I am so screwed!* The earth under my cheek here is so soft and so cool. Just let this be over. What is it they say to do? Play dead? *Play* dead? I *am* dead. . . .

Only a minute has gone by and my initial sense of analytical horror is giving way to some new emotion—I do believe it's *anger. It's time to get those eyes open, girl, and take this in fully—don't just lie in the dirt and die.* About this time, I twist myself around to take a look at the thing that is ravaging me—if it's going to kill me, at least I want it to know I'm watching.

When I open my eyes, there it is—teeth buried in my nose and upper jaw, eyeball to eyeball with me, as close as a kiss. The bear's eye is a dull caramel brown, surprisingly flat, almost dead—like a shark's. Unblinking, emotionless, businesslike.

Businesslike. I think that's what offends me the most. I've been feted by titans and dined with royalty, but I'm simply dinner to this thing. *You can't DO this to me! I've hung out at* Playboy *fer chrissakes! Where's the respect?!* Even in death, I'm beset with sarcasm and irony.

My body is twisted in such a way that my right hand is suspended inches from the bear's right eyeball. *My thumb! I can still use my elbow to drive my thumb into the monster's piggy little eye.* I take a brief look into the unspeakably malevolent thing staring into my own, and something inside of me clicks. *I can fight this!*

Yet even as I'm being mangled, I'm squeamish about doing what I know I have to do next.

One time Andy had knocked me to my knees, sending me sprawling,

THE URSADENT

kicking me in the butt every time I tried to get up. But I just couldn't bring myself to let fly with a back kick into his testicles. I knew I could, I knew it would make him stop, but something inside of me prevented me from letting him have it. *He's not hurting me THAT badly....*

After his kicking propelled me forward onto my face three or four times, I finally did nail him a good one, and he quit beating on me, but I always wondered why I was so reluctant to cause someone pain in order to make *my* pain stop. I'm the same way in heated arguments. I *know* exactly the right nasty thing to say to counter someone's verbal cruelties, but I just can't bring myself to utter them, finding it easier to go numb and simply watch them like they're some bizarre TV performance until they sputter out.

But this time it's for real—it's either this bear or me. I brace my elbow against the creek bed, rare back on my shoulder, and jab at that sullen eye for all I'm worth. And jab again. The bear lets go of my face and I am finally able to yell for my dogs.

"RK!"

The wolfhound will come and the mastiff will follow. I know they will....

I'm not aware of time in any manifestation. I see no white light of neural shut-down, no life flashing before me, no sense of its passage. All I sense is *now*. Just *now*. Then I hear the dogs growling and someone *yiking* in terrified pain. *They've come to my rescue!*

I have a decision to make. Do I stay here and die peacefully, quietly? I certainly want to. Or do I try to get up and face what promises to be a painful and hugely depressing future? I'm so awfully tired of healing from injuries for a living. It's time to give someone else a turn in the proverbial barrel.

Then I think, *If I die here, the bear is going to drag me off into the willows and eat the tasty, soft parts of me. Then the turkey vultures will come, and the coyotes. Then the mice and lizards and yellow jackets and ants.* I've seen what the yellow jackets can do to a dying rattlesnake in the course of an afternoon. Three or four days from now the hillbillies will find what is left of my mangled, decomposing corpse and be hugely grossed out. All the county white trash—the Babbitts and the Baby Jesus people, all the townsfolk who hate me for defying their norms and the petty hypocrites who egg them on—will hear of this and rejoice. I can just hear them cackling over their pork rinds and six packs. "Got just what she deserved. Maybe *now* she'll fear the Lord and the good ol' boys!"

My deliciously grisly death will bring so much pleasure to so many people, I'll be goddamned *if I'll give you all the satisfaction!* I realize I am going to try to survive this, if only for the sake of my vanity.

Then a dog screams again. It shocks me out of my anger, brings me back into immediacy. And when I look over, the bear has my mastiff on his back and is gnawing his belly.

Now I'm enraged. It's bad enough the bear has killed *me,* but he's going after my dog too?

Poor Deke—short for "Decoy," ironically enough—he never signed up for this nonsense. A rescue hound from a dog betting and drug operation down in Bakersfield, this gentle giant is a two-hundred-pound canine Ferdinand; he'd rather smell the posies than fight to the death, but here he is, bless his big old loving heart, fulfilling his destiny—bear baiting. Then I think, *If Deke is willing to die to save me, I can at least honor his sacrifice by getting up and trying to escape.*

The bear is killing my dog. I am terrified it will let go of him and come after me again. Deke is giving me a chance to escape, but I'm momentarily petrified. If I step over them and miss, my femoral artery is as good as gone to the bear's bloody jaws, and then I'm lost for sure. In retrospect, I'm not proud to admit that in this moment, my concern for my poor heroic mastiff is non-existent. *Don't wimp out now!* I tell myself, *or you'll both be dead.*

Then I do the hardest thing I've done in years. I get to my knees, find my feet, take a deep breath through the hole that was my nose, and clamber over the fighting mass of blood and fur and teeth underneath me.

I scramble away and don't look back.

L'EAU DU SCUM POND

Amazed that I am able to stand and stagger from the scene without passing out, there's now a disquieting new sensation to deal with. A lot of my blood is leaking out and I can hear it whooshing from my head, falling in a steady little dribble onto the moist sand at my unsteady feet. I can't actually see this, you understand, because my contact lenses have been lost in the attack and what is left of my already-marginal eyesight is obscured by blood—way too much blood. *But at least my hearing still works!* I sense that there is an immediate danger of the bear coming after me, and begin to stumble away from the spring box where I was just working.

The walls of the narrow pathway are steep and crumbly, the footing treacherous under the best of circumstances. I am skirting the rim of a ten-foot hole dug into the ground; one that thanks to my ministrations this morning is now filled with icy spring water. The surrounding boulders are slippery and steep.

This is insane, I tell myself. *You're going to exsanguinate right here in the mud. There is zero amount of chance you're going to be able to make it out of this one alive.* But my other voice, the perverse one that occasionally creeps into my consciousness and eggs me into doing the damnedest things imaginable, is saying . . . *Oh, why not? If you can pull this one off, you'll be able to dine out on this story for the rest of your life. Now wouldn't that be a hoot? Go on. Give it a try.*

It occurs to me that if I treat this challenge as a project and divide it into a series of manageable steps, I may be able to draw from what I've already accomplished and build from that foundation. Apparently I've escaped the attack; that's a good start. If I can get to the car, I might be able to get to the fire station. If I can get to the fire station, maybe I can get to a hospital. If I get to a hospital, who knows—with a little luck, they may be able to save my life. If they can save my life, maybe they can reassemble me . . .

Oh, what the hey, I'm gonna go for it. I'll deal with the details later.

First, though, I need to even out my breathing. Get focused. Concentrate. Use my diaphragm to push the blood out of my airway and force oxygen into my brain.

Somewhere in the background, Mr. Mendenhall, my high school vocal coach, is telling me to define each breath—exhale it from deep in my center. Relax my throat.

All those years of voice lessons have made the transition from autonomic to measured almost an instinctive thing for me. Conscious breathing has gotten me out of some hairy situations in the past—kept panic from overriding my considered responses. *Don't panic. BREATHE.*

Focus and eliminate all the extraneous stimuli from the scene. It still hasn't registered that I can't actually *see* what I'm doing. *MOVE, MOVE, MOVE!* says the little voice. *Get out of this thicket and into the open—far away from the bear.* But where is the trailhead, so I can find the path back to the car? *Better start walking and keep walking.* (I don't feel at all like walking.) And *DO. NOT. FAINT.*

I negotiate the sandy berm along the spring, following the irrigation pipe like a double yellow line on a foggy highway to make my way down to the trailhead. It must have taken me four or five minutes to get this far, yet I have no recollection of having done so. Later, the forest ranger shows my son a large boulder along the pathway. "She must have stopped her to collect herself," he tells him. It's covered in my blood.

When I get to the fork where the trailhead should be, it hits me that there's a big problem. The recent rains have completely washed away the existing footpath and destroyed all the familiar terrain that usually marks my way out. Without these landmarks, I have no idea where to go or which way to turn, and other than colors and vague shapes, I can't see anything anyway. Even in the best of circumstances, it's easy to misjudge a tree or bush and take a wrong turn into the brambles.

Keep bearing left. Stay out of the ravine! Whatever you do, don't get

L'EAU DU SCUM POND

sidetracked into the ravine or you'll never find your way out.

Well, damn it all, I must have missed the turnoff because here I am, stuck in the goddamm ravine. It's a long, tangled drop of deadwood, wild thorny roses, sage, Manzanita, ceanothus, and assorted spiny cacti, forming a formidable barrier against penetration by anything much larger than a field mouse. Tick-infested and home to territorial rattlesnakes, they call this particular blend of California scrub "The Firefighter's Nightmare" for good reason. Far too thick and thorny for a machete, I'd been waiting to get a dozer up here to tackle the mess and start dragging it all out with chains and cable. Now I must negotiate it on foot—and my heart sinks.

Even deer won't try to go though this stuff. I once watched a young buck double back and rush my dogs rather than jump into the ravine to escape. The one time I ventured in to lay an irrigation line, it tore my leather jacket to ribbons within minutes and left my flesh covered not only in a welter of nasty gouges and scratches but an enthusiastic colony of sucking ticks as well.

I am essentially blind, bouncing off of trees and slipping off of rocks while the thorns tear at my body *again*. The slope is too steep to climb back up without a rope, but I know that if I can somehow keep heading downhill, eventually I will come to the pond . . . and the dirt road leading back up to the trailhead and my car. *Gravity is our friend*, I tell myself. *Just hurl yourself downhill.*

But I can't hurl myself downhill because the scrub is too dense and I don't weigh enough to make even a dent in it—bouncing right back up onto my feet when I fling myself at it. There's no way for me to break through the branches with my diminutive muscles and bones. Nor can I *see* my way out of it. And I'm stuck, literally, impaled by thorns no matter which way I turn or how I try to maneuver myself downhill. I either somehow crash my way though a couple hundred yards of briar patch and dead scrub or sit down and die right here.

My heavy leather shoes have been lost in the attack. *Great! On top of all this, now I'm Rattler Fodder!* It occurs to me that malicious forces are likely laughing their collective asses off at me right now—having foiled a bear attack only to be nailed by a lowly rattlesnake. Cosmic irony. I can't even watch where I step—if I *could* step. . . .

Beyond frustration, beyond mere anger, I throw my head back and give up a long keening wail; a howl of misery tinged with notes of outrage so visceral, so hopeless and heartfelt, that it leaves me in tears. In the course of my life, I've been toyed with and abused. I've been mistreated, beaten, and unjustly prosecuted. I've been victimized and vilified, but I've NEVER been this majorly fucked with. Curiously, this makes me furious. I scream out to the heavens, and this time it's primal.

"FUUUUUUUUUUUUUUUUUUUUUUUUCK!"

I can hear my epithet echoing off the walls of the canyon and out into the valley below, and I'm hoping with all of my heart that someone down there hears my last editorial—and takes it personally.

With this mighty and decidedly *un*joyful noise, I consciously commit everything I have left to getting out of here. *Another do-or-die moment.*

Suddenly I know *exactly* what that means. And so, to spite the fates, I gather myself and wrap my arms around my mangled face, elbows out like pikes, ducking and charging and throwing my body farther down the ravine into the scrub. I am a madwoman, scrambling, half-falling, dodging, stomping, and kicking off dead limbs with my bare feet in a frenzied rage. I am impervious to pain. *I will survive this!*

But I'm not making any headway at all. I am too tiny and the scrub is too thick. I'm stuck, a goner. I begin to cry in earnest.

And then, plowing through the brambles up toward me, yelping and frantic with concern, comes my wolfhound. Maybe it's that ancient alchemy between man and dog, or maybe he's heard my familiar profanity and assumed I'm simply calling him home, but two hundred pounds of galumphing puppy come crashing through the undergrowth like a runaway freight train, his mass clearing a perfect pathway for me to follow to THE POND! "Good boy, RK," I say, putting my hand on his massive head for guidance down the path he's broken in trying to find me. "Good boy."

MUST GET HELP!

As soon as I catch the scent of the pond I know there's a chance. My orientation returns in a flash; I recognize where I am and know what I need to do to get up to my car. My state of mind immediately shifts from that of a frenzied little animal bent only on escape to one of focused determination. My sense of time returns and I am a human being again—thanks to my bad attitude and my good dogs.

Having trudged the path from the pond back up to the car a hundred times, usually laden with tools and supplies for the spring box, I know where the path goes, how much energy it will take to traverse it, and what to expect along the way. True, it is steep—a hot, unpleasant hump under the best of circumstances—but it offers steady footing along a graded dirt track, free of obstacles or obstructions. I walk and keep on walking. I can do this blindfolded. In a sense, that's precisely what's happening.

Just don't faint! If you pass out now, you'll bleed out before you wake up.

A basic backpacker's march is what's needed here. I begin humming a mantra, heavy on the syncopation . . . *tramp, tramp, tramp, the boys are maaar—ching, keep it marchin' up the hill. Breathe in rhythm, in and out, in your nose and out your mouth, keep it going, keep on marchin' up the hill.* . . .

I have no idea where this musical amalgam comes from or why I remember it now, but here is where all those thousands upon thousands of miles of endurance training pay off. Trotting my horse along abandoned tracks and lumber roads, aching, dehydrated, longing for those few seconds of shade we can snatch as we pass under a pine tree, I know if I can just keep myself going, breathing, conscious, eventually I'll get to where I need to be.

CHOMP CHOMP CHOMP

Any distance athlete is familiar with The Wall, but there's another barrier you must deal with after that second wind dissipates—and at some point it always does. When you're at mile seventy-three of a one-hundred-mile race, and your ankles have stopped supporting you, and your bra has rubbed a bleeding sore along your rib cage, and a foxtail you picked up at your last piddle break is working its way along a pathway you are unable to ignore, and you and your horse look at each other and say, "Why? Why exactly are we doing this, again?" *That's* what I have to keep out of my thoughts.

If I worry about passing out or running out of blood, or getting winded, or what has happened to the dogs, or how I am possibly going to navigate a vehicle down that joke of a road without being able to see it, I am doomed. Hence the mantra. It's a distraction from the awful reality, and it keeps me going.

Off in the distance I hear the wolfhound's death cry echoing off the walls of the canyon. I haven't even been aware of him leaving to go back up to help his doomed buddy, Deke. *Damn, it all! I loved those dogs.*

Can't think about that now . . . almost up the hill . . . keep on . . . marchin'. . . .

I'm grieving for my dogs when I finally get to the clearing where my car is parked, so am astounded to see my freaked-out mastiff waiting for me, panting, with spit strings trailing out of his muzzle to the ground.

"I thought you were dead, Deke! How did you get here?" I say, only when it comes out of my mouth it sounds like, "I nyot you ere ed eke."

The poor thing's cringing, but he seems to be okay. Although his vision is not much better than mine, I can tell that the sight, let alone the scent of me, must have him terrified. After the harrowing encounter he's just had with the bear, the big guy is emotionally overwhelmed. (Mastiffs are like that.) I open the hatch for him to jump into the back and tell him to get in the car. "Gnakn ga cungh, Enk."

Deke cowers and begins to slink away, sensing in all likelihood that given my condition, the chances of him arriving back at the ranch in one piece are not all that encouraging. Usually when he tries to sneak off like this, I chase him down, corral him, drag him back to the car, and physically bulldog him inside. That's not gonna happen this time. I am livid—in every sense of the word.

"DAMN IT, DEKE!" I sputter, spewing blood and tissue along with abuse, "If you think I'm going to play this game with you right now, you've got another think coming! I'm going to leave you up here." (*With the bear, you idiot hound.*) Whether he understands me or not, he apparently senses I am serious, because for the first time in his life, he jumps right in.

Now for the fun part! The chances of me making it down this mountain to the fire station are minimal at best, but I've made it this far—maybe I can pull it off!

In a moment of anarchy, I throw caution to the wind and don't belt myself in. *The hell with it. I'm just going to go for it and the DMV be damned! Wheeeee!*

Who knows what a mess I am making of my tranny and undercarriage. As if that matters right now. The awful ruts, the rock and mudslides, drop-offs, and undermined hairpins on the ersatz road are as treacherous today as ever—it's not as if anyone maintains it. So I just basically twirl the steering wheel and stomp on the brakes as the spirit moves me—and hang on. Tools slam around in the back. Poor old Deke is thumping against the sides. I don't care. This is actually happening—except it's *not*. It's like the world's most surreal Disney ride.

I have no idea how I make it to the graded lumber road a mile down the mountain from the spring, nor do I know why, for the first and only time since I've been here, I left the heavy rolling gate unlocked and open when I came up this morning. The unlocked gate saves me the five-minute wrestling match to get it opened again, and I fly right through it, blessing my uncharacteristic prescience, as I fishtail down Piute Mountain Road, trailing dust and gravel like a madwoman, as fast as second gear will allow me, exhilarated, *yes exhilarated*, to be driving like a maniac *with impunity*.

The best thing that could *happen* to me right now would be to run into a cop! (Not that this is likely. I rarely even see another car up this far, and the nearest sheriff's substation is an hour and a half away in Lake Isabella.) I am driving so poorly, in fact, that I'm pretty certain the car will roll or flip off a cliff before I make it to the fire station at the bottom, but *meh*, what are they going to do to me now? What *can* they do?

I'm telling myself to slow down—I am going to kill myself. Then the other little voice tells me to shut up and have fun with it. *You're never going to have a better excuse to drive like a butthead, so GO FOR IT!* Mostly, the car just goes with the road, and I'm hugging the cliff wall as best I can, praying nothing's coming at me in the opposite direction.

Having made it about three miles or so down this suggestion of a road, I come careening around a bend and *NO WAY!* There on a narrow turnout sits a *clean*, white, late-model truck with a round decal on the door. The "clean" part is the giveaway. Whoever's in that truck is definitely new to the neighborhood. *The sheriff? What on earth is he doing up here?* I slam on the brakes, pull a right-angle slider, and hop out, hoping he doesn't shoot me.

The occupant of the vehicle opens his door with great reluctance. I can only imagine what I must look like to this guy—and actually take a small delight in the thought. He's not a local, and he definitely doesn't seem at ease with the zombie woman advancing upon him, gouting blood and shrieking like a crazy person.

"BEAR ATTACK!" I yell, stumbling toward him. He recoils in horror, grows pale. He's not going to be much use to me if he faints, so I bark, "Call the fire station and tell them I'm on my way."

A quick assessment tells me this man is disoriented, obviously a visitor to the area, probably surveying the recent fire damage for the BLM. I already have the momentum going and don't have even a minute to waste trying to get him up to speed; damping the adrenaline at this point would be counter-productive—maybe fatal. I hop back into my car and gun the engine. "Halt!" he orders, "I need to get some information!"

Or what? You'll shoot me?

I leave him standing there on the turnout, literally open-mouthed and gaping after me. "CALL THE FIRE STATION," I yell after him, giving him the number just to be sure. "TELL THEM I'M ON MY

MUST GET HELP!

WAY... and thank you," I add. It never hurts to be polite.

As I drive away, I burst out laughing, imagining what that poor man must be thinking just now. I hope he will be able to get a hold of the fire station so my arrival won't come as a complete shock to them. *Yeech, I hope they don't barf when they see me.*

At this point, I decide to allow myself one teensy little look at my face in the rearview mirror. Just for one second—just to see. So, I peek.

Well, doo dah. I am a mess, and that's the truth. I mostly see a bloody mass of crimson tissues interspersed with globs of black dirt—and the bright green of my eyes. The bill of my white baseball cap is twisted off to the side of my face, and I'm surprised it's still on after all of this. (Later, when I see the photographs they took in the ER, I realize it wasn't my baseball cap after all. It was my scalp hanging off the side of my head.) *You look like the freakin' Italian flag,* I think. My nose is gone. My lips are off. That's about as far as I let myself get.

I squirrel and fishtail the entire last mile, and as I pass the bend in the road where my mare once slipped in mid-gallop and tumbled off the side with me, I'm positively *giddy*. If I can *walk* this last section after a bad horse-wreck, surely I can *drive* it. *I am going to make it! This is soooo amazingly cool! Yee-frikkin' HAH mother-fuckers!*

I do a perfect 270 at the intersection at the bottom of the mountain, slide into the driveway of the firehouse, and come screeching to a stop in the parking lot. I slam the car into park, let my traumatized mastiff out of the back, and stumble into the garage of the station. The guys are there waiting for me and I give thanks for the poor BLM guy's equanimity. "Honey! I'm HOOOOME," I call out.

Then, triumphant at what I just managed to pull off, I let myself collapse onto the cool cement floor of the garage bay.

BACK TO CIVILITY

"Okay," I say, "someone get a pencil and paper. I only have enough energy to do this once, and I don't know how long I can stay conscious."

As methodically as possible, I give them my name, age, driver's license and social security numbers, medical history, blood type, and size of shoe. I tell them my shots are all current, I'm HIV negative, and have never been exposed to Hep C. Rabies, though? I'm not so sure. . . .

I give them my UCLA patient number, next of kin, neighbor's telephone number, and ask if someone could please take what's left of Deke back to the ranch and call a vet for him. I tell them I need an airlift, not ground transport, and that they should take me to UCLA Medical Center, not a local clinic, because it's July when all the new residents come on staff, and a small-town ER is going to be a cluster-hump trying to deal with injuries as extensive and disfiguring as mine. I've come this far; I want as much reconstructive oversight and advanced technology as I can get.

I ask for a sip of water and someone brings me a bottle of Evian, but when I try to swallow, it all dribbles out because my mouth is off and my muscles are shredded. I realize—*for real this time*—that my face *is* gone, and there's no specific feeling where there *should* be—only pain. This is *not* going to be pretty.

The firefighters are very concerned, of course; after all, there is a faceless woman bleeding to death in their garage bay, but they are also extraordinarily sweet, solicitous, and supportive. The kid propping me up keeps telling me, "Hang on, hon, you're doing great," but we both know I'm not.

He's about my son's age and so earnest about all this that I feel like *I* should comforting *him*. "Relax," I tell him. "I promise I won't die here on your floor. We'll leave the extra paperwork to the guys in the helicopter." He laughs. I snort through my blowhole. It's a nice moment.

Our main concern here is that I stay conscious, because if I pass out, they'll have to intubate me, and given the extent of my injuries, no one can be sure of whether or not my trachea is intact, and if it is, where it might be found in all this mess. It just seems better all around for me to stay upright and conscious so I don't aspirate my blood and drown here on the cement floor.

One guy is propping me up and another on the other side is keeping me from pitching forward. *Is this cool or what? How often does a girl get to be the filling in a fireman sandwich?* It's all so cozy, our past legal kerfuffle must be forgotten. Too bad I'm not in any condition to enjoy the reconciliation.

It's only a few minutes before we hear the welcome *chop, chop, chop* of the air-evacuation helicopter coming up the canyon from Mojave. Once again, I bless the BLM guy who called to alert the station to my arrival. Apologizing for the mess I've made of the fire house floor (I know how hard it is to clean up lots of blood), I thank the guys for saving my life and ask that if I don't make it, could someone please tell my son he was loved, and thank him for being such a great kid? I'm thoroughly annoyed with myself that this is the best I can come up with—the last most significant moment of my life, my literal last words, and all I've got is some stupid cliché? Shame on me, and shame on my final ineloquence.

I'm still trying to think of the *mot juste* as they're loading me into the chopper. But then there's this *bea-u*-tiful velvet baritone in my left ear—and it's offering me drugs. "*Hell* yes, son," I tell him. "Keep 'em comin'."

THE AFTERMATH: The Beginning

"Welcome back," says the ICU nurse. "Do you know where you are?"

Well, lookie here. I seem to be alive—one minute I was oblivious and now I'm fully alert and conscious again.

"Yes," I hear myself saying. *Good, my voice is still connected to my speech center.* "Unless you've transferred me to purgatory, I'm at UCLA."

"And do you know who's the president?"

"Unfortunately, yes, but he won't be for much longer." *Hurray! And my sense of snark is still intact.*

This is starting to look encouraging. My mind seems to be functional, and far from being horrified at what I've just been through, I'm thrilled to be back. As the ICU nurse performs her routine interrogation and assessment, I'm dying of curiosity to see what they've managed to do with the lump of hamburger meat the air evac has handed off to them to work with. "How long have I been here?"

"It's been about ten hours since they brought you in."

Wow! "That was fast...." I wouldn't have been surprised if she'd told me I'd been in a coma for the last week. *These UCLA folks sure are efficient, professional. Good decision insisting the air-evacuation crew land me here.*

I hurt, yes, although it's nothing compared to how I felt before I got here. I touch my fingers to my face, exploring, more curious than horrified. My left eye doesn't seem to work, but it's still in there, so at least they didn't have to remove it. And I can see color and movement out of the right one, so maybe there's hope some of my sight has been saved. As I trace the contour of my face I notice there's hardly any sensation—not even of pressure. A small mercy, as it turns out; because the nerves have

THE AFTERMATH: THE BEGINNING

been severed, so has much of the pain they transmit. My lips feel like a baseball glove—huge, floppy, and inert. My upper jaw is a gaping hole inside my mouth, but my brain seems to be working fine, and I can still form words to communicate with my nurse.

"Shall I bring you a mirror?" she asks.

"Sure thing," I tell her. "It's time to see what's become of me."

"I'll go get you one. I'll be right back."

"No hurry. I'm not going anywhere."

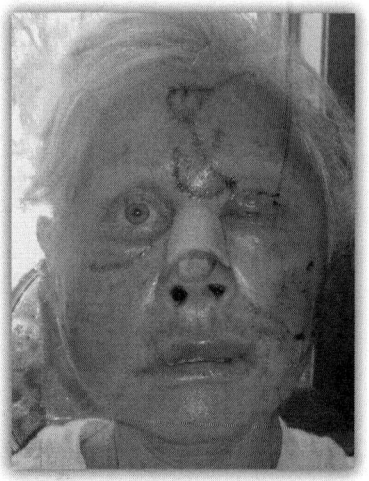

When she returns, she presents me with a hand mirror then takes a step back. I get the impression she's waiting for me to scream and faint dead away, but considering the chipper way I'm feeling, the damage obviously isn't as bad as it might have been. I'm guessing I'll be disfigured, but I'm definitely going to survive.

I notice that the ICU has suddenly filled with people, all milling around, tense and anticipatory. Apparently they've gathered to watch what happens when I first see my new self in the mirror. One of them is holding a syringe. A sedative, perhaps? With all these eyes upon me, and with what must be a grotesque parody of a human face, I feel like Norma Desmond in the movie *Sunset Boulevard*. It only seems right to play up the part for my audience—anything to break the oppressive tension they've brought in with them. Mirror in hand, I strike a pose as best I can and croak, "I'm ready for my close up, Mr. DeMille." I'm greeted with a few snickers from the cognoscenti (this *is* Hollywood, after all).

Without the slightest hint of dread, I hold the mirror up to my face, and try to focus on what's looking back at me. Indeed, I'm hugely aware of the import of what I say next. There's a room full of people, all waiting to take their cue from my reaction. They've worked hard to save me and they're as invested in all of this as I am. The least I can do is be gracious.

CHOMP CHOMP CHOMP

What I see resembles nothing so much as an extremely well-executed patchwork quilt. It's mottled and sutured, with a thousand little black stitches crisscrossing its planes, but amazingly, they've not only put me back together, they've put me back together in a recognizable form!

Whoever is responsible for this effort is a technician of the highest order. When they brought me in, no one had the slightest idea who I was, what my life had been like, certainly not how my roadmap of a face had looked—before. Yet here it is, battered and torn, and swollen up like a puff adder, but still my face! This is *superlative reconstruction*. I don't think anyone is expecting me to look up and say, "Oh my *god*! You guys did such a *good job*!"

Satisfied that I'm not going to lapse into a fit of hysterics, the nurse tells me that my son is waiting outside to see me. "Do you want him to come in?" Unspoken is "with you looking like this?"

Alec has seen me in every state of dishevelment imaginable. When he was a little kid in Malibu, I went to the emergency room for so many horse wrecks that we actually had a secret password so he'd know the paramedics who came to fetch him to the hospital with me were on the level. As *if* some stupid bear attack is going to scare him off!

"Of *course*, "I say. "*Please*. Let him in."

Suddenly, there is nothing I want more than to hug my baby, my link with the real world. Just two months ago, he graduated from college with a degree in history and a minor in classics—utterly useless in this economy, but also the perfect match for his personality and upbringing. Well, *here's* a classic story for you, kid.

"You just had to one-up me," is what he says when he sees me lying there, mangled and broken. During his junior year he'd surprised me with the news that he'd taken up mixed martial arts—and had won his first series of professional cage fights. I guess *this* shows the lad who's the *real badass*. "You just couldn't stand to let *me* have the glory for a change."

It hurts like crazy when I laugh, but I do it anyway.

"They called me out of my improv class," he says. He's been studying stage comedy over in North Hollywood. "When I told them I had to

THE AFTERMATH: THE BEGINNING

leave early because my mom got mauled by a bear, they applauded me for nailing the scene."

"At least you'll get some good material out of all this," I say.

The ICU nurse is observing us from a discreet distance, tissue box at the ready waiting for the inevitable tears and wailing. But we're laughing like maniacs at this latest turn of untoward events. I'm pretty sure she's not seen this sort of mother/son reaction to calamity all that often. Alec tells me that they had a grief counselor waiting for him back in the waiting room. "He seemed kind of confused when I told him I wasn't worried; that we've been through this sort of thing before. The poor guy was so broken up about you *I* ended up comforting *him*."

I'm not eager to broach the next topic, but I have to. Like most animal people, I'm inordinately fond of my doggies, and the memory of their awful last moments weighs on me like a truckload of pavers. I'm hoping someone has found poor RK the Wolfie and brought his body back to the ranch for an honorable burial. It's the least I can do for him. Deke the Mastiff may have fared better; I remember that I was able to get him into the car and let him loose at the fire station. Maybe they were able to get him to a vet in time?

"The dogs?" I ask Alec, choking back a sob. "Have you heard anything?"

"Oh, they're both fine," he says airily. "Augie found RK running around up at the pot farm, and Deke came home on his own." Our neighbor, Augie, may be a pill, but his love for our dogs is undeniable.

"When I got up to the ranch," Alec says, "Augie had already cleaned them off, patched them up, shot them full of antibiotics, and made them a pot roast for dinner. They were all three playing in the yard together when I left to come get you this morning." Awash with relief at this unexpected blessing, I realize everything's going to be okay after all! The Hero Dogs' story must be as remarkable as my own; I can't wait to hear what they have to say about the whole shebang when I get home!

Alec and I are chatting away merrily when the ICU erupts in quiet applause. A young woman makes her way into the room proceeded by a curious aura of girlishness mixed with gravitas—it's almost as if she's surrounded by a radiating energy, such is the electric buzz she gives off. By the deference she's being shown, her identity is obvious. "This is your surgeon, Dr. Lee," says the nurse.

I can't see her face, but the moment she comes into my field of vision my entire body relaxes. There is something so comforting about her, such a cheerful authority, that any anxiety I may have had about my recovery is immediately allayed. Dr. Lee knows my body more intimately than even I do. I've only seen the *outside* of myself for all of these years; she's not only seen the *inside*, she's stitched it back together. Whoever my public self is from now on I owe it to her considerable skill.

Kimberly Lee, MD, is young enough to be my daughter, but right now she feels more like a doting big sister as she sits on my bed and examines her handiwork. Gentle, personal, unlike many surgeons I've known, I can tell immediately that this is more than just "a face" to her. "You did such an amazing job. *Thank* you!" I say.

"After all you've been through," she tells me, "we wanted to give you a face you'd be proud to wake up with." She fusses with the stitching holding my ear to my head, worries over the blood flow to the little heart-shaped flap of skin in the middle of my forehead that she saved from her assistant's over-eager scissors. "It's nearly impossible to match skin grafts, and I'm really concerned that you get a good result," she confides.

She needn't be. We both know that this is a career-making case, and she's aced it. "I was in surgery in the ER when the call came over the PA system," she tells me. "All the staff plastic surgeons were on summer vacation or 'too busy' to take it, so when I heard they needed a trauma team for a facial reconstruction, I came running over here."

It's July, and she just started her rotation as chief resident in the Head and Neck Trauma Department here. I can only imagine how envious all the hyper-competitive Beverly Hills plastic surgeons she works with will be when they find out what a plum case they've passed on to this "rookie"—and a *female* one at that.

Female plastic surgeons are as rare as hen's teeth—it's one of the most rigorous and male-dominated residencies there is. Women are admitted into the ranks only grudgingly, and usually shunted off into the hinterlands rather than made chief resident in one of the world's premier cosmetic and reconstructive surgery hospitals. This lady is in a class of her own.

That she could have come through this good-old-boy's network with her sweetness and compassion unimpaired is every bit as remarkable as the job she's done on my face. I vow right there to be as good a patient for her as she's been a doctor for me.

"So, tell me what happened to you," says Kimberly Lee. And, for the first of what will be uncounted times, people gather 'round and I tell them the story of Goldilocks and the Bear.

BACK ON THE HOMEFRONT

I sleep through the first night at the hospital and awaken the next morning to a scuffle out in the hallway. It seems a camera crew has wormed its way into the corridor in search of an interview with the "bear victim," and has come face to face with hospital security. Ever solicitous of my privacy, the staff has held them at bay so far, but it's the middle of the summer and it's a slow news cycle in Los Angeles; it's only a matter of time until lurking reporters in search of a good human-interest story overrun the facility and make it through their cordon.

Even in my addled state, I can tell that my presence here is disrupting normal hospital activities and compromising other patients' care; I know my condition is stabilized and there's nothing the hospital can do for me at this point that I can't do for myself at home. But how am I going to sneak out without causing a feeding frenzy? News crews are encamped, mushrooming all over the lawn in front of the Medical Center; it's turning into a circus out there.

The Medical Center's media relations director asks if they can give a statement to the gathered reporters—the story's now gone national—and together we decide that Alec and Dr. Lee[*] should hold a press conference. The plan is to sneak me out a back entrance—the VIP route, yet—while the news people are all distracted, then have Alec drive me back up I-5 to Central California before they know I've been discharged. I can come back for follow-up as an outpatient.

We write up a hasty statement thanking the fire station, the air-evacuation crew, and the amazing hospital staff who saved my life, then add

---

[*] Note: For those with a medical interest in the mess Dr. Lee repaired, here is a link to the ER pic. NSFW • http://imgur.com/bew8pqy

BACK ON THE HOMEFRONT

a nod to one of my personal heroes, brass-balled fake-newsman Stephen Colbert, who for years has been warning us about the national threat posed by bears. (*But did we listen . . . ?*) Alec reads the statement and Dr. Lee answers a few questions while I'm quietly discharged from the hospital, hustled out the doctor's entrance and onto the freeway before anyone is the wiser. Thirty-six hours in hospital is enough for anyone—even a bear victim.

When I get home, there are two extremely happy dogs waiting for me. The boys are indeed fine—it never even registers to them that my face is gone.

The horses make no bones about their curiosity. They come right over and gather in a circle around me—cordial, eager to greet me. Sadie, my race mare and trail partner, rubs my lower back and butt with her head, our typical greeting. Bruni, Alec's gruff little Icelandic, cocks his head and nods; he's not big on ceremony. But the least sociable of them, Bearin, sticks his gorgeous Arabian head into my face and slowly begins snuffling my wounds with his velvet muzzle—very methodical, blowing gently all over my face and head along the stitch lines as though he's breathing in my sudden vulnerability. He stares at me with those huge liquid eyes and then he does the most remarkable thing: the standoffish prima donna, who in the whole three years I've had him hasn't let me touch him without flinching, lays his head on my shoulder and lets out a long low sigh of contentment. He *knows*! I'm blown away.

The outside ranch cats come running at the sound of the can of cat food opening. Since it's a special homecoming, they get Mixed Grill. There's no real fanfare here, but Argyle does drip cat spit on me when I scratch his head. He

297

does that when he's happy.

The inside cats are a different story. Eager for reconnection, I invite them to come sit on my lap and purr. Instead, they take one look at my face and flee into a dark corner under the stairs. Manticore, the shyer of the two, actually hisses at me when I try to coax him out. Although his more inquisitive brother comes around within minutes, Manticore resists close contact with me completely. He lets me feed him, of course, but he refuses to even look at me—as though I've somehow betrayed his carefully arranged kitty *feng shui*. I'm vastly offended by his presumptions; if I wanted catty editorials about my appearance, I'd have stayed at UCLA and let the metrosexual lab techs have at me. But his rejection is undeniable evidence that no matter how chipper I may be feeling on the inside, I look like hell on the outside. And that's not about to change anytime soon—if ever.

The first night home, sitting in my own living room, I'm so proud watching Alec on the nightly news. Tall, square-jawed, hair tousled by the wind, though obviously distressed, he reads the statement with dignity and humor above the networks' yellow news crawl. Poor child, he's just graduated from college, ready to face the world on his own terms, but now he will be forever branded as "Son of Bear Victim." "We'll have to make up some calling cards," I tell him. "Alec Newman, College Graduate, Son of Bear Victim." In Hollywood, you have to take any entré you can get.

Our first taste of media snark comes when one local commentator criticizes him for using humor in his statement to the press. I've always disdained the proscribed verbal dance required of broadcast commentators, but if ever there was cause for levity, it's when a little old lady comes out on top of a bear attack. I refuse to let their sensationalist pandering get the better of my cheery outlook—which seems to me to be far healthier than all their doom and gloom. Why not make the public service point (*bears are not our friends*) gently rather than by flogging it for ratings? I'm prepared for some verbal jousting in the press, perhaps even for the hyperbole that's sure to accompany the story for the next day or two, but not for the media barrage that follows.

BACK ON THE HOMEFRONT

The phone started ringing before I even got home from the hospital, and now that I'm back, its incessant racket is tempting me to rip it from the wall and fling it into the chicken coop. I'm the sort of person who picks up the telephone about as often as I leave the ranch—which is to say every couple of weeks or so when I absolutely have to.

Alec has a pocket full of business cards from reporters from all the major morning shows, and poor Elaine in the media relations department back at UCLA is besieged with producers all vying for an exclusive interview. "We'll fly you out to . . . *New YORK!*" says one breathless booker. "And put you up at a four-star hotel for the night!" I haven't the heart to tell him I'd rather stick forks in my ears—ears which are only attached by silk threads at this point. It takes all the energy I can muster just to walk to the bathroom. Driving back down to LA, then sitting on an airplane for five hours, *then* enduring the bright lights and bustle of a television studio would likely do me in right there, live and on camera. Dr. Lee worked far too hard to lose her star patient so early in the game.

I politely decline his kind offer—as I do all the rest of them. As much as I would love to meet some of my favorite talk show hosts, my common sense gets the better of my inner groupie. Besides, Alec's college roommate, David, is coming for a long-planned visit before he starts medical school in a few weeks, and he and Alec are, in my opinion, the finest improvisational comedy team on the planet. I'd far rather sit on my screen porch pumped full of excellent painkillers and laughing my ass off at their wisecracks and rat-a-tat scenarios than negotiate the on-camera ego of the average television personality.

I keep putting off all the calls and email entreaties, but they keep coming, and it's apparent that I'm going to have to give *someone* an interview to shut the rest of them up. It's going to take a lot of strength and focus to get through the reassembly process my doctors have lain out for me, and all this distraction isn't helping my peace of mind one little bit. It's hard to heal when you're beset with other people's agendas.

Alec is running himself ragged trying to stay on top of all the callbacks, and I'm beside myself trying to get off this adrenaline rush and into something more comfortable when the circus culminates a few hot summer afternoons after I've returned home. A news crew from Bakersfield has hopped my locked entry gates, humped their equipment up my long dirt drive on foot, snuck through the yard gates past the two snoozing Hero Dogs, and are now shouting at me from my front lawn. "Come on down. We're from television. We want to talk to the bear victim!"

The bear victim herself appears on the balcony directly above them. They're not exactly standing in a good place to be should a vat of boiling pitch be tipped over the railing, but television reporters are not known for their common sense, let alone their good manners.

"Do you two read English?" I call down to them sweetly. "Do you understand what the words 'no' and 'trespassing' mean?"

"But we're from K***-TV."

By now the dogs have roused and are trotting around to the front yard. It's nearly dinnertime and these two reporters are burly, but they're no match for four hundred pounds of dog-spit factory. More to the point, Alec and David are downstairs playing video games after an afternoon of practicing Brazilian Ju Jitsu take-downs and choke holds on each other in the very spot the reporters have staked out. Then there's the varmit rifle I'm holding across my chest like Granny Clampett guarding the family 'shine.

"I think it best that you two be going now. . . ."

Alec and David interrupt their gaming long enough to escort the bewildered reporters back down the drive, followed by Deke and RK and their merry trails of slobber. I assume that's the last I'll hear from these guys until I get a call from John Nobles, our sheriff. He can hardly control his laughter, but he has to play this one straight.

"We got a call from the station manager down at K***-TV," he tells me. "He says you ran his camera crew off at gunpoint. Did you?"

"Yep," I say.

"Well, he wants me to come arrest you."

"For what? Only posting five 'Absolutely No Trespassing' signs instead of six?"

"Damned if I know. I told him to go pound sand and leave you alone. They've been pestering the fire station all week, too."

BACK ON THE HOMEFRONT

"Well, John, I'd sure love to be in the courtroom when the judge gets to *that* case."

John hoots in derision. "Just take it easy on them, okay, Bear Lady?"

"You betcha, son."

For once, the good-old-boys' network is working in *my* favor. I'm a local hero, and the news organizations of Bakersfield are hardly beloved of some of our law-enforcement personnel. John calls back again the next day.

"Wanted to tell you that after I declined his invitation to come up there and arrest you, the manager got so mad that he called 911 and cussed out the dispatch girl—I guess he forgot that all those 911 calls are recorded." Now it's my turn to guffaw. "We arrested him and charged him with abuse of a peace officer. Just thought you'd like to know."

This small victory cheers me immensely, makes me realize that sometimes there *is* some cosmic justice in the world—that sometimes the right people *are* called to accounts, that money and power aren't always everything. Just knowing that our local community has my back is an enormous comfort to Alec and me, and each morning when I look in the mirror, I feel less and less like a freak and more like an ordinary citizen. In fact, to my mind, these Frankenstein stitches just sort of blend into the person I've always known is inside of my outsides. It's just a matter of healing.

THE FIRST THING WE DO LET'S KILL ALL THE BEARS

There's a whole lot of suffering in the wake of the Ursadent besides just my own. One of the things I've dreaded most has come to pass, for nature, as we know, is circular in its cruelties. We may go into the wild for the peace and at one-ness it offers, but "nature, red in tooth and claw," as Tennyson tells us, dictates that what kills must inevitably also be killed.

I've tried to keep the story out of the press—especially the local press—but too many news organizations have picked it up, and I know my rednecks. One look at the American public's reaction to the 9-11 attacks on the World Trade Center is enough to predict what's going to happen next in *this* little microcosm. First comes the fascinated horror, then compassion for the victim, then the visceral offense, and finally comes the retribution. It doesn't matter who gets the brunt of it, *somebody* has got to pay.

The State of California allows eighteen hundred black bears to be hunted each season—"harvested," as the statute puts it—and permits sell out quickly as bears are killed for trophies, and more sickeningly, their gall bladders, which fetch a handsome price on the Asian market for their supposed aphrodisiac powers. Local ranchers blame bears for killing calves and threatening their livestock, although in my experience bears are mostly scavengers and I've seen them peacefully coexisting with cattle in the same ecosystem.

The upshot is that while killing bears theoretically involves licensure and paperwork, in actuality they are killed with impunity and often on sight. For this reason alone, I've been very hesitant to report any bear

THE FIRST THING WE DO LET'S KILL ALL THE BEARS

sightings up here, and if I do report them, I tend to fudge the location to keep them safe—after all, they live here, too. I've always regarded a bear sighting as a gift; a little bonus for putting up with all the privations and challenges of living in a place as "uncivilized" as this.

The Fish and Game people already spoke to Alec and asked that I call them as soon as I get home; they're hoping for a DNA sample to verify that this was indeed a California Black Bear that attacked me. They recovered my bloodied shirt from the hospital, but wonder if I still have the shoes and cap I was wearing so they can use them for their analysis.

The warden tells me that professional trackers are still hunting the bear with their dogs. I'd given Alec my best description and asked that he relay it to the Fish and Game guys; 200–250 pounds, two to three years old, 26–28 inches at the withers—about the height of my mastiff—with dull, mid-length, sun-bleached brown-colored fur.

Over the years, riding through the various bear "families'" territories up here, I've gotten to know their genetic lines fairly well. I've seen *black* black bears, black-and-white black bears, rust-brown black bears, even red black bears, but never any dull-brown, sun-bleached black bears like the one that got me. Moreover, the local bears seem to have proportionately longer snouts than the short and stubby one this bear had, perhaps the mutant offspring of the three pairs of grizzlies that were quietly relocated to the Piute Mountains in the mid-1970s in an ill-fated attempt to reintroduce the species into the ecosystem.

Alec guides the Fish and Game people to the site of the attack, and together they set up a huge culvert-on-wheels affair baited with bear food, the sort of large animal trap used for wildlife capture and relocation. I imagine this particular bear has already been relocated at least once, and I'm dubious about the likelihood of its re-capture.

Lying at home with my face swaddled in bandages, trying to imagine what the encounter must have been like for the bear, it occurs to me that maybe the creature wasn't some fearsome predator so much as it was simply desperate. Maybe it was a recent orphan, lost and on its own for the first time. Or maybe it was a "problem bear" captured in Yosemite or Monrovia after being found in the vicinity of human beings one time too many, now set loose in the Piutes where there aren't so many opportunities for bear–human "interface"—as the wildlife biologists call such encounters. I find myself identifying with its plight; you can only get run out of so many places before you have to take a territorial stand. Unfortunately ours had "interfaced." Literally.

The warden tells me that after the attack, the bear made its way down the mountain and broke into a weekender's house, rearranged their kitchen, then escaped out a back screen door. Along the way, it killed one of the tracker's dogs before disappearing into the rough terrain. They've been after it for three days now, and the tracker is concerned for the safety of his men. "After all, it's already attacked a dog and tried to kill a human. . . ."

"Let it go," I suggest, imagining this desperate creature fleeing through the rugged mountains pursued by dogs and bounty hunters. "After all this, I kind of doubt it's going to be interested in dealing with human beings ever again."

Now, I understand that it's entirely possible they've shot the bugger to smithereens and simply don't want to publicize the fact to the media for fear of offending some animal-rights groups. But this being Kern County and all, I can't imagine that's too big a consideration, so I'll take them at their word on this.

I'm on the phone doing a follow-up interview with the warden when the other line in his office begins to ring. He excuses himself and puts me on speakerphone so I can hear. The conversation chills me to the bone. The nightmare I've been trying so hard to stave off is starting.

The caller is a woman who's just shot a big bear foraging near her ranch. I can hear her hysteria even as she describes the carcass. It's black, maybe 400 pounds, has white markings. Not the bear that attacked me. But it's one I think I know—a big sow, who's never once bothered me in all the years I've lived here. I've even seen her babies, black and white just like she was.

The warden tells me that another bear's been killed up near Kernville

THE FIRST THING WE DO LET'S KILL ALL THE BEARS

in the last twenty-four hours, too—also not the one that attacked me. And now the weekend is here, and every would-be Elmer Fudd in the county has grabbed his twelve-gauge and headed for the Piutes—loaded for bear.

So many innocent creatures, all just trying to survive, all in the wrong place at the wrong time. Just like me.

APPEARANCES

It's six in the morning and we've been on the road for over an hour already. Alec has bundled me into Honky, his trusty old white Volvo, and nestled me in between the gum wrappers and the discarded fast food containers as he hustles me down to UCLA for my first post-attack consultation with Dr. Lee and the team.

There's something cozy about being driven all over the state by one's kid, reassuring even, in the realization that all those nail-biting moments when he was learning to drive have actually come to fruition. The sweet sense of continuity lulls me, as does the warm early-morning sun into the windows of the car. He's made us a special CD of some of my favorite film soundtracks, traffic is light, and I'm feeling rather normal; in fact, I'm sure my current condition is just a temporary setback.

Alec stops at a coffee emporium for caffeine while I make a pit stop to the restroom. Not entirely comfortable with the idea of being seen in public just yet, I pull my headscarf a little closer around my face, almost hoping some ignorant yahoo at the rest stop will give me grief about being a Muslim or something so I can spring my mangled face on him and shame him into silence. Seeing that the coast is clear, I take a deep breath and head for the ladies' room.

A little girl, maybe four or five years old, is standing at the sinks washing her hands. She's alone, maybe for the first time, and certainly not entirely confident about this independence thing. She's tiny, straining on her tiptoes to reach the faucet to turn it off. Forgetting my new appearance, I smile encouragement at her, and step forward to help her turn off the water. "Here honey, let me help you with that," I say, reaching for the faucet.

APPEARANCES

The child's big brown eyes grow wide and brim with tears. Crying in alarm, she rushes from the restroom without even drying her hands or looking behind her. I take a quick glance in the mirror and the ghoul staring back at me tells me why. (*People, after you've just had facial surgery, never, ever look at yourself in a mirror under fluorescent light. Just don't do it; you'll thank me.*)

The woman in the mirror is green and purple, massively swollen and riddled with stitches. Her smile is toothless and one of her eyes is slit like a reptile's—the other is paralyzed wide open—as big as a golf ball. The bridge of her nose is held off her face by a bandage splint and her lips look like they belong on a Chilean sea bass. *If only I were dressed in chain mail, I'd make a wonderful fantasy game avatar—the one you shoot with laser beams.* I hide in the far stall of the bathroom for a good long time trying to gather my wits about me—to come to grips with my new normal. *Is this the face I'm stuck with? Will I have to go from town to town with a jingle bell and a bag over my head like a medieval leper?*

I've always gone out of my way to smile and make eye contact with those people most of society considers "different," but I know from my own various brushes with disaster that the physically disabled might as well be invisible to most people. Folks in wheelchairs and people with deformities or noticeable afflictions usually pass through their days unremarked. "Even when you're *trying* to reach out," one chair-bound friend told me, "people make a point of ignoring you." (And *he* looked like a rock and roll god, Roger Daltry of The Who.)

Being chatty and effusive makes up for a host of deficiencies, but even my occasionally bubbly personality isn't going to carry me through this one. I wonder if I'm destined to be a non-person for the rest of my life, because it's going to be a *long* while before I'm ready for prime time again.

That morning at the eye center I begin to realize that my story is taking on a life of its own. The chair of the department, a man lauded in the media as "plastic surgeon to the stars," tells me how "inspirational" everyone in his office thinks I am. Truly puzzled, I ask him what he means by that? Getting eaten by a bear is inspirational? It certainly wasn't my intention—I just think of myself as the subject of yet another set of bizarre circumstances.

How is an "inspirational" person supposed to behave? Is there some unspoken code of responsibility my newfound status entails? And what could possibly be "inspirational" about somebody who looks like this?

Later that afternoon, I begin to see a possible upside. We've been at the med center all day, and I'm waiting for someone to give me the third in the series of five anti-rabies injections called for by public health protocol. Dr. Lee has been tinkering with my left ear, *tch tching* until she gets it perfect—or as close to perfect as this stage of my recovery will allow. I'm still waiting for whatever paperwork has to be completed before the specially certified public-health nurse can shoot me full of gamma globulin. Dr. Lee takes this opportunity to torment me some more.

"I'm just not quite"—*snip*—"happy with this "—*snip*—"yet." She can't anesthetize without distorting the tissue, so I just have to grin and bear her perfectionism. And she *is* a perfectionist. Yet I can't credibly whimper without blowing my cred. Bear victims can't wimp out at a few stitches and needles!

Finally, someone comes into the little treatment room and announces that before they can give me the critical injection, I'll need to come up with a $1,400 insurance co-pay.

Now, I've been sitting in waiting rooms all day with people who don't even speak English, and I'm pretty sure that *they* haven't had to come up with $1,400 co-pays for an injection the hospital gets for free from the Centers for Disease Control. Granted, rabies vaccine isn't kept in ready supply, and Blue Cross isn't known for its compassion, but I don't *have* $1,400 lying around—and certainly not for something that shouldn't cost me a penny! Yet the staffer is adamant. "We can't give you the injection until we get the deposit." I feel like running through the wards and biting people, starting with *her*.

"Can't you just call Blue Cross?" I ask her.

"We did, and they told us to collect the co-pay first."

We're at an impasse until I remember that in the interest of efficiency, I finally agreed to do an extended television interview; in fact,

APPEARANCES

I arranged to meet the production crew here at UCLA so they can do a preliminary segment with Dr. Lee and me. They are waiting for us at this very minute out in the visitor's room.

Inspired, I take the billing lady by the arm and lead her to the doorway, pointing down the hallway toward the waiting area. "See that pretty blond lady down there?" I say, "The one with those three big guys holding the light bars and cameras and microphones? The ones that say 'Fox News' on them? What fun do you think they'll have when I tell them that Ronald Reagan Medical Center is withholding my rabies shot because of an insurance screw-up?"

To her credit, she gets the big picture forthwith and scurries off. A moment later she returns with the public health nurse and a profuse apology. Maybe this "inspirational" thing has its perks after all. But I still have to endure all these nasty rabies shots.

ENTER, PURSUED BY A BEAR

I come home from this experience and the thoughtful interview that follows with the realization that "the Ursadent" isn't just my story—it belongs to everyone as part of our human DNA. Being eaten by a wild beast is probably mankind's most primal nightmare, the stuff of ghost stories and campfire tales—as old as storytelling itself. It occurs to me that every generation or so it comes to some lucky staffer to perpetuate the mythology, and that far from being upset when people take such a perverse interest in it, I should see this as an opportunity to do my part.

It's no accident that we remember Shakespeare's Antigonus, who "exits stage pursued by a bear"; or the cautionary tales of the Brothers Grimm, the story of Goldilocks, or the sweetly demented ramblings of the unfortunate "Grizzly Man," Timothy Treadwell, who once visited Alec's little Carden School in Malibu to tell the kids about his life in the Alaskan outback—a life he loved up until the final agonized moments when one of his beloved bears tore him and his fiancée to kibbles and bits.

There is such a splendid symmetry in that someone like me, who tells stories for a living, should be tapped as the millennial "Bear Lady." And irony indeed that said Bear Lady should be a Cassandra who's spent the last decade or so writing about the coming global bear markets typified by the collapse of, ahem, *Bear* Stearns—in the very month before I meet my own nemesis. All the coincidence makes it almost seem *too* fated.

Maybe there's something larger here than just a good yarn about a little old lady who fought off a bear attack and lived to tell the tale? Our whole country got munched by a bear in the summer of 2008. People who once thought their futures were set and secure have lost their homes, their jobs, their retirements, their very faith in their public institutions—they've lost *their* public faces, too. Everything we'd thought we were and had become is gone—*poof*! Vanished along with our suppositions. I'm a national metaphor!

Fresh off this revelation, I get a call from Mrs. Miller, a magnificent woman and a dear friend. During this Ursadent circus, she's had the good breeding and discretion to wait for me to contact her rather than pestering me for details. An ex-Carmelite nun, this remarkable lady also did a long stint as Bob Hope's social secretary then founded what is now an *ü*ber-exclusive private school in Westside Los Angeles. Like many of us up here, she escaped the crush of humanity in the city for the more expansive solitude of the countryside. Unlike many of us, she has taken her early religious vows seriously throughout her life.

When Mrs. Miller was my son's sixth-grade teacher, she had the kids transform their classroom into a Pharaoh's tomb for the semester while they studied Ancient Egypt. Gauze-wrapped dolls became mummies. The kids made cardboard crowns, milk-bottle amphorae, labyrinthine mazes—the room was remarkable, magical. And of course, when they learned about the mummification process the ten-year-olds in her class were enthralled. Their parents, however, were not; our local school board had the one-time nun removed for teaching "Satan worship" to the children.

Egyptian myths apparently contradict Evangelical Christian myths in places such as this. In response, Mrs. Miller and her gentle Amish husband sold their few remaining worldly possessions, bought an old pickup truck, and began a mission. Every morning they would get up and pack the truck full of donated bottles of juice and water, toothbrushes, clean socks, stationary and stamps, and seasonal clothing. Then they'd drive into the Central Valley and make the rounds of the underpasses, the orchards and fields along the highways, the railroad tracks, and parish parking lots to bring supplies to the "blessed ones," as they call their flock, who make their homes in America's hidden places. When they are not bringing comfort, writing letters, or delivering medicines, they are cajoling local citizens and merchants for donations. They have done this for the last decade.

Some of Mrs. Miller's blessed ones have been living in their respective spots for years; some are transients, literally only a few days from death. Many are military veterans or druggies in the last stages of HIV-AIDS. Many have a history of violence. She and her husband know and love them all and care for them as they would their own children, living an authentically Christian life of poverty and service to the poor and the needy. Whenever I can, I put an envelope stuffed with whatever loose currency is hanging around my house into their mailbox. I finally had to ask her to please stop writing me thank you notes for doing this—and save the stamps for her ministry.

A couple of weeks ago, she sent me a lovely card of encouragement with $25 in cash inside. I, of course, sent it right back along with a note telling her I would sooner gnaw off my own elbows (quite a trick—particularly with my lack of teeth) than take a penny from her mission. That's why she called.

She tells me her blessed ones have been so worried about me after hearing of the bear attack, they got together and *took up a collection*. For *me*. And these dear, desperate, hungry, appallingly deprived people have been praying for me, the outspoken atheist, sending thoughts and prayers for my swift recovery.

Well, *that's* humbling.

I hang up the phone, look out onto my enormously self-indulgent rose garden, and weep for a good long while. *They're praying for me? For unkind circumstances? For their own redemption?* No sooner do I wipe my nose on my sleeve than I get a call from the folks at one of the more sensationalist news shows wanting to schedule an interview with me to talk about my "heroism."

I'd have to be pretty dense to miss the irony here, but I think I have a better handle on what I am supposed to do with the strange opportunity that's fallen into my lap. If I am meant to be a national metaphor, by the gods and Mrs. Miller, I'm going to take the responsibility seriously.

"Sure," I tell the bright young thing on the other end of the phone. "When would you like to come up and do the shoot?"

PRETTY AWFUL

Five or six surgeries and five or six production crews later, I'm starting to get the hang of this new routine. My life has become a cycle of fighting Blue Cross for approval for a surgery, psyching myself up for the surgery, recovering from the surgery, writing about the surgery, psyching myself up for interviews, recovering from interviews, and writing about the interviews. Then it's rinse, repeat, and get ready for the next round of financial angst, personal invasion, and self-congratulatory introspection.

At first I'm surprised at the uniformity of the questions the interviewers ask me: "how big was the bear? Are the dogs okay? Did it hurt?" I try to give original answers, challenge myself to remember a new detail or come up with a new way to phrase the same event so I don't sound canned or rehearsed, but with few exceptions, all my musings into the philosophical ramifications of Schopenhauer's irrational universe and Heisenberg's Uncertainty Principle and are answered with taglines that feature the word "chomp," so after a time I just ask them what they want me to say and try to figure out a charming way to say it.

Many are obviously expecting me to attribute my survival to Divine Intervention, and it's here I simply have to draw a line. When they lead with prompts like, "God certainly was watching out for you that day . . ." or "I'll bet you were praying the whole time . . ." sometimes it's hard to refrain from saying that by their line of reasoning, the same Merciful Being that was "looking out for me" also sent a bear to eat my face off, and I'd rather not worship anything as psychotic as all *that*.

Mostly I just counter with a simple "No, *I* was looking out for me," and imply that if there's any God to thank, I'm just glad it sent the bear after someone with my mental toughness, and not some little kid walking home from the school bus stop. Generally that turns their line of questioning into something a bit more thoughtful—I figure they should have known that an ornery little woman who's bested a bear isn't likely to suffer media whores gladly.

One radio host, however, accidentally leaves her studio mike on as she discusses me with her colleague before a show. "Did you *see* the pictures?" she asks her co-host. "She was so beautiful." The other woman, unaware that I can hear them chatting before they go on the air, asks facetiously, "So, when you look in a mirror now, how does that make you feel?" "Oh, you're so *terrible!*" says the hostess.

But far from offending me, her question gives me an idea. When we come back on the air, I have an answer for her.

"You asked how my new face makes me feel when I look at it?" I begin. "Well, Tina [we'll call this interviewer 'Tina'], it makes me feel like singing! Free! Soaring like a bird! Thanks to my sudden disfigurement, I'll never know the slow mounting horror of watching my beauty fade as age takes its inexorable toll—nor will I fear the decrepitude yet to come. You see, Tina, it's already over with! Done and done. I'll never again have to worry about smudged makeup, or bad hair days, or unevenly groomed eyebrows. Lipstick on my teeth? HA! I *have* no teeth! Come Halloween, I've got a ready-made costume with a built-in back story—what a boon on those busy party nights! While other women my age fret over how to pay for their face lifts and chemical peels, I am relieved of even having to make the *effort* to stay young and pretty—because no one expects it of me. And best of all, Tina? I'll never again have to wonder if someone is only interested in me for my looks, or if they're just pretending because they want to get into my pants. Nor will I have to put up with catty comments from women who hate me because they think I'm after their husbands, or husbands who hate me because I am not. The odds are that this is the worst I'm ever going to look, and that as I age and these scars begin to melt into my wrinkles, my face will only get softer. I'm already lumpy, trollish, and disfigured, and the people who love me couldn't care less. You see, I was mauled by a *bear*. So. Tina. What's *your* excuse?"

GRITTING THE PUBLIC

It's amazing how many people see these shows or read these articles and recognize me—on the street, at the store, in the online community. Folks I've never met come up and hug me, touch my hands, examine my face and tell me "how good" I look. "Considering..." is my usual answer. The swelling has gone down enough that my speech, though impeded by insensate tongue and lips, is once-again intelligible, and I've been practicing my facial calisthenics religiously, so while I may not be able to actually *feel* what my face is doing, I can at least isolate and consciously move some of the muscle groups to force it into a smile or a grimace—or the consonant I'm struggling with.

More than a few of my well-wishers, only half-joking, ask me for Kimberly Lee's business card—so I start carrying them with me whenever I go out. She opened a private practice in Beverly Hills, and I want to send her all the referrals she so richly deserves. Dr. Lee's successfully completed *another* high-profile case, this time a construction worker who accidentally shot a bolt gun through his eye socket. She's not only saved his eye, she's put his face back together as skillfully as she reconstructed mine. When I've recovered sufficiently, she's promised to "fine tune" my scars and try to reconnect some of the nerves in my mouth so I can use my lips again. This alone is enough to encourage me to hurry up and heal!

It seems that the people who know me best are the least concerned for my well-being. Alec, my friends and family, all *know* I'm going to get through this with my sanity intact—what other choice do I have? I don't have the energy to waste on feeling sorry for myself or ruminating on my ruined looks. Maybe if all this had happened when I was in my twenties

CHOMP CHOMP CHOMP

I'd feel differently, but I'm pushing sixty now—who cares? Certainly not my dogs and horses. I appreciate the concern of complete strangers, but honestly, it's getting kind of tiresome reassuring them that yes, I'm fine, the dogs are just fine, everything is going to be fine, thank you so much for your kind words.

But when I *do* start to feel put upon, I remember Alex Haley standing in auditoriums and shopping malls, shaking hand after hand for *years*—always with a sincere thank you for buying his book, and always encouraging them to take pride in their children and to work hard to give them a better future. If he could shake a million hands in his efforts to bring his story to the world, I can certainly manage a smile and a good story for disabled veterans, chemo kids, all the shoppers who recognize me and crowd around in the cereal aisle of the grocery store to ask me about the Ursadent.

I begin to understand that I'm doing much more than just reassuring the good-hearted people who take the time to tell me they care about me. Every person who makes contact, or who expresses a thoughtful sentiment on my behalf, takes a little piece of my experience with them, and that enriches all our lives just that much more. More to the point, I realize that what happened to me is more than just a freak accident—it's a *privilege* that's been handed to me. And with that privilege comes the responsibility of administering it wisely.

In my office sits a whole trunk full of cards and letters from people all over the world who have heard the story and want to thank me for giving *them* hope! Each time I read one it brings me a little bit closer to my recovery—besides, responding to them all is good distraction. Given that I can't really see, and I certainly can't get out to do too many ranch chores, at least I'm being useful by keeping up on my correspondence and bringing a little excitement into lonely peoples' summer.

One day I'm standing in line at the grocery store flipping through the *National Enquirer* when I see myself staring back from beside the center staple. There I am on my own page, in four-color newsprint right between John Travolta and Oprah Winfrey. I've never even spoken to a reporter from the publication, so they've likely just cobbled the story together from Internet photographs and reports, and like the source material, the article is riddled with inaccuracies and speculation. The journalist in me is concerned that this whole story is getting away from me.

Not sure whether to be flattered or offended, I remember my dear friend Bonnie Ebsen telling me that she learned of her father, Buddy's, death while flipping through the *National Enquirer* in a grocery line. Maybe there's a rite of passage in here somewhere?

Whatever the case, it's obvious that my fifteen minutes of fame have now stretched into twenty-three and it's way past time to call a halt to all this nonsense. Either I use my notoriety for something useful, or it's time to bow out and let some other *freaque du jour* have a turn in the tabloid barrel. Fortunately for me, the Octomom and her fourteen test-tube babies are waiting in the wings, and it's with great relief that I turn the *chatterati* reins over to her.

Maybe now I can stop reassuring everyone else that I'm going to be okay, and start convincing myself.

REDEMPTION

The sad news has come to me that a fellow bear victim, an RN who twenty years ago endured a horrific grizzly mauling, has taken her own life. One of the smaller fraternities in the world, bear-attack survivors—especially *black* bear attack survivors—tend to be as solitary as their predators, so I hold the three people who have reached out to give advice and encouragement very dear. What haunts me so is that she made it all these years and through all the pain and surgeries only to succumb to her inability to live with herself after being so terribly disfigured. Somehow, I absolutely know why. Maybe we're not meant to survive what is thought to be unsurvivable. Maybe our choice to live contradicts the natural order of things; having once seen death, maybe we're programmed to capitulate without a struggle when it comes knocking again.

But the nightmares I expected to have after the attack have never materialized, and the PTSD everyone keeps talking about only drops in for brief appearances when I'm in the dental chair. There's something about the sound and pressure of drill on bone that's just a bit too close to the sound of bear teeth on human skull, and occasionally it's necessary to ask whoever's doing the drilling and poking to pause until I can

REDEMPTION

collect myself.

But the news of this woman's suicide has left me devastated in a way I could not have imagined. It occurs to me that I've been denying just how much we had in common—and how close to the edge I've come over this last year and a half since the attack.

It's late winter now, and I'm at my wit's end. Never very big to begin with, I've lost a frightening amount of weight, and my energy level is at an all-time low. Because of my lack of teeth and the inability to control my facial muscles, solid food is a luxury I still have to manage selectively. Despite several surgeries, the scar tissue in my mouth is so strictured, and the exposed nerves so raw, that trying to get anything much larger than a straw into my mouth is still not only excruciating, it's also very messy.

Between the paralysis and the pain, I have new respect for teething babies who are learning to use a spoon for the first time. The things simply don't fit into little mouths, and food refuses to stay where it's supposed to, following the law of gravity forward and down the chin instead of backward and down the gullet—hence bibs and baby spoons, which I quickly adopt for myself. I've not eaten in the company of another human being for months, and I find myself hiding my mouth with my hand when I speak lest I dribble—or smile and expose my naked gums.

I've had to learn to speak again too, to move my lips consciously and force my tongue to form the consonants I've spoken automatically for over half a century. And as the nerves in my face begin to regenerate, I'm beset with strange squeamish sensations and sudden phantom pain that leaves me gasping—while the rest of my head goes numb.

The person in the mirror looks reasonably presentable to me: in certain light she's almost normal-looking, but even the reassurances of my friends can't deny that there is a big chunk of flesh missing from my face, that my features are distorted and asymmetrical, and that no matter how much Dr. Lee "prettifies" me, I'm not the person I'm expecting to see when I chance a glance at myself.

Stranger still, I can no longer identify faces. Unless I know someone very well from before the attack, I'm at a loss to differentiate who they are. Watching movies becomes an exercise in frustration, as every new character on the screen looks the same to me; it's impossible to tell them apart anymore. I wonder if other bear survivors have made this odd transference, too? Maybe when it's too painful to recognize the person you associate with being you as *you*, it becomes harder to recognize anyone else, either.

To make matters worse, Blue Cross/Anthem is in full denial-of-services mode, and my finances are shot. The cold, dry winter air has my facial nerves in a tizzy, and I'm so weak and cold-sensitive that simply trying to bring in firewood to heat my little house is an ordeal. Even the horses sense my despair and stop whinnying at me come suppertime. For the first time I can remember, they wait patiently, quietly, until I appear with their evening grain. They must know I'll get there eventually.

When I think of the RN's untimely death, an existentialist angst threatens to overwhelm me. I look to the bear-attack survivors I've spoken with for encouragement, not admission of defeat. A sense of inevitability begins to creep over me.

What's the point of going through all this pain and hassle and expense when I know full well that ultimately—as we humans are wont to do—it will all just come to naught? Despite my best efforts, and those of my doctors, I will continue to get older, more wrinkled, and more mentally incompetent, until I finally deteriorate into oblivion. I mean, seriously—what's the point of all this? If even my insurance company thinks I'm not worth saving, why bother?

I'm in full pity-party mode tonight; in the midst of a snit so profound that even wine isn't helping—though believe me, it's trying. The prospect of dying alone and toothless doesn't bother me nearly so much as the prospect of living out my days in pain and poverty with the awful knowledge of life's goofy futility.

As my state of mind grows more morbid, I think of my baby sister, diagnosed with breast cancer at age thirty-seven. She had a loving husband and three little boys under the age of ten when she found the lump, and certainly had no inkling of what lay ahead for her. For seven years she

REDEMPTION

and her family struggled valiantly against disease and treatment, alternating between hope and despair, before she finally died in the spring of her forty-fifth year. During one remission I'd asked her what she'd learned from her ordeal. What lessons had she taken from the experience?

We were sitting on the sand in front of her beach home at the time, surrounded by family, friends, and neighbors all enjoying a late-summer barbeque. She took a sip of her margarita, looked out at the bay where her beautiful boys were windsurfing, and said, "I learned to really value other people's company."

I'd always thought of my sister Nan as being as insular as myself—not anti-social, necessarily, but not particularly welcoming, either. At first I thought I'd misheard her. Then she went on. "It used to be that when I had some time to myself, I'd go for a run on the beach, or go off alone somewhere and read a book, but since the diagnosis, I've come to appreciate being with my friends—letting them enjoy helping me."

Five hundred people came to her memorial service and they named a children's reading room at the library after her. After she died, I got letters of condolence from people I'd never met. That certainly wouldn't be the case for Alec if I dropped dead up here. . . .

Letting people help me is something I have a great deal of trouble with. My internal accounting system hates to be in anyone's debt, so if someone I don't know well offers to help me out, I either have to pay them for their services or not accept them to begin with. Maybe that's the reason I always used to pay for dinner on a first date—it kept the balance of power in my favor until I could figure out how vulnerable it was safe to be.

This isn't something new for me, either. When my house burned down, the community wanted to get together to throw me a fundraiser. I was *mortified*. "Heavens no!" I'd told my friend Claudine. "Don't even *think* about it!" Now I'm beginning to realize how selfish that had been; sometimes we have a responsibility to *receive*, too. Giving to others makes people feel useful. Giving to others gives people power. Maybe Christ was being ironic when he said, "'Tis better to give than to receive." Maybe I could use *that* one on the bandits at Blue Cross? Fat chance. Their legalese is so impenetrable that even the eloquence of a Bible won't get them to budge.

My telephone answering machine is still blistered from the tirade I launched at it this morning. My "insurer" has left me another denial-of-service notification. It seems that the delicate surgery to reconstruct the contours of my right eye is not considered "medically necessary." True, people have been getting along without their eyes for millennia, but they probably haven't been paying a lifelong contract with Blue Cross to address that issue, either.

"We have reviewed your request and are sorry to inform you that your policy doesn't cover cosmetic surgery," drones the mechanical voice on my machine.

"Of *course* it's cosmetic, you idiots," I scream back at it. "*My face was eaten off by a freaking bear!* It tore my jaw out. It ate my nose. I watched it spit my bloody teeth out into the sand. My *teeth*! I don't have any *teeth anymore*! Do you people understand how isolating that is?"

When you're five years old, having visibly missing teeth is something of a status symbol—a sign you're leaving the social pabulum of babyhood and venturing out into the world beyond the home. But what's adorable in a five-year-old is just pathetic in a grown adult. Especially one who's accustomed to being taken seriously. It's bad enough that the skin of my forearms is knotted with twisted blue veins and my six-pack abs have turned to cardboard; a year and a half of taking my meals through a straw has left me skeletal, my ass looks more like my pelvis, and when I pull on a heavy sweater I'm afraid I'm going to break something. But all that pales when I look at my face in a mirror-and smile. Just as the camera adds ten pounds to one's appearance, a lack of teeth brings the instant loss of forty IQ points.

I'd once visited an antique warehouse that was minded by a statuesque *femme d'un certain age*. Tall, perfectly dressed, her white-grey hair beautifully coiffed, I wondered aloud what such a splendid woman was doing tending the counter in a dusty old shop in Bakersfield. When she answered, her voice was sparkling, modulated, trained. Surely she was an acclaimed actress or royalty of some sort—such was her aura. Then she

REDEMPTION

smiled at me and I noticed the missing canine. I didn't react, of course, but the dissonance was overwhelming. I never saw her again and always wondered why she hadn't had it fixed, whether her elegance was a façade or if she kept the gap as a political statement. Now *I'm* that damaged woman—only orders of magnitude worse—and I finally realize why she hadn't had it fixed. *She couldn't afford to.*

". . . If you feel this determination has been made in error" the machine drones on, "you have the right to appeal. Please contact. . . ." I'm so mad I'm ready to spit. But what would be the point? As Alec is fond of telling me when I scream at the talking heads on TV, "It can't hear you, Mum. It's a *machine*."

If I'm having this much trouble getting treatment with "good" insurance and the medical background to argue on my own behalf, what about all the people who are injured in more mundane accidents? It's only a fluke that my injuries are bizarre enough to attract national attention; had I gotten them in a car crash or in an industrial mishap, the news cycle wouldn't care one whit—and they certainly wouldn't be sending out photographers and makeup artists to interview me for television shows! What about the bicyclist who's hit by the careless trucker, or the guy who goes to his doctor and gets a lousy diagnosis? What about *them*? Does Oprah want them on her talk show? In what twisted universe is getting mauled by a bear supposed to be a *lucky break*?

I've given a fair amount of thought tonight as to how I might do myself in with the least amount of muss and bother for all involved. Do I take the coward's way out with pills and vodka and a plastic bag? Or do I go with the sure thing and swallow a load of buckshot in the shower stall? Either way might have its charms, but neither one appeals to my sense of aesthetics. I was a motel maid once, remember? *Somebody* would have to clean up the mess I've left. Claudine has been my good and loyal housekeeper for fifteen years. I couldn't do that to her.

And what of all the animals? They're good friends, too. Given the lousy economy and the uncertain effect it is having on everyone's finances,

I have no assurance that anyone will take them in and care for them like I do. Just abandoning them to fend for themselves is akin to child abuse in my book.

No, I'd have to take them with me, and that *really* doesn't appeal to me as a prelude to my own demise. How could I look into the eyes of the Hero Dogs and dispatch them in cold blood? Or my house kitties—who sleep under the covers with me every night and lick my tears when I'm crying?

Then, of course, I would have to clear the whole Kevorkian production with Alec, and from what I can gather, he's not terribly keen on the idea. "Don't be an asshole," is how he puts it. He's right, of course. Killing myself would be a totally assholic thing to do, but I'm not feeling particularly charitable at the moment.

So I sit this evening in front of a roaring fire, thinking of my dead colleague and my dead baby sister, and my rapidly deadening soul. Sometimes disgruntlement comes on so hard, it seems like there's not enough gruntling left in the world to pull me out of it. In cases like this, there's only one thing left to do: good wine and bad movies. If I'm going to throw a pity party, I'll make it a good one. There's an unopened bottle of reserve cabernet from my brother Jim's Boothill Vineyard in the back of the pantry. I pour it directly into a one-quart Ball jar, stick in a flex-straw, and start sucking.

Eraserhead is on Turner Classic Movies, David Lynch's dark, troubling, and very funny surrealist freak-fest. Somehow the evening is all falling into place. I sink back into my chair and suck away on my wine, waiting for the young boy who finds Henry Spencer's broken head to take it to a pencil factory. The cat in my lap is puffed up like a dirigible at the images on the screen. The other dances sideways at it. My little viewing room is certainly full of unsettling vibes tonight.

I'm pretty pickled by the time I catch sight of my face reflected by the window in the green glow of the television set. It's even worse than under fluorescents. I look like a ghoul; the crags and scars and hollows of my mangled face stare back at me in the worst lighting possible—and the effect is hideous. It's *so* hideous—and I'm *so* drunk—that I'm able to

REDEMPTION

depersonalize what I'm looking at in the glass of the window. I know it's me, but it's the cadaverous me, the dead me. I'm thinking, *Hmmmm, I could go Goth or vampire with this,* and I start making faces at myself to see if I'm hallucinating.

But I'm not hallucinating; that image I see is for real. I really *do* look like the apparition in the glass. This really *is* my face; I can't go upstairs and wash it off in the bathroom sink when I get tired of it. This is how I'm going to have to go through the rest of my life—as a toothless old hillbilly woman. Maybe the peace I'd felt when I lay my bloodied head in the cool sand of the creek bed was the better option after all—and my friend's suicide seems all the more rational a choice. Maybe it's time to join her.

I'm so tired of being a freak, tired of having people gawk and feel sorry for me. *I'm just going to go find a box somewhere and crawl into it.* As I grow more and more morose, I think back to my most recent surgery. The one that augmented what was left of my jaw so they could put titanium implants into it. Implants for *teeth*. The teeth Blue Cross says I don't need and I can't possibly afford to pay for.

Back on the TV screen, Spencer, his self-identity now utterly destroyed, is being drawn into the final comfort of the Lady in the Radiator's white light as my own mind is drawn back to the abject despair I'd felt after my last facial surgery. When I'd come to, I was weeping. Curious inasmuch as this latest surgery represented another small victory in my struggle to return to a normal life—a triumph of sorts, of will over uncommon circumstances. Upon awakening, my sense of despair was so overwhelming that weeping was all I could manage—the purity of my sorrow oddly comforting. Welcome back, Allena. The surgery was a success.

My first physical sensation was not of the pain, the difficulty drawing breath, nor the bright lights of the recovery room; it was of tears wetting thin little channels down the claw marks that still scarred my cheeks. My consciousness, such as it was as my world came back into focus, was utterly subsumed by defeat.

A nurse hovered nearby, tending to another patient. I didn't want her to know I was coming out of anesthesia, so I made no sound, not even a change in the cadence of my breath. I willed myself not to sob.

Why? Why did you bring me back? I asked no one so much as the cold white tiles on the wall beside me. The tiles were so close I could see the pores in the grouting, and it occurred to me that those tiny imperfections were what gave the surface its integrity, kept the brittle whole intact—like the skin of my reconstructed face, or the matrix in my jaw.

Why did you guys bother with all of this? I don't want to be here. I want to go back!

It had been so peaceful there in that dark, anesthetic nothingness. No people. No emotion. No pain. No me. No nothing; even as the most exquisite nerves in my face and mouth were torn apart and reconnected. Now I had to start this bloody "life" nonsense all over again, and that realization broke me.

My first thought was of Scotty, the young son of a friend of mine, sort of my Charon in all this, rowing me back and forth between the world of the living and the underworld of the dead during all of my reconstructions and surgical tinkerings. He'd left us shortly before he'd turned twenty, having understood the futility of longing for what he could never have, and figured out a way to trump its hold over him. Just a child, really, without the perspective or sense of self to continue the charade, his was the spirit I spoke to when I confronted the shards of my shattered hopes—the ones that beaconed to a path that would free me, and release me from this bizarre sideshow.

Scotty knew what it meant to be completely adrift and longing for a safe harbor; he knew the merciful release of mindlessness, and the peace I had just lost. His last words, which he left on the electric eternity of MySpace, bespoke my wistfulness, and he wrote with the same outraged resignation I'd felt; his sweetness his ultimate undoing. "It's so hard to listen to your parents and all their friends reliving their exploits," he wrote, "and know that no matter what you do or how hard you try, your life will never measure up to their fun, their lovers, their accomplishments...."

We all seek out our small comforts, it seems, even as they destroy us. He'd found the heroin that killed him. I'd found self-pity.

REDEMPTION

Crying uncontrollably now, I'm really getting into it when I hear the ping of incoming email upstairs on my computer. I'm so full of misery that I'm willing to grab any diversion I can get, would welcome a male enhancement commercial, or an ad for a pyramid sales scheme. But once again, my dark musings have lost out to my curiosity. I'll have to do myself in some other day.

The post is from Howard Breuer, a particularly intrepid reporter who drove up here and followed me around after the attack, even poking into the willow copse where I'd been mauled, to get material for the excellent profile he wrote of me for *People* magazine. I've not heard from him in a while, so I'm surprised to read:

"Dear Allena. How are you doing these days? These folks just called me. They are offering you free dental work." Along with his post, he's attached the CV of one Dr. Bill Dorfman, DDS, and provided me with his contact information. Apparently Dr. Dorfman read of my ordeal in the *People* magazine article and decided to help me out. Just like that.

The next morning, I call his office, and it's true. Dr. Dorfman is a famous Beverly Hills dentist with a long list of celebrity clients, but he still devotes a large part of his practice to helping out people like me. Folks who have fallen through society's cracks, whether by chance or by choice.

Well! After I pick my partially reconstructed jaw up off the floor, I start alternately sobbing like a baby and dancing around the room like a crazy woman. I grab a cat and boogie with the poor thing until I drop. Then I run up and down the stairs for a while whooping like a banshee. "I'm gonna get some teeth! I'm gonna get some teeth!" Then I sit down on the landing and cry some more, but they are no longer tears of misery.

More than just an offer of help, Dr. Dorfman's gift is one of *redemption*. Maybe *this* is what I'm supposed to learn from this whole experience. We give what we can give, and in so doing, we perpetuate something larger than ourselves, something that continues on and touches other lives beyond our own. We build on the sacrifices of those who came before.

Just like the resolve I'd felt when the Hero Dogs came to my rescue, just like the resolve I'd felt when I'd vowed to be as good a patient for Kimberly Lee as she'd been a healer to me, I could finally understand that

Madre had been right all along; it isn't "all about me," and there is more to life than just surviving it. That the bear attack was not only a gift, but a responsibility. A responsibility that I *chose* when I chose to survive.

So many people went to such extraordinary lengths to bring me back into the human fold—one gift of self at a time—that spurning them now would be unforgivable. Even *I* wouldn't forgive me if I cut out on everyone now.

The time may come when I'm no longer able to play the hand that's been dealt me, but that time isn't here yet. I sit down at my computer and I begin to write. . . .

EPILOGUE

On the three-year anniversary of the attack, I decide to celebrate with a long ride up to the high country. My face finally having healed enough that I feel ready to risk breaking it again, Sadie and I are trotting along the Pacific Crest Trail up by Robin Bird Springs, just enjoying this fine summer day and communing with the mountains.

As we approach the main meadow, a huge bear, the color of burnished gold, lumbers across our path. This one is magnificent, sleek and powerful, and its golden fur fairly ripples as it moves. It notices me, pauses, and for the briefest of moments makes eye contact. And in that moment I sense connection.

It's only a bear, and I'm only an ornery woman astride a purposeful horse, but of such odd gifts are stories borne. Without breaking stride, it ambles off into the pines while I continue down the forest trail on my way to wherever it is I'm going—we're just two kindred spirits passing through.

And I am home.

Printed in Great Britain
by Amazon